SLAVE HUNTER

SLAVE HUNTER

ONE MAN'S GLOBAL QUEST TO FREE
VICTIMS OF HUMAN TRAFFICKING

Aaron Cohen
with Christine Buckley

Simon Spotlight Entertainment

New York   London   Toronto   Sydney

SIMON SPOTLIGHT ENTERTAINMENT
A Division of Simon & Schuster, Inc.
1230 Avenue of the Americas
New York, NY 10020

First Simon Spotlight Entertainment hardcover edition June 2009

SIMON SPOTLIGHT ENTERTAINMENT and colophon are
trademarks of Simon & Schuster, Inc.

For information about special discounts for bulk purchases,
please contact Simon & Schuster Special Sales at
1-800-456-6798 or business@simonandschuster.com.

The Simon & Schuster Speakers Bureau can bring authors to your live event.
For more information or to book an event, contact the Simon & Schuster Speakers
Bureau at 1-866-248-3049 or visit our website at www.simonspeakers.com.

Designed by Kyoko Watanabe

This work is a memoir. It reflects the author's present recollections of his
experiences over a period of years. Certain names and identifying characteristics
have been changed, characters combined and events compressed or reordered.

Manufactured in the United States of America

1 3 5 7 9 10 8 6 4 2

Library of Congress Cataloging-in-Publication Data
Cohen, Aaron, 1965–
Slave hunter : one man's global quest to free victims of human trafficking /
Aaron Cohen with Christine Buckley.
p. cm.
Includes bibliographical references.
ISBN-13: 978-1-4169-6117-8
ISBN-10:   1-4169-6117-8
1. Human trafficking—Prevention—Case studies. 2. Slavery—Prevention—Case studies.
I. Buckley, Christine, 1972–II.
Title
HQ281.C64   2009
364.15—dc22
2009004957

For my beloved Father

AUTHOR'S NOTE

WHEN PEOPLE FIRST USED THE TERM "SLAVE hunter" to describe my work, I didn't like it. The men who hunted down escaped slaves during the pre–Civil War era were also called slave hunters, but they were bad guys. Yet the moniker didn't go away, and so I started to realize that people simply needed a concrete term to make sense of what I was doing. To the untrained eye, modern-day slaves are not easy to see. I was hunting for slaves. And I was finding them everywhere.

I found my peace with the title.

CONTENTS

Foreword   xi

PART I: **CAMBODIA**

Night Frighting   3

In the Face of Darkness   30

PART II: **CALIFORNIA**

Scream   49

Lollapalooza!   59

Go Sound the Jubilee!   68

Drop the Debt   78

PART III: **SUDAN**

Prelude to Darfur   89

The Time When the World Was Spoiled   107

9/11: Not Good for Business   118

Allez, Allez, Allez!   127

The Freedom Party   136

PART IV: LATIN AMERICA

Si Dios Quiere   151

Sour Lake   165

Tie Yourself to the Mast   186

Ein Sof   212

PART V: MYANMAR

A Simple Twist of Fate   223

Amazing Grace   246

PART VI: MIDDLE EAST

Israel: The Problem with Men   255

Iraq: Their Last Concern   272

Epilogue   291

Get Involved   293

Victim Updates   301

Notes   305

Further Reading   311

Acknowledgments   313

FOREWORD

SLAVERY DIDN'T GO AWAY WHEN IT WAS ABOL-
ished with the Emancipation Proclamation
and the Thirteenth Amendment. It fell off our radar, went underground, and changed its face.

Human trafficking involves the recruitment, transportation,
transfer, harboring, or receiving of human beings through use of
force, fraud, coercion, threats, or deception for the purpose of
forced labor, violence, debt bondage, prostitution, or other forms of
exploitation. In many cases, human trafficking results in modern-
day slavery. This business is tied with the illegal arms industry as the
second-largest racket in the world, after drug dealing. There may be
as many as 27 million people enslaved today—double the number
taken from Africa during the three and a half centuries the trade
thrived there—with approximately 800,000 new victims trafficked
across international borders each year. At least 17,000 of those victims are brought annually into the United States and forced to work
against their will, for nothing more than subsistence. But no one
really knows how many victims there are, since so many are unseen.

This book is dedicated to them.

SLAVE HUNTER

PART I:
CAMBODIA

NIGHT FRIGHTING

PHNOM PENH, CAMBODIA

November 2004

> I don't feel like I can change the world. I don't even try. I only want to
> change this small life that I see standing in front of me, which is suf-
> fering. I want to change this real small thing that is the destiny of one
> little girl. And then another, and another, because if I didn't, I wouldn't
> be able to live with myself or sleep at night.

—**Somaly Mam,** *The Road of Lost Innocence: The True Story of a Cambodian*
Heroine

THE CRESCENT MOON HAS ALREADY RISEN, AND
Venus is shining brightly in the night sky.
I'm following the commander and his men down an unlit back
street. At this hour, the metal gates on the neighborhood's living
room emporiums are all down. The relative quiet belies the not-so-
clandestine activities of the city's shadow world, which bursts into
life after dark. I watch drunken men stagger away from makeshift
street bars and roar off into the dark on throaty Chinese motorbikes.
Children in dirty T-shirts and plastic sandals are splashing in
swampy puddles created by a combination of daily rain and ruts
deep enough to lose sight of a rat, of which there are more than a few.
We pass a small night market, with a cluster of low red and blue
plastic tables and stools where small groups of men have gathered
to slurp soup and homemade rice moonshine. The vendors' candles

3

flicker and cast a dim glow on some of the exotic delicacies on offer. Locusts roasted on tiny coal grills. Duck blood with fresh herbs. Deep-fried tarantulas.

Toward the back of this makeshift market, I spot a dozen or so dogs crammed into cages, ready and waiting for the hot pot. I can hear a few of the puppies whimpering in the darkness, see them chewing at their chains. I wonder if they slaughter them right here, too. No one else seems to notice. We enter our fourth karaoke bar of the night through a door so low I have to fold my six-foot-five-inch frame almost in half to make it through.

The darkened room is long and narrow, with a U-shaped leather sectional facing a large-screen TV blaring karaoke in Khmer, the Cambodian language. A young Vietnamese woman in a short blue dress grabs my elbow and leads me to a spot in the middle of the couch. Other hostesses seat the commander and his men—all in Royal Cambodian Armed Forces uniform—on either side of me. These guys are the Cambodian elite, and I need their approval. Although I'm dressed up in a collared white shirt, I'm suddenly self-conscious about my unruly hair and dark jeans next to their pressed fatigues and linear haircuts.

The images of the dogs don't go away when I close my eyes for a second. I feel for the tiny bottle of green eucalyptus oil in my jacket, shake out a few drops, and slowly rub it into my temples, but it can't prevent the slideshow of canine slaughter scenarios flickering behind my closed eyelids. It's after midnight and there's a full glass of Johnnie Walker Black on the table in front of me, next to a stack of thick plastic binders bursting with photocopied lyrics in six different languages. The table is so low it barely hits my shins.

The rest of the men in the room, whose faces I can't make out in the dim light, are waiting for me to sing. One of them hands me a microphone.

"U.S.A. song," the man in the uniform insists, nudging me. I don't want to sing, not now, not here. I need to focus on the long and ugly night ahead, and it's hard to keep the mood light. But everyone is smiling, prodding me to go on. This is part of the game

I've played for the last few years in a dozen other countries. Now I'll sing "Peace Frog" or "Sounds of Silence," and the commander will applaud, smile encouragingly, and pass me the dried squid as if to tell me not to worry. Life here is like this. Sing another karaoke number to take your mind off reality.

Blood in the streets it's up to my ankles

I'm the only one in the room who knows what I'm singing about—the only one seemingly bothered by the room's crimson bulbs casting a bloody glow over our gathering. I've got to smile, to reassure these men that I can party with them, show them I am not shaken by any of what we've seen or are about to see. No one goes home until the commander says it's time.

As I continue to sing, I notice a young, pretty girl wearing too much lip gloss. She pours more whiskey over a big chunk of ice, picks up the glass with both hands, and offers it to me with a winning smile. I accept it with a nod, then put the glass down immediately and go for the beer instead, which seems more reasonable considering my physical condition. I never get enough time in one place to recover from the jet lag. I haven't fully unpacked my suitcase for a long time now.

The girl with the lip gloss's name is Mai and her English is pretty good. She has been translating for Commander Nam, along with Anh, who's sitting on Nam's other side, feeding him spicy dried peas.

Bloody red sun of phantastic L.A. . . .

Only I'm not Jim Morrison in fantastic seventies L.A. I haven't been home for two weeks now, and haven't had a good night's sleep in even longer.

The commander's men are clapping and humming along to the guitar licks, and I almost start to enjoy myself. But after the familiar Doors lyrics flow out of my mouth, the words of a Cambodian song I heard last night come back to torment my addled mind:

Bright red blood splatters the cities and plains
And over the plain of Kampuchea, our motherland.
The blood of good workers and peasants . . .
Blood spills out into great indignation . . .
Blood that frees us from slavery.[1]

They are part of the national anthem the Khmer Rouge adopted when they took power in 1975, turning the country's clock back to "Year Zero" and unleashing four years of genocidal terror on their people. Yesterday I watched a bootleg copy of a new documentary on the Khmer Rouge's tragic reign that brought all the horror back to the forefront.

Shaken by the resurgence of the film's images and sound, I forfeit the microphone to the soldier next to me, who passes it directly to Commander Nam. He's already programmed in the next song, a thumping Thai love anthem that has the girls shimmying in their seats.

"Cheers!" Nam turns to me, holding up an Angkor beer with a muscular arm and waiting for me to clink my bottle with his. The aged whiskey's presence on the table indicates Nam's high status, as do the abundant tiny plates of salty snacks and spicy dipping sauces. There is an assault rifle leaning up against the sofa next to a square-shouldered bodyguard. The inevitable strains of what seems to be every Southeast Asian man's favorite American song echo from the huge TV speakers:

On a dark desert highway, cool wind in my hair . . .

It's my turn again, and I sing the verses by heart without even looking at the screen, stopping every so often to answer Nam's pointed questions about my past. He listens intently as Mai translates the encapsulated version: my years at the U.S. Air Force Academy, slave retrievals in Sudan, the work with human trafficking victims. I intentionally leave out the part about Jane's Addiction — the proverbial sex, drugs, and rock and roll.

*You can check out any time you like, but you can never
leave . . .*

My opportunity comes during the long guitar solo.

"Commander, I'm going to Siem Reap to retrieve slave girls," I say. "I'd like your authorization, sir, and a unit to back me up."

I can't do this kind of work alone or extrajudicially. In order to escape jail, kidnapping charges, or mafia bullets, I have to put together my own paramilitary team before leaving Phnom Penh. No matter how anarchic it seems to the outside observer, Cambodia still has its own rules—ones that have to be learned and followed. I can't just crash into a brothel on a white horse and break out some girls.

The Cambodian equivalent of a written warrant is an official authorization from within the ranks of the police or the Royal Cambodian Armed Forces, the select corps of men with the access I need. Which is why I have been introduced to Commander Nam.

Nam just nods and makes "Mmm" noises while flipping through the plastic binder, making his next selection. I ask him about a raid my contacts at the American Embassy have told me about in the infamous brothel town of Svay Pak, known to locals as K11—named after its location eleven kilometers from the city center. I've heard there were hundreds of young children enslaved there.

After a long, uneasy silence, Nam makes eye contact with me. Yes, he says, his military unit participated in that bust, which was successful in that most of the brothels there have been forced to temporarily shut their doors. But the traffickers simply found a new location, known as Two o'Clock, which he calls "worse than K11." There's not a lot he can do about it.

One of my friends in the charity world has recommended Nam, so I'm sure he's one of the good guys. Unfortunately, it seems there are plenty of men wearing the same uniform who are not on our side.

Nam watches me consider this, then taps my knee and says in English, "Don't worry, don't worry, my friend, my friend."

Anh is translating now. "Mr. Nam say you want his men help you, you must to do some thing for him before."

"Of course," I say.

"Okay. You get for him girls on video, say what bad things happen, names of who big boss, pictures where the rooms, what look like, where mamasan, where big boss sleeping."

"I can do that," I say. I can start to feel the adrenaline flowing. We're going to do this.

Nam reaches into his pocket, pulls out a silver pen, and writes down a phone number on a paper napkin. "You call Mr. Heng," he says, putting his index and pinkie to his ear as though talking on the phone. Mai and Anh beam at the commander's successful utterance of a complete English sentence. Anh hand-feeds him a morsel of seaweed while Mai pours us both a celebratory glass of whiskey. Both girls take sips from their tall glasses of orange soda.

"Mr. Heng speak good English," says Mai. "Better than me. You call him tomorrow."

"Okay," I say, after telling Mai that her English is very, very good—at least better than my Khmer or Vietnamese—and we all laugh and clink glasses again. Our meeting is over, and—as my military education has taught me to do—I wait for Commander Nam to stand up before me. But first he has a parting song in mind for us.

I recognize the opening bars of a song from my childhood, written by David Gates. It's hard to imagine that while my brother, sister, and I were gathered around our turntable in Southern California singing Bread songs, half a world away hundreds of thousands of Cambodians were being summarily exterminated, tortured, or starved to death.

> There's no one home but you . . . you're all that's left
> me too.

Sappy as the song may be, I'm suddenly singing my heart out, forgetting my surroundings, and drifting away to thoughts of my bedridden father in California. I know he's probably asking Juanita and Maxima, his live-in nurses, how much longer it will be until I come home to take care of him. I miss him, too. Our relationship has grown stronger as his body and mind have grown weaker. Missing him this way, I can't help but sing the song to Papa in my heart.

Commander Nam grabs my arm and shakes me out of my reverie. Concern for my father is rising up in my chest, but I can't let Nam see that my thoughts have drifted elsewhere. He's decided it's time to go, even though the song is only half through. I quietly lay down the microphone and do my best to tidy up the table while I wait for the signal. I'm used to dealing with military men, and have learned how to follow their sometimes capricious orders.

We walk out of the karaoke room through a different door than the one we entered and find ourselves standing in a modest family kitchen. The folding table is sticky with fish sauce and littered with used rice bowls and chopsticks. The karaoke parlor must be this family's living room. Mai and Anh will probably have to wash these dishes and clean up our mess, too. But I can't bother the commander with thoughts like this. He brushes past me and slides up the metal grill, stepping into the empty street. It's 3 A.M. and we both want to get some sleep.

Nam's driver opens the back door of his black Mercedes and gestures for us to slide in. We bump through the side streets of the city for a few minutes before bursting onto the smooth tarmac of Norodom Boulevard. Now we're back in the other Phnom Penh, where shiny SUVs with tinted windows are starting to outnumber cheap imitation-Honda motorbikes. The contrast between Phnom Penh's dusty back alleys and its revamped riverfront is jarring. On the way back to the Phnom Penh Hotel, my tired eyes take in Independence Monument, Wat Phnom, and a shiny, ultramodern shopping mall complete with pop music blasting from outdoor speakers. The display of wealth is harder to swallow when it's juxtaposed with the kind of desperation I've witnessed today. But a small part of me wants to find an air-conditioned bookstore, sit down to sip a chai latte and block out the present for a few moments.

The next morning I wake up in my hotel room with a slight hangover. It's only eight o'clock, but the humidity is already heavy on the flimsy rayon curtain half covering the window. I may still look the part, but at thirty-nine I just don't feel like a party boy in the mornings anymore. Regardless, a party boy looking for underage girls has to appear to be drinking while he thinks—it's part of the image. Guys ordering round after round of Pepsi might as well be admitting they're vice agents.

No matter how exhausted I am, I always make time for my morning ritual. Reading scripture, meditating, and praying immediately after waking centers me and gives me the perspective to face the challenges of days like these. I flip open to the book of Exodus, and reread the passage where Moses confronts Pharaoh and the magicians about the slaves in Egypt, asking them to "let my people go." But today there isn't time for as much study or reflection as I'd like. I've got to move before the heat reaches its peak. I dress quickly in jeans and a loose-fitting cotton shirt and take the back stairs so as to avoid the lobby staff. I'm still not sure whom I can trust.

A *motodop* driver is straddling his motorbike just outside the front door, waiting for me. "Today Mr. A-Ron I take you to Killing Fields! You understand Cam-BO-DYA, you go Killing Fields very important," he says enthusiastically.

Rith was my driver the night before last. He thinks I'm an American tourist here to have a good time—see the sights, maybe find a nice girl to hang out with for a couple of days. He took me to what he called the "best" party places and then waited outside for me for hours, purely in the hope of getting the one-dollar fare home. "I must to eat!" Rith had said with a smile when he saw me nod in his direction. I had just stepped out of my fifth and final karaoke parlor of the night—bleary-eyed from all the whiskey and Cokes—and it was good to see a familiar face. I had paid Rith twice the regular price—so it's only normal he should want to be my escort today at his country's most notorious tourist attraction.

But I wave him off. It's not safe to spend too much time with one driver. I can never be sure if they're working for someone else. At any rate, it's too risky to be a moving target today, so I've promised myself the luxury of a real taxi.

I walk a couple of blocks to the Psar Thmei Market and mix in with the crowd as best I can to make sure I'm not being followed. I spot a white taxi making its way over the potholes, flag it down, and ask the driver to take me to the Killing Fields. Every Cambodian taxi driver knows at least this much English. In a few minutes we've left the polluted city behind and are driving on a paved road in the countryside. The landscape is peaceful and dotted with coconut palms, skinny white cows, and temples. We pass women bent over tending their rice paddies, knee-deep in muddy water. I see men plowing fields with water buffalo and rusty primitive equipment I never would have imagined still existed. It feels like I'm watching a film about life three hundred years ago.

But the tranquil journey has not prepared me for what I see when I walk out onto the fields of Choeung Ek, which used to be an orchard. Inside a Buddhist stupa memorializing the dead, I scan a vast collection of skulls, stacked to overflowing in glass-sided cabinets. My guidebook tells me the stupa holds more than five thousand skulls, although it is estimated that as many as twenty thousand people were executed here alone.

And many of their remains have been left undisturbed. As I walk around the fields, my boots stop short every few seconds to avoid stepping on a fragment of bone.

Between 1975 and 1979, thousands of prisoners being held at Tuol Sleng (a former Phnom Penh high school converted into the Khmer Rouge's infamous Security Prison 21, S-21) were brought here at night and then bludgeoned to death with the butt of a gun, an ax, or any weapon the executioners had handy. Few bullets were used. Babies and children had their heads smashed against the trees. The murderers blasted revolutionary music over loudspeakers to cover the screams of parents forced to watch children meet their violent and senseless deaths. Adults were often sent to their own graves for "betraying the revolution"—manifested by such crimes as wearing glasses, being a teacher, or having learned a foreign language. Tens of thousands more died from disease, overwork, or famine. Over the course of four years, as many as 2 million people, or one-quarter of the population, were lost as a direct result of Khmer Rouge policies.

How can the survivors handle this knowledge? And accept that some of the perpetrators of these incomprehensible crimes still walk among them, and even hold positions of power?

The answer, I think, is that they can't. Only one generation out, Cambodians suffer from depression and post-traumatic stress disorder at rates much higher than the rest of the world.

I crisscross the lumpy earth and mass graves, longing for a shady spot to escape the mean sun that bleaches the sky of its color. I close my eyes and pray for these souls. When I open my eyes again, a small girl is standing there, blinking up at me.

"You buy T-shirt," she says, listlessly pushing her merchandise into my hands. The shirt isn't big enough to fit over my head. And it's covered with pictures of skulls. Not exactly the kind of souvenir I've been thinking of bringing home. But I can't turn her away.

I buy a pack of chewing gum instead, even though I know that the purchase will likely do little to change her condition. She seems drugged and likely belongs to a gang of street beggars run by so-called "aunts" and "uncles" who force children to sell lottery tickets and T-shirts to tourists in exchange for a sleeping spot on the floor and an occasional bowl of meatless broth. She scurries away with a smile, waving the pair of two-thousand-*riel* bills I've given her—roughly one dollar. *With that she can buy a bowl of noodle soup with meat and vegetables,* I think. But I quickly realize my mistake as I watch her run up to a stern-faced older boy, who pockets the bill and barks an order, or more likely a rebuke, at her. My heart breaks for the millionth time.

Back in Phnom Penh, I forget my sadness for a moment as I stroll down Sisowath Quay along the river, looking up at the select buildings that escaped the Khmer Rouge's wrath, and noting their beauty for the first time. After bathing in French colonial architecture for a few minutes, I'm joined by another young girl, not unlike the first—but with wide, intelligent eyes that seem amphetamine free. She's tiny enough to be about six, but I know she is probably closer to eight years old. Generational malnutrition has prevented Cambodian children from growing to their full potential.

Bouncing up and down like a grasshopper as we walk, she slaps her merchandise—a paperback book—against my leg. "You you you! Buy me book!" she insists. I realize that she is not going to let me get away with buying a pack of gum.

Her "book," like most of the foreign language titles sold on the streets and in the bookshops of Southeast Asia, is a pirate edition, painstakingly photocopied and reproduced so that at first glance it appears to be a standard paperback. But it isn't the usual fare: a Graham Greene novel or the latest edition of *Lonely Planet: Southeast Asia on a Shoestring* so eagerly snapped up for three dollars by curious backpackers.

I ask her name, but she ignores me and continues to make her sales pitch: "You buy me book!"

"You're a good saleswoman," I say. "But I feel funny buying your book when I don't even know your name."

"My name Sok Lin," she says.

"*Sues'sday,* Sok Lin. My name's Aaron," I say, using a Cambodian greeting and reaching down to shake her hand.

Lin flashes me a gap-toothed grin now. "You call me Lin, okay. A-ron what mean?" Cambodian people are always asking what my name means.

"Well, it's a Hebrew name that means 'high,'" I say, pointing at the sky as Lin's bright eyes blink back at me. "And my last name, Cohen, means 'priest.' In the Bible, Aaron was the high priest of Israel, Moses's brother and prophet . . ."

I stop here, realizing that Lin's vocabulary won't permit us to have this conversation—at least not yet.

I look down at the book in her hand, which is titled *Sex Slaves*.[2] She gazes up at me, and is apparently oblivious to the impact those two words have just had on my mental state. My left brain insists it's just a coincidence that this child—at the prime age to be targeted by human traffickers—has handed me a book about the very subject I've come to Cambodia to address. But my intuition tells me to be careful. Could this tiny angel also be delivering a message for someone else, someone who's been clocking my every move since my arrival in Phnom Penh?

Seeing my hesitation, Lin switches tactics. "You buy me food," she says, driving home her request with an unmistakable hand-to-mouth gesture. Always a sucker for feminine wiles, I tell her I'll take the book *and* buy her lunch. She's beaming as we cross the street together. No one can smile like Cambodians, and they all seem to engage in the act of smiling unconsciously and utterly without guile. The effect these smiles have had on foreigners is legendary in expatriate circles. Some expats claim the smiles alone are what keep them here.

We sit down at one of several canteens along the quay serving up everything from banana pancakes to pad Thai at prices only Westerners can afford. But Lin seems to have been here before and knows exactly what she wants.

"Hamburger, Coke!" she orders with authority. I sheepishly ask for a plate of stir-fried vegetables and coconut juice, waxing reflective for a moment on Westerners' predilection for healthy Asian food compared to the local tendency to seek out our junk food at any opportunity.

Lin begins to devour her burger, which is three times the size of her tiny hands. At the same time she keeps up a steady stream of small talk:

"How old you, Mr. A-RON?"

"Why you come Cambodia?"

"How much money you get one month?"

"How big you house?"

"You have big car?"

"Why you long hair, like lady boy?"

And, most importantly, "Why you no girlfriend?" Lin stares right through me as she waits for an answer to this one.

I have become used to this form of interrogation from everyone in Southeast Asia. In their culture, pointed personal questions are not considered intrusive, but rather necessary in order to place each person in the grand hierarchy that makes society fathomable.

I do manage to learn that, like many girls in developing countries, Lin does not go to school. "No time, no money, honey!" is her sassy answer. But she deftly manages to avoid responding to my own questions about her life, and so I struggle with the answer to her last one.

Lin's not the first person to ask why I can't seem to keep a steady female presence in my life. The short answer is that most women have a hard time accepting that I spend my time in brothels looking for underage sex slaves. The long answer is more complicated.

Moving from brothel to brothel gathering information, finding lost or enslaved children, and taking care of my ailing father are the only life I've had for eight years now. In many ways I am responsible for an extended family of trafficking victims all over the world. Women who express an interest in me quickly figure out that I am already married to my own father—constantly thinking of him, making sure he is comfortable and has everything he needs. I moved back into my childhood bedroom and became Papa's live-in caretaker three years ago. The fact that Papa's been spared a nursing home sentence is enough for me to forget, most of the time, that I have no real life of my own. This is more than most women can accept.

Sok Lin's question also reminds me that I've got a lot of emotions simmering on the back burner, continually being pushed away to deal with "later"—as soon as I know Papa is comfortable, as soon as I get back from the next trip, as soon as I'm sure the last group of girls are safe. I know that the daily traumas of my existence preclude a "normal" life with wife and family, but that simplicity is something I long for.

For now, little Lin, there's the mission to concentrate on. Then Papa will inevitably be calling, wanting reassurance that I haven't forgotten him.

Midway through our lunch, we are joined by a boy Lin introduces as her younger brother. Eyes permanently focused on his worn plastic sandals, he sits on a tiny stool next to Lin, who offers to share her hamburger with him. I tell him to order what he likes. Another hamburger is on its way when another brother magically appears, followed a few minutes later by Lin's mother with another girl. Everyone politely requests hamburgers except her older brother, Snar, who orders a steak. They consume their food in silence, thank me, and leave as quickly as they came. All except Lin. She hasn't finished talking.

"You know," she says, draining her second Coke. "Here not good place for you to eat. You should go F-C-C." I don't know what she's talking about.

"FCC where all important foreigner go!" she explains in disbelief. "You go there, talk business."

What kind of business Lin imagines I'm in, I'm still not sure. But she obviously knows what's good for me. She takes my arm and leads me down the quay to a magnificent French colonial building and points to the second floor, which has big arched windows overlooking the river.

"That FCC," she says. "Now I go working. You bye-bye." We wave to each other as I mount the stairs. I'm sure she'll have no trouble finding me again.

After several days of breathing in the raw sewage and other indescribable odors on the capital's dusty sun-baked streets and spending my nights trolling brothels and squalid karaoke parlors, the airy sunlit interior of the Foreign Correspondents' Club is a bit of a shock. It immediately feels to me like Rick's in *Casablanca*—a mixture of the exotic and familiar, a refuge from the chaos.

I take a seat at the horseshoe-shaped bar and order a beer, which is a daytime beverage in this impossibly humid climate. An entire wall of the restaurant is completely open to the riverfront. Ceiling fans are turning overhead, and for the first time in many days I feel a relaxing breeze on my sticky neck. Birds are chirping in unseen trees, and I can hear the chatter of pet monkeys down on the pavement, entertaining passersby for their supper. As if to complete the jungle scenario, an elephant saunters by on the street below. He's being led by a young boy who makes his living selling bags of peanuts to well-dressed Cambodians—who giggle as the elephant snuffles unshelled nuts from their children's palms.

Although I've walked up and down this promenade a dozen times, I haven't really looked at the river or thought about its significance. I'm looking down at the confluence of the Mekong and the Tonle Sap, and from up here the fabled river shimmers, seeming placid and almost swimmable. Rustic wooden fishing boats float by, painted in bright colors to ward off evil spirits. It's a bucolic scene.

But dip just below the surface, and there are wretched currents and whirlpools that can drown a man in a matter of seconds. I'm watching the river that enables millions of Cambodians to move their fish, rice, and vegetables down to Vietnam and all the way up through Laos and Burma to China. Looking out at those boats loaded down with coconuts and dragon fruit, I find it difficult to turn off my X-ray vision. The kind of vision that, even from this distance, can see the guns, the heroin, methamphetamines, and human beings packed into the hulls, silently and lethally making their way to their intended destination. There is blood on the rocky banks of this river.

I sip my beer and take in the crowd at the FCC: mostly non-Cambodians—nongovernmental organization (NGO) policy wonks, U.N. employees, and a handful of men and women with the distinctive look of intelligence agents trying not to look like intelligence agents. I chat with a couple of Caucasian guys smoking cigars at the bar. One's a British police officer here to show his Cambodian counterparts how to conduct a human trafficking investigation. His Australian colleague is training Phnom Penh police officers. Both tell me they're being paid via an international grant processed through London's Metropolitan Police Service.

On my other side, a distinguished-looking gentleman from Vienna turns out to be a prosecutor for Cambodia's War Crimes Tribunal, which is finally going after the few remaining Khmer Rouge cadres who oversaw the four terrible years of execution, torture, forced labor, and starvation that deprived nearly 2 million Cambodians of their lives. They're only three decades late.

Although on the surface the atmosphere is relaxed, I can't completely enjoy myself at the FCC. Despite the decade-long presence of the United Nations,[3] this country still seems to exist in a state of lawlessness and immorality. Many of the influential foreigners in this room have come to Cambodia with the best of intentions, but I sense the chaos has corrupted far too many of them.

I start to feel the full weight of the terror campaign over which Pol Pot and the henchmen of Democratic Kampuchea presided. Although a quarter century has passed since their fall from power, the dread they instilled in the populace still hangs in the air. I turn away from the conversation, which has devolved into an analysis of the "lovely ladies" the men know at their favorite bar, Heart of Darkness. They seem oblivious to the connection between their work and their extracurricular lives. Soon they are animatedly rehashing a recent gunfight that left several people dead on the street outside the bar. The banality of violence in Cambodia is such that decent people seem to have lost their capacity for moral outrage. Tonight I just don't have the energy to make small talk with these gentlemen, no matter how amiable they seem.

I take my drink and move to a seat by the open windows, where I can watch the riverfront action. Beggars, their limbs missing or stunted from run-ins with mines, work the crowd along with tiny street urchins selling single cigarettes and flimsy paper lottery tickets. Like me, a few other foreigners are lined up on barstools, drinking with abandon and looking down at the tableau. No one on the street returns our gaze. They are far too busy worrying about where dinner's coming from to concern themselves with the leisure class. Thirty-five percent of Cambodians live below the national poverty line. In other words, more than a third of these people are forced to live on less than forty-five cents a day.[4]

Two well-dressed European women come in and sit nearby. I recognize one of them as Nina, a French aid worker I met yesterday at the Hagar Shelter, where she coordinates vocational training programs. I go over to say hello, and am introduced to Nina's friend, Juliette, a willowy French beauty.

Juliette is an administrator at a Phnom Penh shelter run by Agir pour les Femmes en Situation Précaire (AFESIP), a French NGO known in English as Acting for Women in Distressing Situations. They've just won a grant to care for and rehabilitate victims of sex slavery. Her sentences are the kind that can only be constructed by a humanitarian. I tell her I'm heading up north to research temples—a story I use with everyone not directly related to the mission.

"Naturally," she says dryly. She gets it. But I still have to keep up my cover. She gives me some useful information about the Vietnamese and Chinese Triads and their involvement in human trafficking in the region, and then slides her card across the bar.

"If you have some luck up north," she says, "then it's possible we'll wind up taking care of some of the girls you find at our shelter." Most of the shelters in Phnom Penh, she explains, are full—and even if they're not, Vietnamese girls are often turned away from Cambodian shelters. Despite the fact that they are usually brought into the country against their will, they are still considered illegal aliens and therefore treated as criminals once they are "liberated" from bondage.

Her face twists in emotional anguish as she describes how these girls are sometimes deported to Vietnam, only to get sold back into the system.

"Be careful," she says with a motherly look. She doesn't have to say any more.

We finish the last of our drinks and simultaneously let out audible sighs, which lighten the mood at last. I give Juliette a hug and my card, and head out into the street where the sun is setting behind the National Museum.

I wander the streets for a while and end up in an Internet café, numbly checking emails from friends back in California. While they love and support me, most of them live in a world vastly different from the one I now inhabit. My old friend Darrel Adams tells me about a few high-profile parties I've been missing, and it sounds like he's still ruling a stretch of turf from his native Huntington Beach all the way up to West Hollywood. The old Wedge crew guys—

Phil, Tom, and Mel—describe the unseasonably big waves they've been surfing this week, and tell me to hurry back to get in on the action. At first, their funny, lighthearted emails cheer me up a bit. But well-intentioned questions like "What's going on over there?" only increase my feelings of alienation. I can't explain. So I send back reassuring notes making light of my work and insisting, "I'm fine." It takes a lot out of me.

I step back out onto the quay and watch a small city of fishing boats bobbing on the water, biding my time until it's early morning in Orange County. Then I go back inside to call Papa from a computer cubicle in the back. His voice, once fierce and determined, now sounds like a child's. I've woken him up, and he's upset with me.

Although my sister Ruthie (an expert at keeping Papa laughing and optimistic) is spending a few days with him now, he is still devastated by my absence.

"Why did you leave me again?" he says weakly. "You said you would never leave me, but I need you now, and you're not here!" His childlike manner is heartbreaking, and I lean my head down on the desk to hide my emotion from the other customers. I try to reassure him. "I love you, Papa, and I promise I'll see you soon. Don't forget about me."

It's almost time to head north.

I sleep restlessly, and am awakened by the sound of motorcycle traffic on Monivong Boulevard. Children are yelling and playing badminton on the side street, and adults in exercise gear are walking briskly in pairs, getting their daily gossip fix. It's 5:30—still dark—and it feels like I'm the last one out of bed.

I spend a couple of hours reading and meditating. I pray that Papa will be comfortable and emotionally stable so that I can finish my work without having to race back to the hospital. If I'm gone for longer than a week now, Papa will often refuse to eat or take his medication—without me, he starts giving up, and so does his body. I've already had to rush home from trips to Sudan and Central America after Papa was suddenly hospitalized. I don't want the same thing to happen again.

Once I've gone through my prayer list, I pick up the worn paperback copy of the Tao I've been meditating on lately and lose myself for another hour in the wisdom of ancient China. But I'm quickly distracted by my own anxieties.

Before a journey like this, I have to come to grips with fear and mortal terror. The cliché is true to a degree . . . When death is near, your life's big and small moments flash before you until everything comes to a closure of sorts. It is finished.

My big suitcase is waiting for me in the Bangkok hotel I plan to pass through on my way out of here, so all I have to do is pack a small tactical backpack. By force of habit, I can perform this task in a couple of minutes. I'll be wearing the clothes on my back for the next few days. Along with socks and underwear, I take a low-light digital camera, bulletproof vest and plates, two thousand dollars in cash, flashlight, painkillers, and a GPS unit.

This is the first moment I've had to reflect on what I'm about to do. My first few days in Cambodia have been busy—shaking hands with diplomats at the U.S. Embassy, visiting victim shelters, and meeting bigwigs in the local police.

I've had difficulty with the latter task, since it is obvious that some of the men I've been sitting down with are no foes of human trafficking. In fact, the local NGOs have evidence that many of the authorities here are directly involved in the trade—in a country where there are still few, if any, enforceable human rights laws. Corruption is built into a system where salaries are low and a family man is forced to find alternate methods to pad his income.

One of my main objectives is to learn what happens to Vietnamese girls brought into Cambodia. I have been told that although many of these girls are working in the capital city, even more can be found enslaved in Siem Reap. Most tourists pass through Cambodia's second-largest city when visiting the Angkor Wat temple complex. The increase in the number of tourists making temple pilgrimages has injected much-needed cash into Siem Reap's economy but has been accompanied by a spike in sex tourism—with thousands of underage and unwilling children from Vietnam or rural Cambodian settlements as its victims.

Some are sold to traffickers by destitute parents, while others are kidnapped or tricked into the trade. Once these children fall into the black hole of the traffickers and criminal gangs who control them, it is extremely difficult to help them find their way out. I dream of retrieving some of these young women and getting their testimony on tape—evidence that might motivate governments and regular citizens to do more to combat the trade.

My room at the Phnom Penh Hotel is paid up for the next several days, so I leave the rest of my things scattered around the dresser and desk. If anyone comes looking, it will appear as though I've just gone out for a few hours. Plenty of foreign sex tourists don't have time to sleep in their hotel rooms, anyway.

Instead of calling a taxi from the hotel phone, I flag one down at the market again and ask the driver to take me to the airport. Taking out the paper napkin Nam gave me, I make my second call to Commander Heng and let him know I'm on the move. Law officers by day, Heng and his colleagues command two hundred dollars each for a night of special ops work. Moonlighting of this kind is profitable, but extremely risky. I've asked for four off-duty policemen and soldiers to help me take on the armed guards the Triads pay to protect their brothels and valuable human merchandise inside.

Heng gives me the names of the other men who will join us on the raid.

"We meet you hotel Siem Reap," he says. "Eee-leven clock."

Three hours later, I'm sitting in the lobby of my new hotel, pressing a cold welcome washcloth to my forehead when a slight man with smooth skin glides silently toward me and shakes my hand. His fingers are perfectly manicured. At first Heng seems so delicate and humble, it's hard to imagine him commanding a brigade, not to mention heading up a slave retrieval. But as he warms up, his English gets better, and louder. "You pay now," he says matter-of-factly after asking about my flight and the quality of the air hostesses.

I tell him I can pay four hundred dollars up front and the rest as soon as the girls are turned over to the authorities, and he nods in agreement. I check in, and then get into Heng's truck for a ride to another hotel where he has preregistered my name. I go up to the room, ruffle the sheets, and leave behind a couple of inexpensive personal items to make the place look lived-in. We repeat the process at two more hotels, and Heng explains with a slight smile that anyone following me would have to assign four guys to watch all these rooms—which would put somewhat of a strain on their manpower.

Our last stop is for lunch at the Royal Angkor Resort, a five-star hotel with a sparkling lobby opening onto a gigantic swimming pool. Taking in the splendor while sipping tropical fruit juice, my mind drifts to the young girls I can imagine being kept barely a kilometer away in the most inhumane conditions. The well-heeled foreign tour groups rolling their matching luggage through this lobby will spend three or four days visiting temples, possibly catching a traditional dance performance or cruising Tonle Sap Lake at sunrise. They'll leave with fond memories of the hotel restaurant's spicy fish *amok*, the plushness of its white terrycloth bathrobes, and the genuine smiles of its helpful staff.

These are not the kind of tourists that frequent the 555 or the Tokyo, two of the city's most infamous brothels. They are too polite to ask questions about uncomfortable subjects, and the staff at Royal Angkor has been trained to keep away the kind of taxi drivers that might offer to show unsuspecting visitors such places.

Heng's men are waiting for us in the café. Despite their efforts to blend in by wearing civilian clothes, their rigid posture and serious demeanor give them away. I shake hands with each one, searching for something to trust in each pair of eyes. I stop just short of asking, "Can I put my life in your hands?" But each man squeezes my forearm with both hands and returns my serious gaze. This I take to mean that he in turn is entrusting me with his own life.

After resting and showering at one of my four hotel rooms, at dusk I hit the streets alone, posing as a sex tourist and starting the process I've come to call "night frighting." Finding the brothels in Siem Reap turns out to be as easy as finding a *motodop* (motorcycle taxi). The first driver I ask understands very well when I shake my head at the first few brothels he shows me. "Girls not pretty. Too old," I say. "Where are the pretty Vietnamese girls?"

Just as in any other city where underground prostitution is rampant, taxi drivers are offered incentives for connecting sex tourists with their prey. For every client delivered to a brothel's front door, Siem Reap *motodop* and taxi drivers usually earn a voucher good for a tank of gas.

This driver nods and takes me out of the central city, down a long dirt road and into a shantytown. Here the houses are even more rudimentary than the city's concrete apartment blocks—many are simply a few rotten boards covered with corrugated iron or sheet metal, and I can see that most have an earthen floor. Nearly every home has a telltale blue light glowing from the main room. Although few have electricity, I've been told that people hook their TVs up to old car batteries. There are no streetlights. Only the blue glow and the occasional human form trudging forward in the dim light. Homeless.

We pull up in front of a dilapidated two-story house, and the driver nods in the direction of an armed guard leaning on the door frame. There is no sign. The guard stares at me coolly and steps back to let me pass. His eyes are cold, empty of emotion.

I walk into a small living room, its only furniture a long table serving as a bar and two card tables with plastic chairs. One older man—a Westerner—is slumped behind one of the tables, lost in his own thoughts and sipping an Angkor beer. He looks like the kind of sad-sack, aging backpacker one often sees in Asian capitals. The only light comes from an overhead fluorescent strip that gives the room a purplish tone.

I am met by a hideous sight when I walk up to the "bar"—a dead vulture hanging from the ceiling next to a woman I take to be the mamasan, or slave master. Bald patches and long, greasy hair make her look sixty, although she is probably somewhere in her late forties. Her haggard appearance and pasty skin tell me she's a heroin addict, but there's a glimmer of fire in her yellowed eyes. She must have been beautiful once, I think—a lifetime ago. Whatever beauty she once possessed has been twisted into a mask of resentment and bitterness.

"You like girl?" she says, tapping on the bar with her claws. Up close I can see that the vulture has been ritually sacrificed. There are talismanic trinkets in its dried claws. This mamasan probably uses witchcraft and superstition to control the young women kept here.

"Yeah," I say, surprised at how high my voice sounds. "Not so many, though. Just the pretty ones." I break into a sheepish smile, as if to say, "You know how it is," and absentmindedly finger the Star of David amulet around my neck. It makes me think of home, and the friends who are praying for my safety.

The mamasan nods and disappears behind a flimsy curtain into the rest of the house.

I've met dozens of madams like this one, and most of them have gone through the same hell they put their captives through. Once they get this far, they're dead inside—no empathy or compassion remains. Only a drugged-out empty shell.

When she pokes her head through the curtain again, I say, "First, I want to invite *you* to have a drink with me."

"*Me* have drink with you?" she says quizzically, almost blushing.

"Yeah," I say, flashing her my most charming smile and stepping close enough to feel her alcoholic breath on my neck.

"Okay," she says, disarmed, and pours us two tiny shots of Black Label. She doesn't wait for me—just tosses hers back with her eyes open and slams the glass down on the bar. As I drain mine, I hear the sound of engines revving outside. A group of young men with tattoos and punked-out hair burst right through the door on their motorcycles, still gunning their engines. Vietnamese motorcycle mafia. They park their bikes haphazardly around the front room, sniggering meanly at an inside joke. Several push past me, swarming the bar area and grabbing beers by the handful, like a victorious football team in a beer commercial. A few of them disappear into the back room. Probably going to get their rigs—supplies for shooting up heroin. The look in their eyes is all too familiar.

One of the beer drinkers notices me and comes over to try out his English.

"Whassaname?" he asks me, screeching with laughter as though it's the funniest thing anyone's ever said. Out of the corner of my eye I watch the Western man in the corner slink out the door. He probably senses potential trouble.

The gangster's wiry form is teeming with unnatural energy; his eyes are wild. I take in his dragon tattoos, chains, and long fingernails. I tell him my name, but he's decided on a better one.

"Why Rambo come Cambodia?" he asks, chugging his beer in long gulps before burping loudly.

"I love Cambodia," I say. "It's my first time here, and the girls are very beautiful."

He laughs bitterly, spitting droplets of beer on my shirt. "Noooooooo," he says, staggering. "Cambodia lady no bi-you-ti-ful." He squints and waves his hand in the air. "Vietnam lady very very bi-you-ti-ful. Here . . ." He shakes his hands around dismissively to indicate his distaste.

I wonder what he means, suggesting it's no good here. He and his pals seem to be having the time of their lives. We finish our beers together and talk about music. He's never heard of Jane's Addiction, but tells me he likes Britney Spears—very bi-you-ti-ful. I nod and smile and make small talk to make him feel comfortable. No matter how repulsed I am, I can't afford to arouse his suspicion.

The mamasan matter-of-factly places a bowl on the bar—full of condoms and blue Viagra pills. A couple of the gang members step up and help themselves. When it's my turn to select a girl, I follow the mamasan through the curtain and down a hallway to the back of the brothel. We enter a dark waiting room where a dozen little girls with numbers on their shirts are standing behind a glass wall. I'm sure all of them are less than sixteen—a few look half that age.

In the four years I have been doing research into sex slavery, I have never seen so many young girls in one place. Not to mention all in one room, sacrificing their bodies to men twice or three times their age. And here they are, in my first brothel of the night, on my first night in Siem Reap, without even having to put much effort into the search. I feel like I've descended into a netherworld.

I tell the mamasan I'd like to meet the group of three young girls standing together, and she brings them out to me, leaving us alone in the corner. I speak to the smallest one first, bending in half to reach her—she's only about four feet tall. I hope she can speak English. "How old are you?" I ask.

"Eighteen," she responds in a tiny voice, looking at the ground.

"And who's this?" I ask, indicating the girl next to her, who is slightly taller.

"Sister mine," she says. Her accent and facial features indicate she's Vietnamese, not Cambodian.

I touch the shoulder of the tallest of the three, who comes up to my abdomen. "And is this your sister, too?"

The youngest one nods.

I ask the middle girl, "And how old are you?"

"Eighteen," she responds.

"So you're all sisters, and you're all the same age—eighteen?"

The youngest girl nods.

I tell the mamasan I'll choose her, and we go upstairs. There's no door separating our partition from the others—just a bunch of sheets hanging from the ceiling and bamboo mats on the floor. The unventilated room smells of sweat, sex, and the green eucalyptus oil often used to treat minor ailments here.

Once we're alone, I take my cell phone from my pocket. The little girl doesn't look surprised. Men may have videotaped her before, for other purposes. She is probably about nine years old.

"You're a beautiful girl," I say.

She smiles her innocent smile and looks at the floor again.

"What's your name?" I ask.

"Chau," she says, pronouncing it "Trau." A Vietnamese name indeed.

"Can I take your picture?"

She nods, and I start asking questions about how she got here and where her parents are. Does she have a debt? Does she know how much it is? What does she want to do when she gets older?

I speak quietly to avoid arousing suspicion. But I'm not too worried about the mafia guys. From what I can hear coming from behind the other partitions, they are temporarily distracted. And I've already won over the mamasan.

If I can get a child to express her dreams, then I know the traffickers have not yet managed to completely break her spirit. Chau's life has been full of savagery, but hope is still locked in her soul, and she believes that someday she will have a real life outside these walls. It kills me that I can't help little Chau make that life start right this minute. But I have to be patient. No retrieval without evidence.

Luckily, in a few minutes I have all the proof I need for the authorities to start a trafficking investigation. I get her on tape explaining what she will do for money—the solicitation. To get a trafficking conviction, prosecutors also have to prove the presence of coercion or intimidation. Chau's age alone makes it pretty clear that she has not come to the brothel of her own accord.

Chau goes on to tell me she hopes to leave here someday, as soon as her debt is paid off. "Má need money," she explains, using the South Vietnamese word for mother. Chau says she was brought to Siem Reap from Vietnam by boat, with many other girls. She was given pills to make her sleep, and she doesn't remember much else.

It's a classic case.

When we've finished the interview, I send the photos and audio I've recorded to my second cell phone, which I've stashed in the closet in one of my hotel rooms, ready to receive the download.

I remove the memory chip and replace it with a blank one, concealing the used one in a hidden pocket.

"I have girlfriend," I tell Chau, reverting to my own form of pidgin English. "I lonely. Maybe we just sit and talk, okay? Just massage." I put my phone in my pocket and sit next to her on the mat.

Chau looks surprised and relieved. She stands up to reach my shoulders, and starts rubbing them. I close my eyes and memorize the layout of the place.

After twenty minutes, I give Chau a big tip and tell her to share it with her sisters. Downstairs again, I have a Heineken, tip the mamasan and security guard, and walk out with a nod. They nod back. In their minds, I'm a satisfied customer who may become a regular. They have no idea I'll only be back for the raid.

I repeat the same drill in four more sex bars—each worse than the last—and get back to one of my rooms at daybreak. I want to rinse the smell of these places off my body, but first I set up my video camera in one corner. The video journal is perhaps the hardest part of the night—reliving the horror and putting it in words. What I've just seen and heard is too appalling to tell another human being—but it's my responsibility, and the camera takes it all in. I talk until I finally feel sleep coming on. But my dreams are haunted by the faces of the three Vietnamese sisters, condemned so young to a life in hell. Their lives are ruined.

On my subsequent nights in Siem Reap I meet many more children like Chau and her sisters. When I get back to the hotel I take a sleeping pill, the only way to free myself from the real-life nightmares I keep living. Looking out at a sky filled with stars, I wonder how many slave girls are gazing out at the same sky through their barred windows. Thousands more I will never know, servicing man after man, night after night.

IN THE FACE OF DARKNESS

AFTER THREE DAYS OF NIGHT FRIGHTING, I'M rescued by a call from Mikel Dunham, an American acquaintance who happens to be in town. He's an artist and author of *Buddha's Warriors*, which tells the story of how the CIA helped turn peaceful Tibetan monks into resistance fighters.

Over dinner, Mikel tells me he's thinking of writing a book about the sex-slave trade in Cambodia. He asks if he can accompany me on my investigation tonight, posing alongside me as a sex tourist. I ponder this for a second. Mikel's a fairly rugged guy, but his round glasses and caring eyes make him a rather unconvincing sex tourist.

On the other hand, he's spent years interviewing CIA agents for his book and understands the stakes. He's tough and smart, and I trust his judgment. Besides, it will be nice to have some company. I tell him he can come, but that if things get hectic, he should find a way to leave without making a scene.

Our first stop is the 333 Massage Parlor, right in the heart of Siem Reap's tourist district. Somewhat classier in appearance than the other brothels I've seen in this country, from the outside it looks like an Asian restaurant you might find in an American strip mall — with a neon sign and cheap vertical blinds hanging in the window. The bar and waiting area have a few token plants and a smiling red ceramic cat dispensing toothpicks and mints — completing the "I'm just a restaurant" vibe.

The energy emitted by the men I see here is palpably different, too — more aggressive and affluent than the dejected middle-aged backpackers I've seen frequenting the shantytown brothels. A few

European businessmen sit drinking and talking at a table and a couple of lone Cambodian and Chinese men in casual wear are hanging out at the bar. There is even a group of young Australians toasting the bachelor party they are about to kick off. I've seen this all before.

What *is* noticeable are the conversations and handshaking going on at the opposite end of that same bar—young Vietnamese gangsters in hip-hop gear exchanging business cards with older guys in business suits.

Vietnamese gangs have long ruled the drug business in Southeast Asia, but in the last few years they've been diversifying into human flesh, which is just as profitable and easier to hide than guns, drugs, and precious gems. But to move people across borders you need powerful contacts. I'm pretty sure that the suits are representing foreign Triads interested in Vietnamese women, renowned for their beauty. I take in as many details of these men as possible while avoiding eye contact.

The mamasan brings Mikel and me Heinekens and leads us to a long table with benches on one side of a darkened room where we can view the merchandise. Here, too, the girls are kept in a glassed-in box and are wearing paper numbers pinned to the front of their skimpy T-shirt dresses. It's not unlike a perverted reversal of a police lineup. The madam lets a few of the captives out of their enclosure, and they rush over to us, flirting and caressing our legs and giggling nervously like the girls they are.

When one of them suddenly grabs Mikel's crotch, he looks helplessly at me. I imagine he's thinking about his own children. He may be tough, but he can't handle this. He was expecting to see prostitutes, but these are very young kids. He murmurs to the child something that sounds like "sorry" and picks her up like a baby before placing her on the ground. I know he'd love to put her under his arm and take her away from all this. So do most decent men who see this up close. But it's not so simple. There are layers of hidden barriers in the way.

Without a word, Mikel stands up and moves toward the door, making brief eye contact with me. We don't say good-bye—he knows I can't leave yet and he doesn't want to jeopardize my chances of getting the information I need. He simply walks out, head down.

A group of girls have gathered around me, and I have to choose one of them to take upstairs. I select a child in a blue Hello Kitty shirt wearing stud earrings. She has huge eyes and thick straight hair. She looks to be ten years old. I try not to worry about Mikel and think about how important it is to get evidence on this place so I can return with backup and get these girls out. I have to go on.

Taking the little girl's hand, I lead her upstairs in the dim light and stumble over a pile of garbage—potato chip wrappers, used condoms, discarded tissues, and needles. None of this is new. But thinking of Mikel's face, I can feel the disgust rising in my throat. It gets worse when I pull back the first curtain and see a naked old man thrusting himself into a girl half his size. She and I make eye contact as I let the curtain fall back into place. I can do nothing for her now, and I hate myself for letting my mind do what it needs to in order to go on—instantly start to erase the image of the old man with the hairy back desecrating her, the little girl with the wide, frightened eyes. *He is killing her soul.*

The chamber next door has just been vacated. It reeks of green medicinal oil and sweat, and from the entrance I spot blood and semen on the floor. There's a heap of soiled towels on one side of the dirty mattress. I go into the next available stall—which is somewhat cleaner—and try to focus on my mission. I tape the girl on my cell phone as she tells me her story.

But my mind wanders back to Mikel. Here's a man who understands much of the way the world works, who's far from cloistered—too sickened by what he's just seen here to stick around. Have I become that immune to suffering? How can I keep coming back to these places? What does this say about me?

Upstairs in the privacy of the sex room it is safer and easier to conduct the interview with the little girl. I go through my standard script: I have a girlfriend. I'm lonely, and I don't want to have sex. I turn around for her to give me a shoulder massage; I fiddle with my phone and clandestinely snap her picture. Then I record the audio of her solicitation:

"Yum-yum thirty dollar. Boom-boom fifty dollar."

Yum-yum is oral sex. Boom-boom is intercourse. For twenty dollars more a man can have unprotected sex with this child. Her free will has been removed from the equation.

By the time we finish our talk, I am ready to go home. But I force myself to go to several more brothels—memorizing their layouts, their exits, the placement of the guards. The sadder and more disgusted I feel, the more energy I find to walk up those stairs and pull back the next curtain.

Walking back to the hotel in the predawn cool, I try to look for the charming details my guidebook points out in these tree-lined streets. But all I can see are men who might well be traffickers, and children who I imagine are just steps away from becoming their next victims. It's like a zombie nightmare where everyone seems corrupted.

Back in my room, I call Commander Heng and let him know we have everything we need. He tells me to get some sleep, but to keep my phone on.

A few hours later, it rings. It's Mikel, calling to ask if I'd like to come with him to Ta Prom, a temple hidden in the jungle. He's going to take pictures, and he thinks a walk will be good for me. "Come and surround yourself with beauty," he says. Neither of us wants to talk about last night. I hope he's able to block some of it out.

The time spent outdoors does do me good—we talk about Mikel's son, a musician. It's clear that he loves his kids very much and that last night was really rough on him. He is quick to change the subject to what happened to these temples and the jungle during the Khmer Rouge era. Most of the antiquities, he tells me, were looted. A lot of those statues ended up in museums—not in Cambodia, but in France, the onetime colonial ruler.

We marvel at the craftsmanship of the ancient temples nonetheless, simultaneously awed by their beauty and saddened by their condition—some reduced by war and neglect to little more than a pile of stones. While Mikel takes pictures, I take deep breaths of fresh air and sit in the shade of massive banyan trees with root systems as ancient as the temple ruins. Counting six breaths in and six breaths out, I remind myself that all is one and that it is okay for me to sit as long as I like under these trees.

The jungle has overtaken the man-made temples, and we begin to wander deeper into the old growth. Mosquitoes hum around our heads and I shoo them away, trying not to kill any. Twisting and swatting, I barely notice a large red *X* in faded red paint on a nearby tree. I'm just about to inspect it more closely when someone yells out from behind me.

"Careful!" I swivel to see a young security guard with a kind face pointing to the tree. "Danger," he says.

I've been told that the mines left over from Cambodia's four-year war with Vietnam in the late seventies still remain a threat if you wander off the beaten path. In my sleep-deprived state I might have stepped on unexploded ordnance.

Shaken, Mikel and I walk back to the temple so he can finish his photo shoot. As the sun decreases in intensity, I start to feel progressively calmer. Mikel and I make it back to town by dark and have an early dinner together. "Tomorrow," he tells me between bites of *lok lak*, Cambodian-style steak, "we'll do the main temple at Angkor Wat." I agree readily, looking forward to seeing one of the greatest wonders of the ancient world. Angkor has become a symbol of the country itself. Cambodians swell with pride when they talk about the temples, built in the twelfth century. One of the first Westerners to set eyes on the main temple called it "grander than anything left to us by Greece or Rome."[1]

I watch night fall from the window of my hotel room. This is always the hardest part of my missions. With the night frighting over, there is nothing to do but wait for the raid. And pray. I make a phone call to Papa, telling him I will be home soon and that everything will be okay.

"You won't forget about me if I'm gone another week, will you, Papa?"

"I'll never forget about you, honey," he replies in a haggard voice.

He is eighty-seven years old and feeling insecure that I've been gone so long. Hearing his voice fills me with emotion. I tear up and tell him everything is okay, that I love him, and that I will be home soon.

I think of the kind of letters soldiers write home to their wives, husbands, and parents: "I'm going into battle, but don't worry—I'll make it home alive. I always do!" It must be hard for these women and men not to become bitter when their loved ones *don't* come home alive. When this is the last letter they'll ever receive from their beloved.

I walk back to my hotel room and fall into a dead sleep, exhausted from the miles of walking through abandoned temples overtaken by the jungle. I'm awakened three hours later by a call from Commander Heng: "Two units ready, Co Hai," he says. "We send truck now."

Co Hai is a corruption of the Vietnamese for "oldest sister," which, thanks to some initial phonetic confusion with "Cohen" mixed with a bit of Southeast Asian humor, has been my code name on these missions. The inside joke with the Cambodians and Vietnamese is that I resemble a tall, skinny, long-haired girl.

I splash some water on my face and put on black boots, fatigues, a black T-shirt, jeans, and my bulletproof vest. In the time I have left, I sit on the edge of the bed and meditate on what is to come. I am going into this raid unarmed, at Commander Heng's request. I ask the Almighty to watch over Papa, who needs me, or is it me who needs him?

I pray that all goes well for the children; that the slaves will be set free. Grabbing my gear, I go downstairs to wait for the truck to arrive in the darkness, still meditating and flashing through the images of the children in my mind.

I go into these raids already dead—resigned to the idea that we are on automatic pilot now. G-d is in charge. I close my eyes and wait for the military units to arrive. It's just before 3 A.M.

I wake Mikel with a call to his room, telling him that the commander has authorized the slave retrieval and that I can't catch sunrise with him at Angkor Wat—but if all goes well, I will find him there later this morning. He grunts in groggy affirmation.

Once we're in the pickup truck, Heng lifts up his shirt and shows me an extra 9 mm handgun tucked into the waist of his pants. The other men laugh, telling me that if things get hot, Heng will throw me a niner. I try to smile back.

The second unit follows in a van. There are ten of us altogether—two units of four men each, and two drivers. Our first stop is a tiny shack with a palm-frond roof where street vendors gather to sell their fruit during the day. It's empty at night and will serve nicely as a staging area. The victims will be temporarily safe here until we can get them to the drop-in center near the police station. In the brief respite, I whisper a verse from Job:

These men turn night into day; In the face of darkness they say, Light is near. If the only home I hope for is the grave, if I spread out my bed in darkness, if I say to corruption, You are my father, and to the worm, my mother or my sister, where then is my hope? Will it go down to the gates of death? Will we descend together into the dust?

The guys call out to each other in Khmer over the walkie-talkies. My heart rate picks up. Then we're on our way to the first brothel, where the three little sisters live. We arrive just after four o'clock, and the place is dark. All of the customers have left and everyone else appears to be asleep. Heng orders his men to take their places at the other exits. I follow him through the front door to confront the mamasan, who is sleeping on a mat just inside the door next to a slew of motorbikes. She rubs makeup and sleep from her eyes as Heng speaks calmly to her in Khmer.

There are two ways of doing this, he tells her. If she resists, he will come back later with a bigger team and see to it that she is prosecuted for her crimes. If she cooperates and lets us buy the girls' freedom, then she can avoid going to jail right now. But he offers no guarantee that the Cambodian police won't come back and arrest her once they have a chance to look into the case. The mamasan looks coolly at me and agrees to the sale in one word.

It is as simple as that. The lives of eight little girls are worth five hundred dollars each.

Then Heng hands the mamasan documents to sign—statements that will keep us from being charged with a crime and prevent the mamasan from accusing us of kidnapping. We will have to ask the girls to sign as well. Since the brothels usually have at least one mafia family on their payroll, and because the gangs buy influence with the police, we have to protect ourselves. As the investigation proceeds, our critics will express outrage at the fact that we have handed money over to the industry at all. They'll suggest we are indirectly supporting it in this way. But at least for now, the money will keep the mafia from threatening these girls' families. And the children will be safe for the time being. It's not a perfect solution, but it is better than the alternative.

We agree to pay the mamasan as soon as the girls get to the shelter, and our men go upstairs to find them. Initially our weapons are drawn, but once the commander makes a determination that there is no resistance, we put them away. I follow the team up the stairs until we find the children sleeping together in one room, curled up together on a row of double beds. At this brothel, the captives are all Vietnamese, which makes them more vulnerable than Cambodian children in the same situation, because as foreign nationals they cannot legally be housed in Cambodian shelters. I have contacts with an NGO that can assist them. But first we need to get them to the safe house.

The female counselor, a Vietnamese-American named Linda, approaches the girls and shakes them gently awake one by one. In soothing Vietnamese, she begins to explain to them what is going on. Some are too young to understand what is happening, and several begin to cry out of fear of the unknown. There is no way for me to explain to them that we are on their side. If they have ever known kindness, they have long forgotten what it feels like.

Linda attempts to ease their concerns and tells them they will now be able to go to a school (subsidized by overseas donors and members of the NGO community). Some of the girls permit themselves a smile at the thought of studying everything from math and history to science and vocational programs in their own language. Linda explains that their lives are now in their hands. They may later be asked by the police to testify, but even if they choose not to, they can still go to school. Either way, tonight they are leaving the clutches of their mamasan.

My heart is still racing as we help gather the few bits of clothing and possessions in the room. Linda leads them out the back door into our van.

One of the guards stays behind with the girls in the staging area while we move on to the next place on our list. We raid four brothels that night, saving the 333 for last. In less than three hours, the tiny shack is full of bewildered slave girls about to be transferred to police custody. As soon as they've been interviewed and signed their statements, they will be safely in the arms of people like Juliette and her colleagues at AFESIP or with Stephanie Freed at the Rapha House Shelter.

Watching the girls be processed, I can't help but think how easy it all seemed. No matter how screwed up Cambodia can be, in a few hours we have managed to start turning the wheels of justice. The girls are in protective custody and no one has gotten hurt. I organize the victims' personal statements and prepare evidence for the police commander back at the station, and wonder how long it will take them to go out and arrest the men who have caused all this pain. For now the kids are safe, but I can't help wishing there were more of a unified resolve on the part of the Cambodian authorities to protect Vietnamese and their own children—not to mention prosecute the bad guys.

Heng drives us back to town and we all laugh at how nervous some of the men were during the raid. Regardless, now they are elated—experiencing the kind of rush I used to get after riding a big wave at the Wedge in Newport Beach. They also know they are about to be paid. I ask Heng to drop me off at Angkor Wat. Although the sun has already risen, it may still be early enough to catch Mikel at the main temple.

In a few minutes, the silhouette of Cambodia's crowning accomplishment takes shape on the horizon. We are all moved to silence by the ornately carved towers of the vast temple, seeming to burst out of the jungle ahead of us. The sky gets brighter as we approach Angkor itself, reflected in nearby ponds rich with lily pads and lotus flowers just opening up to the morning. A look of serenity comes over the men's faces as we approach one of their greatest sources of national pride. One of them nudges me playfully, pointing out the impressive sight: "You see, Co Hai, you see Angkor?"

Yes, I assure him. I see.

This monolithic temple complex—originally dedicated by the Khmer king Suryavarman II to one of the Hindu gods—has been holding court in a stand of lush jungle for nine centuries. It's gone through several incarnations since becoming Cambodia's national symbol—representative of a more prosperous era.

Calm at last, I return to my reflection on Job as we approach Angkor:

> Have the gates of death been shown to you? Have you seen the gates of the shadow of death? Have you considered the vast expanse of the earth? Tell me if you know all this. What is the way to the abode of light? And where does darkness reside?

Blue butterflies flit past the window, and my exhaustion helps me slip into an almost meditative state that is all too quickly interrupted by a crackle from the old police radio one of the men has attached to his belt. The disembodied voice barks an order in Khmer, which seems to rattle the team. They look at me with frightened eyes and then back at the radio.

The order comes again—this time I can clearly make out the words "Co Hai." Someone at the police station is giving an order related to "Co Hai"—me. And the men who were slapping my back and congratulating me a few minutes ago are now shifting in their seats and muttering uncomfortably to each other. I can even sense the tension coming from Commander Heng, still solidly at the wheel.

One of the men bangs several times on the roof of the truck with his fist and then flings open the door as Heng slows to a near stop.

The soldier shoots me a panicked look and yells "Me no die!" before jumping out of the truck, rolling out into the dusty road before getting himself up and tearing off in the opposite direction. I didn't know he could speak any English.

"What is going on?" I ask Heng.

"There are orders to bring you in," he says coolly.

"Bring me in?" I ask. "Why? Do they want to debrief me?"

"No," he says, looking at me in the rearview mirror. "They want to kill you."

At this, a second guy leaps out of the truck, also offering "Me no die!" as an explanation.

Mercenaries don't run off before they've been paid. Not unless they really believe their lives are in danger. I look at Heng for help, but his face is noncommittal. I quickly hand him the amount of money we agreed upon for the operation.

"You go now, or police find you," he says, slowing down some more and pulling to the shoulder. The man next to me opens the back door and tries to shove me out.

"Leave Cambodia today!" says Heng insistently.

Stunned, I step out of the car and watch him pull away without looking back. I've been abandoned by my unit, and there's nowhere to hide. But at least they haven't turned me in.

The sun is higher now, light bouncing off the pools in front of the ancient temples. I begin to run in the direction of Angkor Wat, just a few hundred yards away now.

Some drink vendors are setting up their stands, and they look at me strangely. I see a police car parked near the temple ticket booth, and slow to a walk. Trying to be inconspicuous here is impossible when you're a tall white guy with long hair, so I try to play it cool and buy a bottle of water from one of the vendors before turning and walking quickly in the other direction. In a few minutes I hail a taxi and ask him to drive me to the center of town. I get out, speed-walk a few blocks, and hail another taxi. I repeat this evasion tactic a few more times and make sure no one is following me, but I can't shake the feeling that I'm a dead man. I just hope they aren't after Mikel, too. The sun is up now, and I feel as though all eyes are on me.

I rush into Mikel's hotel, hoping that somehow he has gotten up late today and missed the sunrise at Angkor. It's a big relief when I find him finishing his breakfast in the café inside.

"How much time do you need to get packed and out of here?" I ask without explanation.

"A minute," he says, reading my face and simultaneously standing up to pay his bill. "Most of my equipment is already in the trunk of the car outside," he says, explaining that he's just been out for a sunrise shoot. The driver is waiting out front to take him to see more ruins.

"Great," I say, thinking quickly. "I've got to leave Siem Reap now."

After Mikel grabs his bag from upstairs, we jump into the backseat of the car. Mikel tells the driver to forget the ruins and take us the airport instead. "No!" I say, filling him in on what's happened in the last hour. In the meantime, I've gotten a cell phone call from Heng, who's informed me that there are thugs looking for us at the airport. He's instructed me to turn off my cell phone and remove the battery and SIM card. I've got to find another way out.

I explain to Mikel that he, too, might be in danger, and he courageously agrees to travel south. He's already cast his lot with me.

"Drive us to Phnom Penh," he says to the driver, whose face lights up at the prospect of the fare on a six-hour drive. He starts to call the trip in to his dispatcher, but Mikel stops him. "No!" He pulls a hundred-dollar bill from his wallet. "I need your phone to make some calls." The driver nods and hands Mikel the cell without a word.

We both flatten ourselves in the backseat so as not to be seen leaving the hotel. But as we reach the outskirts of town, I realize that I have forgotten to photograph the exterior of the 333 Massage Parlor. I need that picture in order to link the place with the wretched crimes I've documented inside.

"Mikel, we've got to go back into town," I say, afraid he will refuse.

He looks at me as though I'm mad, but immediately directs his driver to the 333. Mikel's been inside this hellhole and he knows how important it is to expose the people who run it. The driver stops just long enough for me to snap a couple of pictures. Then we both scrunch back down in the backseat and get on the road to Phnom Penh, taking turns to look behind us to make sure we are not being followed. Every time a car gets too close, we ask the driver to pull over at a noodle stand or make a loop through a village.

Mikel's experience with Buddhism is very helpful to me during this long, stressful car ride. He manages to distract my mind from mafia assassins by telling me about his adventures in Tibet. He helps me find my breath again, and for the first time during the journey my heart is beating normally. I follow my breath and become mindful of my surroundings. Then I use Mikel's cellphone to dial friends and colleagues who might be able to advise me on what to do next.

I try to reach Michele Clark in Vienna, who knows all about the risk of taking on traffickers—no answer. Then I ring R., my contact at the Pentagon, but his voice mail tells me he's out of the country. I finally get through to my point person in Phnom Penh, who tells me to make my way to the Thai border near Poipet, where some mercenaries sympathetic to our cause might be able to smuggle me across the border. But that means driving back toward Siem Reap . . . which seems like a reckless idea right now.

Instead I decide to call another police commander I know in Phnom Penh—Sok, my highest-ranking connection to the Royal Cambodian Armed Forces. We have met only briefly, but he may be able to help me find a way out. Sok is my last solid hope. He confirms that we are in very real danger. The 333 Massage Parlor, he says, is run by a Vietnamese Triad with direct connections to corrupt police officials. I pray we have not awakened the "sleeping dragon," Cambodia's national police commissioner, Hok Lundy.[2]

"If order comes from sleeping dragon," Sok explains, "all hit men come after you. Must leave Cambodia very fast."

Sleeping dragon or not, each one of those girls we freed tonight would have earned her captors up to one hundred thousand dollars a year. Our actions have probably roused more than one gang boss tonight with some very bad news. By taking back nearly thirty girls, we have just cut off the bad guys' cash flow to the tune of about $3 million. That's something we can feel good about, no matter what comes next.

Ten hours after leaving Siem Reap, Sok is waiting for us in front of the Sunway Hotel in Phnom Penh as promised. Commander Nam is there, too, and both are armed.

Sok touches Mikel on the shoulder and tells him not to worry. "You safe in this hotel no problem." The mafia is looking for a man of my description, not Mikel's. Luckily he didn't stay long enough with me at the 333 to be recognized.

Mikel and I hug good-bye and wish each other luck. We will see each other back in Los Angeles. I watch him walk into the lobby. Commander Sok shakes my hand, and we get into Commander Nam's BMW once again.

For the first time in twenty-four hours I feel secure, surrounded by these guys. Nam's driver takes us directly to Phnom Penh airport in his SUV, flanked by four military cops on motorbikes.

Nam and the other soldiers watch me buy a ticket to Bangkok before Nam walks me to the gate alone. He waves solemnly as I board the plane. There will be repercussions for him now.

I sink into my seat and look out the window at the Cambodian earth. I take a final photo for Papa, who hungrily soaks up the details of my trips with as much relish as he relates his own stories of flying missions over the Congo. I wonder what would become of him if I didn't make it back from this one. Juanita and Maxima would do what they could, but he would have to go into a home eventually; that would kill him. I have to keep it together so Papa can stay with me.

I've got a missed call from Juliette, who I presume will be helping to find places for the victims at the AFESIP and other shelters. Before the plane leaves the tarmac I listen to her message. Her voice is still only a few miles away, but already seems to belong to a distant world. "It looks like the girls are out of immediate danger," she says simply. "Now let's pray they can start a new life. Merci, Aaron."

Bayon Temple, Siem Riep, Cambodia

Sok Lin, age nine,
selling books on the streets
of Phnom Penh

Shot with my camera phone
the night I found Jonty at a
karaoke parlor/brothel. She
was only thirteen and terrified.

Singing karaoke out
on a night fright

Preparing for a slave retrieval

Aaron in the tuk tuk,
leaving Angkor Wat

Angkor Wat temple complex

PART II: CALIFORNIA

SCREAM

PERRY FARRELL: "We're trying to make adults sick."

KURT LODER: "Do you think you've succeeded?"

PERRY: "Yeah, I'm sure of it. My father won't talk to me."

—MTV interview with Jane's Addiction at the "grotty storefront space where they were living with a large chicken," just prior to the 1988 release of _Nothing's Shocking_

THE FIRST TIME I SAW PERRY FARRELL WAS ONSTAGE with Jane's Addiction at Scream in downtown L.A., circa 1987.

I was a junior in college, and I used to cruise up to Ninth and Grand a few nights a week with my friends Colleen and Dave to hear what was probably the best underground music in the country. We weren't aware of it then, but we were smack in the middle of the end of Southern California's punk heyday. Whether you want to call it postpunk or pregrunge, all that the three of us knew was that it was a great time to be young and on the live music scene. A lot of the local bands we were seeing at holes-in-the-wall for next to nothing—like TSOL, Fishbone, and the Red Hot Chili Peppers—were on their way to becoming big international acts.

By age twenty-one I was a head taller than everyone I knew and obsessed with playing the guitar, growing out my hair, and my attitude. Up until then, I had been the obedient middle child in my family of five. At Costa Mesa High School I was a water polo All American who, at my father's urging, had earned a spot at the U.S.

Air Force Academy. Not submitting to Papa's authority had been out of the question.

Although I had struggled with the rigorous requirements and ambience in Colorado Springs, I wanted to please my father and did everything I could to take the academy's "Integrity First . . ." motto to heart. I relished the long hours spent reading, writing, and gazing at the mountains, and I learned to love the camaraderie and orderly aspect of military culture. At the academy, everyone had a defined role. Just as it had in high school, being a part of the water polo team made me feel protected and taught me patience. I thrived under pressure, working with my teammates toward a common goal.

After a water polo injury sent me to the hospital, the academy doctor took my height and weight and offhandedly told me that I had grown too tall to eject from a plane. My lifelong dream of being a fighter pilot like Papa was shattered in an afternoon. Although I considered pursuing a career in military intelligence, I decided to put my energies toward fulfilling a second goal: playing for the U.S. Men's National Water Polo Team, an opportunity I'd been denied at the academy. My father, who had long regaled me with stories of his World War II glory days flying in and out of Casablanca, was devastated by the news I had lost my pilot qualification and maybe even more unhappy with my decision to leave the academy to pursue water polo and another dream: music.

My best high school buddy, Phil Castillo, helped me land a full water polo scholarship at Pepperdine University, close to home and the waves in Malibu, California. There I got to play for two of the country's best coaches—Terry Schroeder and Rick Roland. I lived out my water polo dream there, scoring goals, becoming an NCAA all-American, and eventually being selected for the U.S. national team by legendary coach Bill Barnett.

Burnt out by my years with the Air Force, at Pepperdine I played hard but still threw myself into academics and became the editor of the campus literary magazine. Working out with the National Team twice a week and making college team practice twice a day while carrying a full academic load would have been exhausting unto itself, but I made time to improve my guitar playing and tune in to political activism while listening to U2 and Bob Geldof.

By my second year at Pepperdine I had launched a standard late-adolescent rebellion—against my middle-class upbringing by a religious mother, militaristic father, and straight-arrow older brother, Arthur. I grew my hair out, wore mostly black clothes and combat boots, and cared more for playing guitar and writing punk rock than anything else.

Around this time, my father told me that if I didn't cut my hair and get serious, he would stop speaking to me. I think Papa's exact words were "Either you go back to military intelligence in the reserves and give up this music crap, or we're finished."

But I had become a good guitar player by then. Music was in me—and no matter how much I wanted my father's respect, it wasn't something I could just "give up." Hanging out with my friends Dave, a.k.a. Hairball (for his matted hair that he rarely washed), and Colleen (who changed her hair color about as frequently as most people look in the mirror) was much more about the music than the drugs they had started using. My friends were starting to get into heavier things like heroin, but I was a reluctant participant. I wasn't buying my own.

That would come later.

The night I first saw Perry was also the first time I had been to the Scream club downtown. Colleen, Hairball, and I roared up on motorcycles and made quite an entrance in the wake of Colleen's purple hair. The decrepit hotel lobby made us feel as if we were walking onto a vampire film set. Inside, I remember being mesmerized by the black light paintings on the walls and the avant-garde audience. Every woman looked like someone I wanted to know. And the Goth guys were a coven of stylish vampires, a far cry from the detached punk aesthetic I'd been perfecting over the last few years. But still, I was edgy enough to blend in. Which was unusual for a kid from Orange County.

From a surfing perspective the O.C. had it all, but when you live in Los Angeles, Orange County was (and still is) largely written off as bourgeois white suburbia: the antithesis of cool. What the Alternative crowd didn't know was that the O.C. had a hard-core and punk scene that rivaled L.A.'s. From age fourteen, I had been following an older crowd of surf-riding punk rockers to a club called the Cuckoo's Nest. While my mom thought I was at the movies with other kids my age, I was thrashing around to the sounds of Dead Kennedys, 999, and Black Flag. I was still in the process of shaking off the Orange County image while living in Malibu; the long hair and combat boots helped. But any insecurities I might have had faded away when Jane's Addiction took the stage.

It wasn't the music that got my attention first. The singer totally captivated the audience from the outset. The other musicians—Stephen Perkins on drums, Dave Navarro on guitar, and Eric Avery on bass—were supertight, but all eyes were on Perry Farrell. He didn't play an instrument, but he didn't need to. His look, his presence—his sovereignty—conveyed it all.

People around us were smoking pot, eating mushrooms, and shooting up right there. It was already a pretty hedonistic scene, and then suddenly here was this strange alien being onstage, just pouring everything he had into the performance. At first he came out wearing a woman's camisole and bondage gear. One second he was a praying mantis, rocking side-to-side on his raptorial legs in a soulful dance as he sang a sad song about losing a friend to a drug overdose. Then he'd be staring into the eyes of individual audience members, singing: "*Oh baby, I know about war . . . But I just want to fuck! I know about pain and suffering and being cold, but I just wanna . . . Fuck . . . The pig is led to the slaughter . . .*"[1]

Colleen and I looked at each other and let out a cry of freedom, joining the audience in a feverish dance. Her joy stemmed from the proximity and sex appeal of a soon-to-be rock star. What got me were Perry's honest, heartbroken lyrics. They reminded me of my own struggles.

When the set was almost finished, Perry went offstage and came back out totally naked, except for some strategically placed sheer pantyhose. Then he stretched out his arms and lost the pantyhose, shocking us all. I can still hear the collective gasp that went through the crowd. Next he stepped directly off the stage into the mass of people, as though he were the Messiah walking on water. This got Colleen and all the girls in the room into a frenzy. Some of them even rushed the stage, crying and reaching out for Perry, scream-ing his name. While most people were in awe of the spectacle, a few seemed outraged by it. With my religious upbringing I couldn't help visualizing Sodom and Gomorrah—it all felt so forbidden. I remember thinking, "Man, if my brother saw me here, he'd dis-own me."

After that night, Jane's Addiction started headlining at Scream. I spent many Saturday nights there, usually with one or both of my best friends. As time went on, I watched the drugs and drinking take a toll on Colleen and Hairball. More and more people were coming to see Perry perform. The occultism and sense of danger that he evoked with every brooding move sent people into states of euphoria. None of us had seen someone dance and sing like that. Even his name, a play on "peripheral," conveyed the kind of life we were all leading, or wanted to lead . . . on the fringes. The bound-aries were where it was happening, and Perry's dark omens and out-rageous visions took us there. He was king, and no one could touch him. Seeing that kind of freedom of expression was a revelation to me. The energy I took home from Scream every weekend started to inform and inspire my own writing. More than that, I was develop-ing a new sense of tribal identity. I wanted to be a part of something bigger than myself.

It didn't take long for people in my wider circle of friends to start showing the effects of the drugs and excessive living. But I had fallen in love with another Pepperdine student, Rebecca Young, and con-tinued on the path to graduation. I poured my creative energies into writing prose poetry for her. With Becky and Colleen's encourage-ment, I eventually got up the courage to enter a creative writing con-test. My submission was a short story I'd written about a father and son who can't get along. A few weeks later, Colleen came running up to the pool after water polo practice to tell me I'd won the prize.

"You did it!" she squealed, smacking the top of my wet head with the Pepperdine student paper, which had run an article about the contest. A few days later, my award was mentioned in the Malibu newspaper as well, and Colleen said, "Cool, just think how many shows we can get into with your prize money!"

Later that night at Scream, Colleen—whose hair had gone from purple to jet black—met a musician and left me stranded at the club without a ride home. Hairball had wandered off to an after party and had probably gotten himself into trouble. I took the Wilshire bus all the way to the beach at Santa Monica and then hitchhiked the rest of the way home to my dorm. All the while I was composing poetry in my head, full of ideas for the future.

Becky loved music, too, but the club scene started to cause a rift in our romantic relationship. She hated me being around druggies and temptation in the form of alt-rock girls. I loved her so much that I thought I would do anything to make her happy. But fear of commitment pushed me into doing the opposite. That summer— without consulting Becky—I said yes to an offer to play semiprofessional water polo in Buenos Aires. The gig would give me money to travel around the continent, learning about music and magical rituals in Peru, Argentina, and Bolivia. I found myself surrounded by new music and beautiful people, but I stayed in shape and told myself I would eventually go home and marry Becky. Yet having no clue of my plans, by the time I got home in the fall she had already moved in with another guy and wouldn't speak to me. I was devastated, and used the pain as an excuse to experiment with drugs.

I'd only been back a couple of weeks when I got a call from Ted Gardner, who identified himself as the road manager for a band called Jane's Addiction. Had I heard of them?

I couldn't believe it. Ted had seen the article about my writing award in the Malibu paper a few months back and had managed to track me down. He said Perry Farrell had asked him to find a partner for an upcoming film and a few video projects. He wanted writers who could think visually—outside of the box.

"Yeah, of course I know the band," I said casually. "I love the music."

So Ted set up an appointment for me to meet Casey Niccoli, who was then Perry's girlfriend and creative collaborator. I waited for an hour at a café near their place in central Los Angeles, but she didn't show up. The next day I got a call from Perry, who apologized for Casey's blowing me off.

"I'm so sorry about that—she and I've got problems," he said. "Can you come over tonight?" They were then living near Sixth and La Brea. I went over wearing my Air Force Academy jump boots and long black military shorts. I got the sense that Perry liked how odd I was. Originality was really important to him. It wasn't high fashion or spending money on clothes that he valued, but rather a sense of personal style and following one's own instinct. He hated conformity.

His and Casey's apartment made that ethos pretty obvious from the second you walked in. It looked like the cross between a fashion designer's studio and the chaotic backstage of an experimental theater. I tripped over a papier-mâché sculpture on my way in the door. Wild costumes peeked out of black garbage bags, and the floor was covered with cans of spray paint and other art supplies. In the kitchen, ants were crawling on a mound of candy that had been left on the counter.

Perry was pretty mellow at that first meeting, but Casey was standoffish and spent a lot of time grilling me. At that point, Jane's first studio album, *Nothing's Shocking,* had been out about a year and had spent more than six months on the charts. Sudden fame was simultaneously energizing and exhausting, and so the band was taking a bit of a break from performing to work on songwriting and ideas for future projects. Perry told me that he and a filmmaker friend were putting the finishing touches on a *Nothing's Shocking* documentary called *Soul Kiss.* The next thing he and Casey were working on was a semiautobiographical love story they had tentatively titled *Gift.* They were in the process of lining up the funding and production people, and planning to star in it themselves. I could tell these two loved each other, but I also sensed some serious tension.

"And then there's our new album; that'll be out next year," said Perry. "But what I want to know is, what can you bring to the table? What kind of stories do you want to do?"

I told them about what I had learned in Argentina and Peru. My heartbreak over Becky had driven me into researching love-related ritual magic. "Man, there are witchcraft stores and Romeo and Juliet–type love potions, spells, and rituals that would just blow your mind," I said. I thought all of it would make a great storyline.

"I see two people battling each other with magic, essentially to win each other's love. Instead of bringing them together, the magic ends up bringing about the woman's death. When he finds out, her lover commits suicide."

"I love that," said Perry. He was really friendly and open to unorthodox ideas. And even though I had expected him to behave strangely, he surprised me by being remarkably articulate and thoughtful. By that point it was getting late, we had already finished a bottle of wine, and Casey was about to go and score some white (cocaine) and black (heroin)—the ingredients for a speedball.

Just before she left Perry said, "Hey, I'm working on this new track; it's really cool. Check it out." He had the rhythm down, and he played it for me. "Can you play that?" he asked. I smiled. Because I could.

So Casey got me a guitar, and we started jamming while Perry tried out the words to a new song he was writing. It was called "Then She Did," and would later make it onto the *Ritual de lo Habitual* album. I knew a lot of people who could sing and play guitar, but Perry's voice, rhythm, and timing were phenomenal.

"That's about my mom," he said quietly when we had finished playing. "She was an artist, and we used to do really cool projects together."

Perry's mother had died tragically when he was three. I got the sense that the lyrics he was writing were helping him reconcile with his past. My poems and songs had been helping me do the same.

I was in the midst of a difficult phase with my family then. Papa was still angry with me for having left the Air Force Academy, and my mom was worried that I had lost my moral compass.

My "normal" brother and sister both thought I was a freak. But I couldn't imagine what losing your mom at such a young age would do to a person. We ended up talking about a lot more than music that first night—everything from Jewish families to surfing to spirituality. Perry was more or less estranged from his dad at that point, which was why I think my short story had resonated with him. The more we talked, the more we found we had in common. I hadn't bonded with another human being like this in so long—maybe ever. I think we each felt we had found a soul brother. And I know Perry appreciated that I was treating him like a regular person, instead of a rock star.

When Casey got back with the drugs, they offered to share them with me, but I begged off, since the red wine had already put me in a pleasant place. I had never shot up, and wasn't about to do so in the midst of what amounted to a job interview. The two of them disappeared into a back room for a few minutes while I got accustomed to Perry's guitar.

Then Perry came out again, looking energized, and asked, "Do you have anything you can play for me?" I immediately thought of a song by a Cuban revolutionary musician that I had dismantled and made my own. It was going to be hard to play without thinking of Becky—I'd planned on coming back home and playing it for her. But here I was with Perry Farrell, and I wasn't going to mess this up.

"Silvio Rodríguez is kind of like Cuba's John Lennon," I said. "He was a hero of the Latin American Left, a favorite of Che Guevara's. A bunch of Latin American dictators have even banned his music." Perry's eyes lit up at that thought.

"It's a sad song about two lovers, and one of them's painting a picture of the other, but he's not happy with the way the picture's turning out, so he keeps changing his perspective. He's painting this picture but the woman's just not going to make it, and instead he ends up just watching her die."

Perry was paying close attention now. Casey had plopped down on the floor with her score and was listening attentively.

"But it's really a metaphor for the relationship between the U.S., represented by the man . . . and of course Cuba and the other Latin

American countries our government has manipulated over the years are portrayed as the woman," I explained.

My guard totally down, I sang this tragic love song for them. Rodríguez's composition is musically sophisticated and requires classical picking. I wanted to show Perry what I could do. By that point my voice was warmed up, too, and I nailed it. The last line, which roughly translates as "While once I cried for myself, now I cry watching her die," was thematically linked to the suggestions I'd just made for the film Perry and Casey were brainstorming. It all seemed to click.

I held the last note as long as I could, relishing the moment. I could tell we were all on the same wavelength and that we were about to start a working partnership. Perry and Casey started cheering and then rushed toward me and tackled me together, guitar and all. We fell into fits of giggles.

"Can you work again tomorrow night, man?" Perry asked, still grinning.

I was about to join the circus.

LOLLAPALOOZA!

VENICE, CALIFORNIA

Winter 1989

L ISTEN KIDS, YOU MAY THINK THAT YOU'RE Picassos . . . but this is a business. I'm giving you this money so that we can make more money, not so you can make art. If you make art, and make money at the same time, that's fine, but I do mind if you make art that doesn't make us any money."

After a few months making the rounds at the studios, we'd finally gotten a half-million-dollar budget from Warner Bros. Records to make Perry and Casey's gothic love story, *Gift*. Landing the funding from a major label was a big moment for all of us. I was still in college and starting to feel as though I'd been plucked from planet Earth and dropped onto a celestial body spinning much faster than I was used to.

Sitting in the executive's office, I remember the thrill of realizing that we were really going to make the movie. In a few short months I'd learned a lot about the music and film business as well as my own abilities and limitations. But I couldn't ignore the nagging concern that the wild antics of Perry and his crowd were going to make for a bumpy journey. Of course we nodded our heads vigorously at John Beug's directive to make money for them. And then went off to make art.

I'd gone to work for Perry that fall, after my last year at Pepperdine. I'd drive up to Los Angeles from Malibu and work all night brainstorming ideas with Perry, spending many nights crashing on his couch.

I eventually moved into the Park La Brea Apartments in Los Angeles with a couple of friends. Soon after that, Perry introduced me to heroin. He seemed to think of my place as a sanctuary whenever he and Casey were fighting, which was often. At first he would come over to get high; we'd smoke weed and work on videos and ideas for the movie all day. At night we'd go to the studio, where Perry was recording and mixing several tracks for the upcoming *Ritual de lo Habitual* record. One day, after we had already made some progress filming a few video scenes, Perry showed up at my place alone.

"Aaron, I hope it's okay that I came over," he said. He looked disheveled and upset—a sign that he'd been fighting with Casey. "I just thought I'd see if you were up for partying with me."

"Of course, Per, come in, man."

It was my first time doing heroin, and it was euphoric, at first. I don't remember getting any work done that day, but that night Casey came over with a pair of cutting-edge female musicians and a few band aids (groupies) who wanted to stick themselves all over Perry. I had been high since the afternoon and by that time wasn't feeling well. My skin was itchy and I felt nauseated. I just wanted to feel normal again.

I ran into the bathroom, vomited for a while, and eventually crawled back into bed. The next thing I knew, my roommate David Imbernino was shaking me and frowning at the two girls, curled around me in a groggy pretzel formation. We had inadvertently crashed in David's bed instead of mine.

"Aaron!" he yelled. "Rock stars out of my bedroom, please!"

It was only 2 A.M., so I invited everyone into my room, where we did more drugs and played strip poker. My head was spinning and I was down to my underwear, but somehow I didn't care. Perry, Casey, and I eventually left the others passed out in my bed and drove downtown to score more drugs. We stayed up all night, playing music and driving around shooting video.

A few months after Perry and Casey left Hollywood for Venice,

I took their advice and moved out to the beach myself. Perry considered himself a regular guy, and even when his fame grew he resisted the urge to move up to the Hollywood Hills to live behind a security fence—not his style. His new place was just a short drive from the studio on Venice's Abbot Kinney Boulevard. That studio, and the alley behind it—Electric Avenue—were consistently packed with swaggering rock stars and fawning groupies. Perry's fans, in particular, had a tendency to fall in love with him to the point of madness. One of my jobs was to keep the stalkers at bay. The studio offered a neutral environment where band members could mingle with their family and friends, and it turned out to be the home of the wildest parties of the Jane's days. If things got too crazy, Perry could always sneak out and catch a ride back to his house.

Wild parties came with the territory. But I quickly vowed to tone down the hard drugs so I could concentrate on myriad aspects of the business. I felt I had no choice. It was clear that everybody around me was falling apart. I wanted to see the *Gift* movie get made and finish the *Ritual* album, which I loved but could see was suffering from the double distraction of drugs and groupies.

These girls came in droves. At one of the Jane's shows as many as thirty women begged me for access to Perry. Swept up in the music, they would throw themselves at him and the other band members. I worked hard not to treat the "band aids" like an expendable commodity.

I also figured that if one person could just give Perry the attention and stability he needed, we could have a hit record. So I started to take on every role and responsibility I could. Over the course of the next few years I would play the translator, on-tour road manager, best friend, and all-night recording buddy. I'd eventually become the executive director of Perry's business. The other two people holding everything together were his managers, Trudy Green and Adam Schneider.

When Trudy, Adam, and I were around, one of us would connect the dots and make things work. Jane's Addiction was a pretty volatile band. We were able to smooth things out for Perry and help everyone keep up with the dynamic pace Perry's creativity dictated.

By that point I had moved into 803 Oakwood, about a mile from Perry. A colony of Jane's people rapidly sprouted around us—all of us working and partying together. In many ways it was like a circus or fraternity—there was always someone around, sleeping on the couch or walking into the kitchen to make something to eat or grab a beer. I had almost no privacy, since there was no real separation between work and home. My living room was also the office, and from nine to seven every day Perry's assistants, producers, and all kinds of other creative people came flowing in and out. After dark we would transition into studio or party mode—sometimes both. I prided myself on being able to resist the drugs and temptations of that environment, but I was taking sleeping and anxiety pills on a regular basis to keep up with the workload I had created for myself. Still, in the beginning everyone was excited and inspired to get started on *Gift*, and for a while that energy held everything together. When we came home from the Warner Bros. meeting with the news that they'd given us a budget, spirits were soaring.

During that period we'd been making music videos for a hundred thousand dollars. So suddenly having five times that amount to play with was fantastic. The only problem was that almost everyone was so strung out on drugs that we found ourselves spending thousands a day on crew and unused rental equipment while the cast lay around drug-sick. I found myself with the responsibility of having to score drugs to get the cast "well" enough to film. Once the studio people realized that a fair amount of our budget was gone with nothing to show for it, they decided to bring in an outside producer. He wasn't the world's most creative guy, but unlike me, he knew how to say no to Perry.

Over the course of the first few months I worked for Perry, we became like brothers. He started asking for more of my artistic input, and Casey seemed to grow progressively more hostile toward me.

In an attempt to relieve some tension, I brought in a rock video director friend of mine, Mark Racco, who I thought might add a little inspiration to the film project. Mark was a handsome filmmaker who rode a Harley and ran around with guys like Axl Rose and Kurt Cobain. He and Casey hit it off, which freed me up to concentrate on working with Perry.

I very quickly found myself demoted from producer to filmmaker, along with Mark. He and I pulled together the film logistics and chose locations in Mexico, where my Spanish came in handy. Casey and I tangled over her insistence on hiring a real Santería black magic priest to perform the rituals they wanted to film.

"Casey, I don't feel comfortable with this," I said. "This is real life and we're not simply hiring an actor to play a role here—we're talking about somebody who has made a deal with dark powers and can do things that we don't want to be involved in."

She didn't want to hear what I had to say. Her response was "All right then; you're fired. You don't have to work on this film anymore."

Perry defended me, pointing out that I had come up with a lot of good ideas. Casey seemed blind with rage and jealousy, and although she backed down for the moment, I felt she had it in for me. The situation was painful, since I believed she was a talented artist with a great sense of style. But I got the feeling that her insecurities extended to anyone who dared to break into Perry's inner circle.

I stayed in the hotel while they filmed the black magic wedding sequence, and in a few days we traveled to Mexico City where Jane's was scheduled to give a concert with the popular Mexican band Los Hijos del Quinto Patio. The first night in town, Los Hijos showed us a bunch of trendy nightspots, but Perry and Casey couldn't enjoy the scene because they were sick and needed more heroin.

"You're the one that speaks Spanish," they begged. "You've gotta score for us."

The next morning Casey came up with the idea to go to the emergency room, pretend that she was having a miscarriage, and ask the
doctors to give her something for her pain. She needed me to translate, of course. So we went through an elaborate script, and Casey
managed to talk the doctors into giving her what she wanted—morphine and syringes. She was a brilliant actress. Perry high-fived us
on the way out as Casey mumbled, "We got lucky because I was so
convincing, not thanks to Aaron's Spanish."

I said nothing. By then I was used to people taking credit for
my work. I didn't need or want the recognition for a drug score,
anyhow. This was a pivotal realization, although it would take
me years to act on it. I was still young and had not yet found the
confidence I'd need to do something more universal with my
abilities.

Later that afternoon, as the band was preparing for that
evening's concert, I walked out of my room to find Eric Avery in
the hallway jamming on his bass. He was such a virtuoso, and I sat
with him for a while just listening and admiring his talent. After a
while, Eric started confiding in me some of his frustrations with the
band—mostly that he wasn't getting enough recognition. I simply
listened and tried to be a friend. Since it was still a few hours until
call time, I invited Eric to come shopping with me to take his mind
off the situation.

When we came back, Perry shot me a look of betrayal. There
was an unspoken understanding that I was *Perry's* friend, and my
loyalties rested with him. Yet I saw Eric as a brilliant musician—his
natural leadership simply drove him into conflict with Perry. The
fact that I was now bonding with Eric was incompatible with being
Perry's best friend.

I took a couple of days off and drove down to meet the film
crew in San Blas, where they were supposed to be shooting a surf
sequence. But it turned out there were no waves, and so they hadn't
managed to shoot anything. Perry still had some liquid morphine
left and was happy and animated when I arrived. I told him and

Casey, "It doesn't matter that there's no surf. Let's just have fun on the beach."

If they weren't going to shoot the surf sequence, we were at least going to make sure we went home with *something* to show for our time. Mark grabbed the Super 8 camera and went out to film the young couple trying to throw each other in the water and frolicking in the waves. Their unmistakeable love for each other translated beautifully onto film. The sequence ended up being one of the classic scenes in the movie. But after looking at the dailies, Casey announced that I would now be the camera operator—yet another demotion.

Here I was once again being punished for doing things right. I still kept my mouth shut, but the handwriting was on the wall. As we flew home, I saw myself from the outside in: a guy struggling to be sober surrounded by people on drugs acting like adolescents. Yet I couldn't imagine giving up my commitment to Perry, who despite his weaknesses still respected and valued my input. And we needed to finish the film. We were missing a shot of Perry getting "tubed," and there were no waves on the Southern California horizon. Just as I had so often done in my high school days, I stayed by the TV watching the satellite picture until I noticed a swell in southern Mexico.

"We should just fly down there and nail the sequence," Perry suggested, and next thing I knew we had chartered an aircraft and were on our way down to Tijuana, our final destination being the virgin airstrip on Isla Navidad—Christmas Island, halfway down the Baja Coast.

But first we had to stop to pick up drugs, and by the time we took off, everyone except the pilot and me was high. I was getting tired of having to pack everyone's bags and babysit them afterward. Once we landed, Perry and Mark were basket cases. They were coming down off the heroin and there was no more to be had.

So there we were on a deserted island, ready to shoot the surfing sequence. But when you're coming down off heroin, the last thing you want to do is get in the water. You've got hot and cold shivers. On top of that, before we left Venice, the tension between the band members and the rest of the entourage had just about reached its breaking point. I had become the unofficial ambassador between Eric and Dave's clean club and the junkies, led by Casey and Mark. Perry wavered between wanting to be high and wanting to do a good film. He cared deeply about the art but was too sick to concentrate.

Mark and Perry and a few of their friends went into the village to wander around, but I stayed behind with the pilot, feeling disillusioned and trying to connect to nature. In those couple of hours, head-high waves started rolling in. I jumped happily in the surf and rode until I could push my job worries to the back of my mind. But we still missed our chance to get the tube shot. By the time Perry came back and got in the water, the surf had died down.

After two days of waiting for the waves to synchronize with Perry's rare moments of sobriety, we were all suffering from the heat. That night we decided to sleep in the open air, all lined up under the wing of the plane. We'd already spent $150,000 with nothing to show for it, and the following morning was our last chance to film the sequence before we had to fly home.

We were awakened at dawn by a loud metallic "Bang!" that reverberated through the shell of the empty plane.

Someone had sat up and banged his head on the wing. The airplane resonated like a drum, evoking a tribal rhythm. Lined up next to Mark and the pilot, I looked over and saw Perry sitting on his sleeping bag. "Lollapalooza!" he proclaimed, rubbing his head. We all laughed at the one word that managed to sum up the confusion and frustration we were all feeling.

On the flight back, I started to tell Perry about my anxiety. The Jane's Addiction roller coaster was taking me in directions I didn't want to go, but I didn't want to quit. I knew there was so much more we could do together. Perry understood, and told me that the previous night he'd dreamed about running away and joining the circus. "Lollapalooza's the perfect name," he said, "for what we're going to do next." Something outstanding and exceptional.

He explained that the constraints of being in a band were too much for him, too, and that he wanted to work with a wider range of musicians within the freer format of a music festival.

Back in Los Angeles that afternoon, Perry talked to his road manager, Ted Gardner, who went to Marc Geiger at Triad Artists. Lollapalooza had just been born.

GO SOUND THE JUBILEE!

VENICE, CALIFORNIA

1991–1996

[The Jubilee Debt Campaign] embodies aspirations and values shared by peoples of all faiths. It echoes the trumpet call of Jubilee first heard in the ancient scriptures of the Jewish and Christian faiths: when those enslaved as a result of debt are freed, lands lost because of debt are returned and communities torn by inequality are restored. It is the call to let the oppressed go free.

—Jubilee Debt Campaign

THE BIRTH OF LOLLAPALOOZA SIGNALED THE PEAK of Jane's Addiction's fame as well as Perry's drug use. Casey checked into rehab soon after *Gift* and the *Ritual* album were finished, but even after she had left the scene it was virtually impossible to engage Perry in meaningful dialogue. He was doing so many drugs that he almost seemed possessed. Yet even in that state he wielded an intense curiosity backed by an arsenal of creative and spiritual gifts—most of which intimidated people who didn't know him well enough to understand his talent.

It felt like the end of an era, and I finally gave up trying to heal my friend. I was weak and tired and wanted to stop thinking so much. After eight months of being clean, I dove full throttle back into drugs one night, joining Perry on a big run downtown to score with his new girlfriend, Kim. Then we drove back to Perry's place and went crazy. Shooting up cocaine and heroin speed balls can generate delusions and even psychosis. The user often hears voices or feels monsters coming after him. Injecting heroin with the cocaine evens out the paranoia, so that one can withstand the gallery of monsters. It sounds crazy to say that this state would have seemed in any way desirable, but alongside Perry I saw myself as an addict-artist; a character in a supernatural horror story who needed to experience this kind of transformation in order to feel alive. I even managed to convince myself that my drug problem was a kind of "research."

We were slaves to the drugs together. Perry's managers were having a hard time convincing him to give up his study of black magic, which had brought out a side of him that rightfully frightened everyone else away. Speaking in tongues and channeling dark spirits while sitting cross-legged on the floor, he resembled the mysterious praying mantis he had tattooed on his upper right arm.

Often we'd spend days hiding out at his place, exploring the darkness. One night, Perry walked out of his closet after shooting up and I noticed blood running down his arm. He had been mixing so much cocaine into the hits that he was having convulsions. When he was like this, I would take care of him, as he had done for me. We had learned to support the other when one of us was too far gone to clean up the nine bloody needles on the ground or take the gun out of his own hand. Anyone who saw us during those days ran away in fear or disgust.

Our frequent drug binges were getting expensive, and they lasted longer and longer as time went by. Most runs lasted three or four days. But sometimes we would lock ourselves into separate rooms and get high until we ran out of drugs or burst out paranoid and hallucinating. Weeks like this became months, and then a year. Perry was so spooky and mystical that he had chased most of his entourage away. Aside from an occasional phone call, I had virtually cut off contact with my family.

One afternoon, Perry was down at the beach and came upon some dead seagulls. He arranged their carcasses along with pieces of scarlet yarn and magic symbols at the entrance to his apartment complex. To him it was an inspired art project. The neighbors, however, took it to be some kind of powerful satanic ritual and called the police.

Although I was high myself, I tried to explain Perry's artistic perspective to the cops, who had no idea who he was and were not impressed by my reasoning. Instead they looked at me as though I was crazy, too, and started to ask a lot of questions. After handcuffing Perry and looking around a bit, they agreed to leave as long as we agreed to remove the sacrificial collage from public view.

I knew I couldn't keep going on this way. Then one morning the living room phone rang. It was Papa. We hadn't talked in a while, and I was surprised to hear the raw emotion in his voice. "I know things are bad between us, Aaron," he said. "But I need you to put aside our differences." I braced myself for what was coming. Another lecture about coming down to earth and getting a regular job.

"I'm not perfect and neither are you," he said, "but I'm going to control my temper, and you're going to quit those drugs and stop hurting yourself."

I started to protest, but he went on.

"We need you here. Mother's cancer is back," he said, with tears in his throat.

I couldn't believe it. The illness that had largely dictated the terms of my childhood had returned. My mother, Lynn, was first diagnosed with breast cancer in 1967, when I was still a toddler, and by 1969 had suffered through a double mastectomy and hysterectomy. In a few short years L.C.—as I liked to call her—had been transformed from a fashion runway model into a cancer-ridden mother of three. In the process, both of my parents' hearts broke. Virtually abandoned by her husband, L.C. clung to her baby boy like a life raft.

I had asthma from an early age and was dependent on inhalers and pills to control my breathing—an addiction my mother inadvertently encouraged because it kept me at home, where I became her confidant and emotional codependent. In the past, Papa was unable to handle her illness and had responded by withdrawing emotionally and having affairs. By 1972 he had virtually moved into a rental property he was managing in downtown L.A., where he could find his "peace and quiet." When he did make an appearance on weekends, he was verbally and physically abusive, especially to me, his whipping boy. I learned to provoke his anger—preferring he heap it on me instead of my mother or sister. My siblings dealt with his betrayal in their own ways.

Arthur took over as father/enforcer. Even though Ruthie was the youngest, she became the mother/cheerleader while L.C. and I were relegated to playing the roles of docile children. My brother, a model student, was also the one making sure the trash was out, the lawn was mowed, and Ruthie and I had done our chores. L.C. and I were emotional wild cards who could get out of anything by invoking our respective illnesses. If I didn't want to go to school, I simply wouldn't go. Nobody would doubt the veracity of my asthma attacks. Meanwhile, Ruthie had developed a stand-up routine that we thought rivaled Carol Burnett's. One of her favorite jokes when she was about five went something like this:

"What did the zero say to the eight?" (comic pause before the punchline)

"Nice belt."

Then she'd make the sound of a rim shot and take a bow. Somehow she made the three of us believe that with a little laughter, everything was going to be all right.

My earliest childhood memories are tinted with the blue glow of the television as my mom and I sat huddled in her darkened bedroom under our blankets. Back then, my favorite days were the ones that started with a heavy dose of my asthma medicine, to which I had been addicted since the age of six. Arthur and Ruthie would have already gone to school. Mother and I would stay in bed all day watching television programs about the Bible.

L.C. had always been a woman of faith, but became more zealous after she befriended a faith healer, whom she largely credited with keeping her alive after the first cancer diagnosis. So she had me studying and debating biblical prophecy from the get-go. The best way to spend time with my mom and see her happy was to sit with her and study the Bible.

Initially, Arthur took to Bible study more readily than I did. Our mom's miraculous remission had transformed him into a sort of adolescent biblical authority, which caused serious problems between us, because I refused to allow him to manipulate me with the scriptures. He meant well and I really needed guidance, but I was young and damaged from my relationship with Papa. As I got older, I became a more reluctant scripture student, especially after I discovered surfing and punk rock.

My mom refused to define her religious denomination with any one term. "I'm a woman of faith," she'd say when my father, an avowed "reformed agnostic," would tease her about her devotion. He'd courted a Hollywood "it" girl, and now he saw himself as married to a terminally ill religious saint. My mother responded by loving him even more. "Because I love the L-rd I can forgive your father everything," she used to say.

Now in a tragic way, my mother was giving me the perfect excuse to leave Perry and the rock star mess behind. Papa handed her the phone. L.C. did not waste time expressing the main thing on her mind. "I want you to come back and study Hebrew," she said.

Within a few weeks, I had given Perry notice and moved back into my old bedroom in Costa Mesa. I enrolled myself in a master's program at nearby Vanguard University, taking classes in Hebrew, Middle Eastern studies, and the books of Genesis, Exodus, Leviticus, Numbers, and Deuteronomy.

Two instructors at Vanguard changed my life. The first was Professor William C. Williams, my strict but benevolent Hebrew instructor who for some reason decided to tuck me under his wing. I was so excited by the course load and my transition home that I stopped doing drugs altogether. Within a few weeks of my departure, Jane's Addiction split up and Perry left Casey—but their drama already felt so far away from my new reality that I barely paid attention.

My classes were so inspiring that I looked forward to waking up early for the first time in my life. We began each Hebrew class by singing a few classical songs, which stirred my soul to the point that I'd take the sheet music home and learn to play the ancient melodies on the guitar. When the time came to sing them with the rest of the class, I felt like I was a part of a new band, freed from the demons that had long haunted me.

It was around then that I met Professor Murray Dempster, who led me to my thesis subject: Jubilee, which I first took to calling "peace through music." Dempster dressed in a suit and tie, yet wore a beard and his hair long. His patience and vision had earned him the wholehearted respect of both faculty and students. Dr. Dempster never tired of my questions, and constantly steered me to new resources. He was my first intellectual mentor.

With Dr. Williams's and Dr. Dempster's help, I began to develop a vision for what the Jubilee could be: a framework of time to set things right, restore life to suffering people, and revive a sense of hope that we were all one people. At a modern Jubilee festival there would be no discriminating mind; no pity. No one would ask for help and no one would "help" in the traditional sense—because no one single person would be seen as being "in need." I came to see that we were all in need. Once we entered the realm of nondiscrimination, we were free to love and be loved.

The word *jubilee* means "to blow the ram's horn." The shofar was a trumpet used in ancient ceremonial festivals during which captives were set free, debts were forgiven, and land that had been seized was restored to those who would preserve its environmental integrity. Jubilee was also a year of reckoning and a time for prophetic revelation. In the Hebrew calendar, a Jubilee period (fifty years) was made up of seven blocks of seven years each. The first year of each seven-year period was known as a *shmittah*, a sabbatical year of rest. After seven *shmittahs*, or forty-nine years, the following year was known as the *jubal* year, or "Jubilee"—a time to celebrate and be jubilant, for the land and people were at peace. This period was celebrated with music, feasting, the freeing of slaves, and the forgiveness of debts.

The deeper I dug, the more meaning and hope I found in Jubilee. Leaving behind a fast-paced life of music, travel, and excitement for middle-class suburbia at age twenty-seven did not always feel like the best bachelor move, but for a while I successfully shifted my focus from music and parties to books. Those first two years back at home became a spiritual and physical rehab for me. As I was healing myself, L.C.'s condition began to stabilize, and I spent a lot of time sharing my newfound knowledge with her. We bathed in books and delved into the significance of what I came to label Jubilee 101, peace through music, and Jubilee 202, dropping debts and freeing slaves.

By my second year at Vanguard, L.C. started fading away again. She lost the use of her right arm and suddenly needed all of her meals cooked and served to her. My brother and sister had children and lives of their own, and my father was working full-time to cover the medical bills that were stacking up. Afraid that my mother's illness would frighten my father away as it had before, I left school to become her round-the-clock nursemaid.

I felt as though I had fallen back into the unhealthy relationship L.C. had established for us during my childhood—only this time it was me counting her breaths as she developed pneumonia and slipped further into the abyss, pulling me with her. I started to resort to the same tactics I had sought for protection as a child. It started with her Vicodin pills and graduated to stronger painkillers and sleeping pills.

As this pattern established itself, I realized I desperately needed a creative outlet, and found it playing guitar and singing with a pair of talented local musicians, Daniel and Andy. They had a studio a mile from my house, and in our jam sessions I finally found the release I'd been craving. Soon after that we met Scott, who could play bass, piano, and sing backup, and all of a sudden I had artistic partners again.

The trouble was that these guys were dabbling with heroin, and I slowly fell back into drug use. It was partly a way of dealing with the pain of my mother's pending death, for which I'd been preparing myself for so long but was still not ready to accept. Soon I was taking one type of pill to go to sleep and another to stay awake and keep watch over her. I was diving back into the escapism of the past, getting high late into the night and ghosting around the house while my mother's lungs struggled for each breath.

Perry had started reaching out to me, sending me emails and calling periodically. He missed me and I missed him. He loved the idea of having a friend who didn't need or want anything from him. An actual friend.

I became that friend again. Perry and Stephen Perkins had formed the group Porno for Pyros in 1992 and were already putting the finishing touches on their second album. Whenever they had a big recording session, Perry would invite me to come down to the studio. I'd go down there and he'd be all tripped out on drugs, so I'd take care of him for four days while he laid down a hit record. He didn't need me creatively. I was there because I cared about him as an artist and a friend. I saw Perry as a kind of king, and I just wanted to make sure His Majesty was okay. I had my own artistic path now, and hoped I could inspire him to launch the Jubilee movement with me.

Perry's estranged father was very ill then, too. I remember driving up another time to spend a weekend with him in Venice. My brother had come out to stay with our mother, so I was free to take off for a little while. Perry had just finished a recording session at a studio near Zuma Beach, and we went to Malibu afterward to surf. He told me he was writing a song for his father and asked my opinion of the lyrics.

"Should I sing 'Good gods' or 'Good G-d?'" he asked me.

"Good G-d, good G-d," I said.

But he just shook his head, smiled, and ignored me. Then he sang a bit of the new tune for me, right there on the beach.

I was still amazed at Perry's ability to distill an emotion so perfectly into song, ghosts and all. It was the right moment to tell him about peace through music and the Jubilee. About all I'd learned. He listened intently. It turned out he'd been looking into the same thing himself.

"Hey man, we've got to do something with that, then, huh?" He paused thoughtfully. Jubilee was our new common ground.

"As soon as we take care of our parents, right?" Perry put his arm around my shoulder, and told me he was praying for my mom. We sat in meditative silence on the beach for a while. It was time for me to go be with my mother.

My father, brother, sister, and I were all reunited around L.C.'s hospice bed as she lost consciousness and slowly left us. We sat quietly together for a few hours, cried, and faced the reality of her death.

I went back to the empty house and played a John Lennon song over and over: *My mommy's dead, I can't get it through my head . . .* That night I passed out in my clothes with my shoes on, and woke up only to cry some more.

With her death, I lost my sense of purpose. For three years I had been doing nothing but studying abstract religious texts and taking care of my beloved mother. I didn't know what to do next. I sat in the empty house for weeks and mourned before getting a call from my surfing buddy Phil Castillo, who understood how much I was suffering. I forced myself to drive down to Newport Beach and the Wedge with Phil, where our old friends Terry, Tom, and Mel let me have all the best waves that came in. The water was incredible that morning, and as I faced the awesome force of nature I thought more deeply about forgiving debts and setting captives free. I came out of the water baptized, energized, and fully broken.

Still, I spent the next months grieving for my mother and lamenting what I had become. As a tribute to L.C., I drove up to a family reunion in Big Sur to see my cousins Brendan and Randy. They made me feel loved, and staring down at the sea together we said it seemed as though we had arrived at one of life's turning points.

On the way home, I found myself steering toward Venice.

I stopped by Perry's. He was sitting in the kitchen, putting the finishing touches on a song. He had plenty of new music he was excited to play for me, and I had a bevy of poems and short stories I wanted to share about my mother's last days. But when he expressed interest, I changed the subject and decided to keep the poems for another time. He walked over and gave me a hug, as if to say, "Don't worry about it, Aaron, we don't have to talk about it now."

We had work to do.

"Per, we've got to go sound the Jubilee!" I proclaimed, smiling while tears found their way down my cheeks.

"Yah! My old friend is back!" Perry said, with a huge smile.

I looked at him and felt a lump in my throat. "I've got some ancient melodies to share with you, Peretz," I said, using the Hebrew name I had not pronounced for too long.

I started tapping my foot and humming to get the tempo right. For the first time in months, I was singing again.

DROP THE DEBT

Millions of lives are being lost for the stupidest of reasons . . . money, and not even very much money. So let's not play "who are the good guys" and "who are the bad guys."

—Bono, explaining why he was willing to work with George W. Bush on solutions to global poverty[1]

PERRY AND I STARTED STUDYING THE KABBALAH and Jubilee more intensely soon after my mother died in 1996. I moved back to Venice so we could work together on what was going to be our most important collaboration yet. Porno for Pyros was dissolving, and when Dave Navarro took a break from the Red Hot Chili Peppers, Perry and Stephen Perkins pulled together a Jane's reunion the following year, with Red Hot Chili Peppers bassist Flea replacing Eric Avery. The six-week Relapse Tour produced an album (*Kettle Whistle*), a documentary (*Three Days*), and forced Dave and Perry to struggle with their drug demons once again.

I went along for the tour, only this time I didn't slide back into debauchery. Having our Jubilee studies to focus on helped Perry stay afloat as well. On stage, he started to casually preach to fans in between songs about the Jubilee, presenting it in terms they could understand: "You know, this is a Jubilee year coming up, and that means all debts are forgiven. Can you dig that, can you try that? I'm gonna try it . . . like, think of the cat you hate the mother fuckin' most. You don't gotta love him, cause that's too fuckin' hard, but just say, 'All right, you know, we can share the same lunch table,' and all that."[2]

By 1999, Perry was working on a solo album and had more time to devote to studying with me. Finding a way to turn the Jubilee principles we'd been examining from abstract biblical concepts into concrete practice was going to take some time and effort. I thought that if we could teach other musicians what Jubilee was about, we might inspire them to get on board.

So it seemed like a sign from the universe when Ann Pettifor, the executive director of the Jubilee 2000 Coalition, called from London. Ann and her colleagues had proposed the cancellation of $100 billion of unwieldy debts owed by poor and developing countries to creditors like the World Bank, International Monetary Fund, and commercial banks by December 31, 2000. Offering "a fresh start for millions of the world's poor," Jubilee 2000 had begun as a grassroots movement and was gradually gaining strength as the new millennium approached. These were our kind of people.

Ann had seen an interview Perry and I did with *Playboy* explaining what Jubilee was and the various ways it could be celebrated. We knew that Pope John Paul II had started sounding the Jubilee earlier that year, lobbying for debt cancellation and preaching in the name of global justice and tolerance. Theologian Ched Myers had been inspiring activists of all faiths to call for debts to be dropped in time for the Jubilee year, which Christians were preparing to celebrate in 2000. The Catholic Jubilee coincided with Jesus's two thousandth birthday celebration and the pope's apology for the role the church had played in the Holocaust. Perry and I were waiting for the Jubilee to arrive in 2001, the year the Orthodox rabbis of Israel had set aside for national study of Jubilee.

The Jubilee Coalition had done a good job of reaching the faithful—now they needed a broader appeal. So the Jubilee 2000 organizers asked if Perry and I would share our Jubilee inspiration and knowledge with the musicians and activists in the Jane's Addiction and Lollapalooza circles. We were honored to oblige. By that point Perry had already started talking about Jubilee in interviews;[3] now he took out his Rolodex and started putting in calls to Lenny

Kravitz, David Bowie, Bono, Bob Geldof—everybody he knew in rock royalty. Perry would set up the contact first, and if they were interested I would follow up with a fax containing more detail about the ancient festival and what it could mean for the modern world. For the most part, the more people heard about Jubilee, the more they wanted to know.

A few weeks later I met Bono and the Edge backstage before a Jane's show in Miami. Bono had already lent his name and support to a range of human rights causes and was interested in learning more about what we were planning. We talked before the show about the layers of hidden meaning in Jubilee—forgiving debts, addressing poverty, and freeing slaves. But then the house lights went down, and all eyes were on Perry.

That was when I got the feeling there was something beyond a healthy rivalry going on between these two rock giants. Perry gave a peak performance that night, nailing his high vocals and dancing as only he could. Bono's eyes were riveted on Perry as he suddenly climbed up on a stack of speakers and fearlessly executed an elegant dive, landing on the stage two feet from Bono, holding his high note from *Nothing Shocking's* "Ocean Size" all the while. After making his gymnast's landing, he was up on his toes, arching his back and finishing the song:

>   *In the sky lives a spy*

I felt like Perry was sending a message to Bono with this display: "You're a pretty good singer, man, but can you do this?"

As the crowd applauded and screamed for more, I looked over and saw Bono acknowledge the move to the Edge. U2 had achieved global renown, but Perry's performance was hard to rival. Even after all of his career ups and downs, he had clearly not forsaken his title as the godfather of alternative rock. He went on that night for several encores.

After the show, we all went back to the Delano Hotel in South Beach and talked about the upcoming Jubilee 2000 campaign. Perry referred a lot of the questions to me, and I shared what I knew with

Bono, who was well informed on the economic side of things but, like many people, less attentive to what we had to say about the Jubilee's prophetic implications regarding the nation of Israel. Still, by the time we said good-bye that night, we were all excited about the Jubilee.

Back in California, Perry expanded our effort by recruiting politicians, movie stars, and bankers into the movement. One of the most important calls we made was to Inter-American Development Bank president Enrique Iglesias. Bono was soon on his way to meet Iglesias and start talking about how to reduce Latin American debt. The word was getting out. More and more musicians began to take an interest in the Jubilee movement, and I knew we were making headway when people started calling *us* to ask what they could do to help. That was where I came in. I fielded calls from managers and followed up with visits to Gwen Stefani from No Doubt, Nirvana bassist Krist Novoselic, and Dave Grohl from the Foo Fighters. Our Jubilee study group of two had turned into a movement people were asking to join.

One morning Perry told me expectantly he'd just gotten a call from Bono, who was finally home in Ireland and wanted some more details on Jubilee. "Can we send him that three-pager you've been working on?" he asked. I faxed it over, and an hour later, Bono joined our Jubilee study session on speakerphone. Perry and I had already spent hundreds of hours doing research and challenging each other to find modern interpretations of the ancient texts. So it was a joy to be answering Bono's questions together.

Over the next several weeks, we dissected the Jubilee by phone while Bono listened and occasionally interjected. These brief sessions led to a few discussions with Bob Geldof, who was committed but, like Bono, preferred to focus on the details of the campaign rather than the mysticism of the ancient festival. That didn't worry me. While Bono and Geldof were talking Jubilee 2000 up in the media, I turned my focus to preparing talking points for the other musicians who were going to help us gather signatures for Drop the Debt, an offshoot of the Jubilee Coalition. We were planning to deliver the world's largest petition to relieve Third World debt at the Group of Eight (G8) summit, the annual meeting for leaders of the planet's top eight industrialized democracies.

Perry and I went back to his Rolodex. After securing sponsorship from House of Blues, which had a venue in many American cities, we got in touch with every major musical group touring the country and asked them to present a Drop the Debt petition at their shows that fans could sign. Perry was on the phone to everyone in the business—from road managers to the folks at MTV—to make sure every show signed up. Bono and Geldof took the lead and did the same, and we soon had a grassroots movement on our hands. Meanwhile, Ann Pettifor and her people were covering Europe.

As the leaders of the Group of 8 (United States, United Kingdom, France, Canada, Germany, Japan, Russia, and Italy) gathered for their annual forum in Cologne, Germany, that summer, Perry and I flew over to meet Bono, the Edge and Bob Geldof along with Radiohead's Thom Yorke and Youssou N'Dour, who had since joined the effort. With the help of thousands of human rights activists and music fans, we had managed to gather an impressive 24 million signatures encouraging the world's richest countries to forgive the debts of the poorest. Bono walked onstage and handed the giant petition to German chancellor Gerhard Schröder as the rest of us looked on. I looked to Perry for signs of that old rivalry, but he just smiled. It didn't matter who got the credit. We had all worked together to make this historic moment happen.

At the press conference, Geldof answered questions like a prince, with grace and eloquence. Whenever the question dealt specifically with what Jubilee was or how it was being implemented, Perry and I would handle it. Later on, we joined hands with the crowd in a fifty-thousand-strong human chain. All of the fans screamed and cried when they saw Bono. He had an amazing power to connect with people and get them to hear his message. Thom Yorke, who'd been cracking jokes with me all day, gave me the signal to head back to our hotel. After a long day of meetings and rallies, we deserved a few beers. Thom and I sat at an outdoor café and toasted the more than $300 billion in debt reduction that had just been announced. Even though that sounded like a crowning achievement, Ann Pettifor pointed out that the agreed-upon sum merely offered "crumbs of comfort" to the poorest of the poor—although it looked like a lot, the debt relief the bankers had negotiated amounted to a bag of rice per year for the average person in that group. We still needed to do more.

Nonetheless, our Drop the Debt experience had given us the proof that the music world was willing to put some momentum behind our efforts. And the public wanted to help—they just needed to be given a head start. I knew we still had some difficult subjects to grapple with, because understanding global poverty and enslavement was a process, not an event. Sitting there with Bono, Geldof, Yorke, and Farrell—guys who understood that—I believed that peace through music was becoming less of a fantasy and more of a possibility.

But the Drop the Debt campaign was just one pillar of the Jubilee dream. Everyone had already started to call me "the Jubilee guy," and I now felt it my responsibility to push further and explore the more esoteric aspects of my subject. It was time to motivate an entire new group of musicians and celebrities to free the captives.

With U2's The Edge at the G8 Summit,
Cologne, Germany, June 1999

Perry and Bono at a café during the
G8 Summit in Cologne

Playing music with Perry at a Jubilee
festival in San Francisco, 1997

With Perry Farrell and Thom Yorke (background),
at the G8 Summit, Cologne, Germany, 1999

Standing on Capitol Hill,
the day I went to a hearing
on Sudan to testify about
what I'd seen there

Senator Sam Brownback testifying
about slavery in Sudan to the Senate
Foreign Relations Committee,
September 2000

PART III: SUDAN

PRELUDE TO DARFUR

LOS ANGELES INTERNATIONAL AIRPORT

Winter 2000

> There is perhaps no greater tragedy on the face of the earth today than
> the tragedy that is unfolding in the Sudan.
>
> **—Colin Powell, newly appointed secretary of state, speaking at a House**
> **Foreign Affairs Committee hearing, March 6, 2001[1]**

Y OUR BAGS ARE OVERWEIGHT," SAID THE AIR-
port desk attendant flatly. I was carrying
too much food. Having already given up any hope of fashion
sense, I'd left my second pair of shoes, jeans, and a dress shirt at
home. But my childhood surfing buddies Tom and Phil, who were
now experienced outdoorsmen, had filled my pack with trail mix,
protein bars, and self-heating meals. I was ready for a long winter on the tundra! As I shifted some heavy things into my carry-
on and handed a few packets of nuts over to a woman in line who
was greedily eyeing my snack food, I could barely believe I was
actually headed for Sudan. Africa's largest country is more than
twice the size of Western Europe.[2]

Months earlier I had turned on the TV to a PBS report on
modern-day slavery in the Sudan. At that point I had some vague
notions of the country's famines and widespread poverty, but was
still blown away by the images I saw. Human beings were being
used as the spoils of war—raped, killed, or torn away from their

families and forced into lives of servitude under inhumane conditions. The documentary both horrified and educated me. My new inspiration started to take shape as I sat watching Colorado schoolteacher Barbara Vogel talk about how shocked she had been to learn that the most unspeakable of man's crimes was thriving in Sudan and Mauritania. Like most fourth-grade teachers, she'd been telling her kids that slavery had ended with the Civil War.

Vogel's class raised enough money in 1999 to free hundreds of people from chattel slavery in Sudan through Christian Solidarity International (CSI), a nonprofit organization based in Zurich, Switzerland. The kids had started their own awareness campaign, STOP: Slavery That Oppresses People, and prompted their congressman, Representative Tom Tancredo, to raise the issue with then-Secretary of State Madeleine Albright.

Sitting on the sofa with Papa that night, it occurred to me that if a handful of Colorado fourth-graders could free slaves with proceeds from their lemonade stand, then a group of influential musicians and concert organizers like the ones I had worked with on Drop the Debt could certainly make some waves. The next day I drove to Venice to see Perry. He listened, nodded his approval, and went off to write music. I started making phone calls.

In the fall of 2000, I learned that Vogel and a few members of her class were on their way to Washington to testify in front of the Senate Foreign Relations Committee about their grassroots efforts to combat slavery. So Perry and I followed. We knew that many of the key players in the emerging abolitionist movement were going to be in one room. And we wanted to find a way to collaborate with them.

I couldn't have imagined that on that trip I would meet the two individuals who would become my lifelong mentors: John Eibner and Sharon Payt.

Since 1995, Eibner, a human rights activist, had been conducting slave redemptions in southern Sudan's war zones under the auspices of CSI, the charity Barbara Vogel's class had chosen to support. He showed pictures and spoke candidly about the slave redemptions CSI had been conducting, which at that stage numbered around six thousand, according to CSI estimates. The Foreign Relations Committee's attorney in charge of human rights, Sharon Payt, was a bundle of energy and brains. She excitedly explained the exhaustive slavery evidence package she and her congressional colleagues had been working on for years. The testimony we were about to hear, she said, would be incorporated into landmark legislation known as the Trafficking Victims Protection Act (TVPA). If passed, not only would it make human trafficking a federal crime, it would become the most comprehensive antislavery legislation since the Emancipation Proclamation.

By the time we arrived on Capitol Hill, the committee was about three months into the hearing process. So it was a much more laid-back affair than I'd been expecting, at least until the senior senator from North Carolina zoomed in on his motorized wheelchair. It was none other than Jesse Helms, then well into his seventies. Over a five-term Senate career, Helms had opposed the Civil Rights Act, school integration, and the Martin Luther King, Jr., holiday— but here he was chairing a committee on the abolition of a new manifestation of slavery!

Although I could tell he had to really concentrate to stay awake during the hearings, I admired Republican "Senator No" for standing up for the TVPA, which had very little political capital at the time. Along with Senators Paul Wellstone, Democrat of Minnesota, and Sam Brownback, a Republican from Kansas, Helms had gathered support from both sides of the aisle by trying to keep the TVPA discussion focused on human rights, not politics. It seemed we were seeing a true bipartisan effort in Washington. It was a historic day, and Perry and I were dressed for the occasion. It wasn't often you could get either one of us in a jacket and tie in those days.

Perry and I listened intently to testimony from Barbara Vogel's students as well as Francis Bok, a former Dinka tribesman who had spent ten years as a slave in northern Sudan after being abducted as a child by an Arab militia during his country's second civil war. He was the first escaped slave to speak before the Senate Foreign Relations Committee. Two years later he'd become the first of his kind to meet with a U.S. president—at the signing of the Sudan Peace Act.

After returning from Washington, we teamed up with the American Anti-Slavery Group's Charles Jacobs and started raising funds for a fact-finding mission to Sudan. We were ready to put our resources toward CSI's Sudan program, and I wanted to see how it worked firsthand before fully committing.

I immediately got in contact with Eibner, and described the kind of concert series we might be able to set up to benefit his work. I asked if I could accompany his team on a redemption trip, in the hopes I would come back with video testimony I could use to show my people what was going on in Sudan and get them behind the fund-raising effort. From the outset, Eibner was a man of few words—tough but fair. He asked me to prepare a two-page vision statement explaining how my participation could increase the visibility of the victims and how I would keep that focus in mind as we designed the project.

So I did. In a matter of weeks Adam Schneider and I had hired promoters and signed up groups like Hole, Goldie, Femi Kuti, Foo Fighters, and a reunited Jane's Addiction for the Jubilee 2001 Tour, which would start the following fall.

I called Eibner back and told him what we had so far. "One dollar from every ticket we sell on this tour will go to the Sudan program," I said.

"Very well, then, Aaron," he said calmly. "You'd better come to Sudan, then."

I was not used to John Eibner's dry sense of humor. It took me a few seconds to seize upon the fact that this antislavery pioneer was inviting me along on one of his rescue missions.

"Hallelujah!" I said. I didn't sound too much like the music industry wrangler Eibner must have initially taken me for.

A week later, he sent me a list of things I'd need for survival in a war zone: tent, sleeping mat, sleeping bag, walking shoes, ready-made lightweight meals, a water filter, first-aid kid.

"There are no roads where we're going," he specified in his succinct email. "No bottled water—nothing except what's on the list. Pack like you're going on safari in a forward area."

It was the first time I had a second to worry. I remember thinking, *What will happen to Papa if I don't make it back?* He had recently been diagnosed with shingles and lost the use of his right arm as a result. Since losing my mom four years earlier, he had been struggling to prove his love for her by obeying her dying wish—to help me pursue my Jubilee dream. It was as though by repairing his relationship with me and finally showing his financial and emotional support, he was finding a way to make peace with my mother. As I left Papa in his bedroom prison, I realized that my reports from Sudan would become his lifeline. He had always told me vivid stories of flying sorties over Bône, Algeria, as a World War II fighter pilot and walking through fields of cobras—now it would be my turn to captivate him.

It was strange to think about going on the trip on my own, without Perry. He was too busy with songwriting to fly off to Sudan, although I could tell he wanted to be a part of it. He urged me to go without him, but I think the pending trip exacerbated the tension that had been growing between us. I was starting to spread my wings and think about leaving the Venice crew for good. If forced to choose between music and human rights activism, I was going to take the latter, and we both knew it. I'd been successfully blending the two for a while now by following the Jubilee, but my soul longed to find a concrete expression of my own dreams.

Nevertheless, agreeing to that first trip with Eibner felt like jumping off a cliff. Perry and I had worked together on and off for the last ten years, and in the last four we'd spent almost every day together, for twelve-hour stretches—surfing, praying, studying, singing, debating, and helping each other kick drugs. We would always be spiritual brothers. But we both needed to move on.

So here I was actually going to Sudan. After being forced to leave some of my food behind at LAX, I flew to Switzerland and spent a long afternoon in a snowy Zurich contemplating the upcoming trip under the influence of Van Gogh's *Sunflowers*. The contrast between the city widely considered to possess the world's best quality of life and the devastated region I was heading into would be as indescribable as my first glimpse of Sub-Saharan Africa.

Eibner and his technology specialist, Gunnar Wiebalck, a middle-aged German whose sense of humor was arguably drier than Eibner's, had offered Sharon Payt and me their business-class seats. So we emerged from the plane in Nairobi, Kenya, refreshed and ready for what lay ahead. Not that we'd slept. Sharon and I had met only once before—at the TVPA hearings in D.C.—but I felt as if I were reuniting with an old friend. I had so much respect for this woman—whose intelligence and compassion had not failed to escape the notice of most of her male colleagues.

"It's you!" she'd hollered with a huge grin across the Zurich terminal as soon as we spotted each other. Sharon was coming to Sudan to get a few more interviews to help wrap up her TVPA evidentiary package for Senator Brownback's office. The TVPA had essentially been passed at that point. But she explained that staving off political bullets from critics who claimed there was no reliable evidence took vigilance—each case of slavery had to be carefully documented and verified. We'd spent the last eight hours talking excitedly about everything from fractal math and cell division to number theory.

Eibner's selfless gesture took me by surprise. I had gotten used to the "me first" world of Hollywood, and here was a human rights giant I barely knew using his frequent-flier miles to make sure I was comfortable. It all sunk in as I watched my first sunrise over the African continent from the single-engine plane we'd just boarded. Rock stars never gave new roadies their first-class seats— only the famous got special treatment. But Eibner and Wiebalck, two rock stars of the burgeoning antislavery movement, were different. They were focused on doing whatever they could to fight injustice and protect the vulnerable. And they were treating me like one of their own. As I looked out the window at the sunrise over the alien landscape, flat and punctuated with the kind of trees I identified with *The Lion King,* it was impossible not to feel awed. And very small.

In Nairobi, John, Gunnar, Sharon, and I met up with the rest of our team: a CSI volunteer called Marcus, physician Dr. Luka Deng, and a field coordinator/Dinka translator named Dominic Deng.

Freelance photojournalist Lucian Niemeyer was along to take pictures. Majok, a grinning Sudanese People's Liberation Army (SPLA) commander, was the last to board the plane. He would be in charge of our regional security.

The SPLA and its accompanying movement had been born in 1983, out of protest against Khartoum's long record of human rights abuses and neglect in its southern provinces. The rebels' relations with the northern government had worsened since President Omar Hassan al-Bashir's declaration of sharia (Islamic) law and consolidation of power behind the political organization National Islamic Front (NIF). Bashir and the NIF had not made much of an effort to hide their overreaching goal: establishing an Islamic state by dividing the country along Arabic and African lines and ridding it of all but the few Arab tribes from which he and the ruling elite descended.

The Sudanese president had been achieving that objective partly through his Popular Defense Force (PDF), composed of volunteer *mujahideen*, holy warriors recruited from all over the Arab world who had been told they were waging a justifiable *jihad* against southern animists and Christians.[3] Although Western NGOs and media had largely interpreted the Sudanese war along religious and ethnic lines,[4] the less visible conflict was over oil and water resources.

To back up its PDF, Khartoum had been funding the *murahaleen*, proxy militias made up of nomadic Arabs descended from some of Sudan's poorest tribes, who had historically shared scarce resources with African southerners. Suddenly armed and given free rein to rape, pillage, and plunder, these raiders were guided less by ideological warfare than by simple economics. The Dinka and other African tribes had something the Arabs didn't: cattle and land. Yet the cattle's value paled in comparison to that of the oil beneath southern and northwestern Sudan.

SPLA leader John Garang had meanwhile united fractured rebel groups under the stated goal of establishing a democratic Sudan, with the SPLA in charge of the southern region and its oil and water resources. Although he would later be criticized for conscripting starving refugee children dubbed "The Lost Boys," Garang, a

Dinka, maintained that his troops' courage came from "the conviction that we are fighting a just cause. That is something North
Sudan and its people don't have."[5]

I sucked in my breath as we flew low over Mount Kilimanjaro,
taking in the sight of volcanoes, craters, and massive herds of
migrating wild gazelles. There were no commercial flights to Sudan
in those days, so we were first taking a private charter bound for
Lokichokio, near the Kenyan-Sudanese border. Our pilot was
Heather Stewart, a spunky blonde Brit in her mid-fifties who'd
grown up in South Africa before settling in Nairobi to run her charter business. Dressed in a crisp white captain's shirt and pants and
full of breathless stories about flying missions out of Somalia, it was
hard not to fall in love with her just a little bit. I was sure I wasn't
the first, and Heather let me down lightly. "Remember, I'm a happily married woman with a son not that much younger than you,
Aaron!" she laughed over her shoulder.

Loki, as it was known to the locals and NGO workers who had
swollen its population in recent years, finally appeared on the horizon after a half-day flight and a refueling stop. Heather's company
had its own base camp here, which seemed luxurious compared to
what I'd been expecting. There were a series of large permanent
tents anchored to the ground, complete with running water in the
bathrooms. We were the camp's only inhabitants, and although it
felt as though there were miles of raw bush between us and the near-
est road, our dinner plates were still bursting with green vegetables
that first night. We slept on cots under soft mosquito nets. In a few
days I'd be looking back on these amenities with nostalgia.

Over breakfast, Eibner and Gunnar, identically dressed in blue
button-down shirts, khaki pants, and hiking boots, briefed us on
what to expect. "We're in no-man's-land right now," Eibner said.
"But in a few hours, we're going to be in a war zone." He filled in
some details on the Sudanese government's scorched-earth campaign against the rebels. He reminded us that Khartoum had so far
managed to effectively depict the nearly two-decade-long north-
south "civil war" as a battle between tribes, and it was becoming
increasingly clear that Bashir and the NIF were intent on ethnically

cleansing the civilian population. "Don't talk to anyone about our plans or business," Eibner said sternly. "Not the SPLA officers, and definitely not the U.N. folks or anyone from a northern militia. We consider ourselves neutral," he said. "But not everyone else is."

I was still pondering his statement a few hours later. We were standing on an airstrip in Lokichokio, in the northern province of Kenya—our last fuel stop before we reached our final destination. Everyone was groggy, quiet, and lost in his or her own thoughts. Knowing this would be my last chance to buy any food, I snapped up anything I could find, even though I wasn't yet hungry. As a former athlete, I knew how much fuel my 225-pound body required to function. I was embarrassed when Eibner suddenly strode over, nodding wryly at my sandwiches and bottles of Coke. "Health food, huh?"

"What did you mean, John, when you said not everyone's neutral?" I responded, eager to change the subject.

"Well," he said, "some of the NGOs think that redeeming slaves exacerbates the problem. I guess they'd rather have us do nothing."

I nodded.

"Everyone knows that extermination of the non-Arab tribes is part of Bashir's master plan, Aaron," he continued. "There's no question they're well on their way, with thousands of documented cases of slavery, rape, and murder. Yet UNICEF and others have been going along with the government's official version—there is no 'slavery' in Sudan, they say, only 'abductions.'" Eibner sighed and gave me a weary smile. "Anyway, in a few hours you'll be able to decide for yourself what is actually occurring here."

It was hard for me to process Eibner's words, since I'd always been a believer in the power of multilateral diplomacy. But it was also impossible to ignore the United Nations' track record when it came to Rwanda, where as many as 1 million people were slaughtered while U.N. blue helmets—unable to take up arms—looked on helplessly; or in Bosnia, where nearly eight thousand unarmed Muslims were massacred by the Serbs at the U.N.'s "safe haven" in Srebrenica.[6] When the government itself is causing the problem, U.N. agencies, which are obligated to work with their host governments, often find their hands tied. In their need to accommodate their hosts, certain U.N. representatives have even become complicit in the denial of facts—and indifference to human suffering—that have preceded atrocities such as the ones committed in Rwanda and Bosnia. By the time the U.N. has gotten around to crying "genocide," as it did for the first time in its history in the case of Rwanda, it has been far too late.

Here's what I'd quickly learn in my first few hours in Lokichokio: it's pretty near impossible to stay 100 percent neutral in a conflict zone, because security needs are inextricably linked to politics and special interests. Eibner explained that CSI had found a way to operate in SPLA-controlled areas without compromising its integrity.

"Without the SPLA we'd have no security," he said. "So we have to work with them. But we never give our money directly to the army. We pay for our transport, lodging, food, and security in Sudanese currency instead of dollars. We can be sure that this money stays here to help the victims."

"It sounds like you're constantly walking a tightrope," I said.

"That's about right," Eibner replied.

Part of me got the sense that he thrived on this tension. Over the next couple of days I'd watch Eibner turn down a whole host of SPLA requests. Through our translators, I'd hear him respond:

"No, we will bring in the currency ourselves . . . no deposits with the general. No."

"No, you can't have this food. This is for victims and refugees."

"No, the medicine is for civilians who need it."

"No, you know I can't take you on our plane."

He would never apologize, flatter the military commanders, or bother to rationalize his decisive answers. It was better not to make too much small talk with John. I had never seen anyone command so much respect from everyone around him, even in my days at the Air Force Academy. Just as I'd learned to do there, I decided to keep my mouth shut. I'd put my head down, leave my ears open, and do what I was told. This was a good way to deal with the very real fear of going into such an unstable war zone. We departed Loki, made a few refueling stops on dry river beds, and continued north into Sudan.

After another two-and-a-half-hour hop, we landed in the settlement of Malual Kon, about four villages back from the war's front line. From the plane I could see a large Dinka compound—a big group of *tukul*s, traditional one-room huts made of mud with conical thatched roofs scattered around bits of scrubby vegetation. As we approached I counted a handful of cattle, but not as many as I'd expected, considering that the Dinka and Nuer tribes are credited with having introduced cattle to the area south of the Sahara beginning around 3000 B.C.[7] Then I remembered what I'd been told about the logic behind the destruction of southern Sudanese villages by the *murahaleen* raiders—kill the men, rape the women, and enslave the children. Destroy the rest, leaving them no means to rebuild.

Depriving Dinka of their cattle was like depriving someone of his livelihood. A cow was a Dinka family's most valuable possession, and the factor that made a nomadic herder's lifestyle sustainable. Without their cattle, the Dinka and other tribal people not only lost their livelihood, they lost their link to the past. Still by far the largest tribe in South Sudan, the Dinka had so far suffered the worst of the government's wrath, followed closely by the traditionalist Nuba people of the north, who inhabit strategic mountainous territory closer to Khartoum.

As we landed, a mob of ragtag soldiers and villagers came rushing up to the airplane to get a look at us. And I immediately heard my first Arabic word in the Sudanese dialect—*khawaja*, which I assumed meant either "foreigner" or something like "white people in strange clothing," since the word was obviously being applied to us—but not unkindly. It literally felt like we were Martians landing our spaceship on Earth for the first time, and the Earthlings were curious to find out what we *khawaja*s were all about.

I had to try hard not to look at these people in that same way. Some were naked and others wore little more than rags. I noticed the signs of war immediately—trucks and guns, cannons and SPLA soldiers carrying body bags. The scene quickly became chaotic, as the soldiers rushed up to John to ask if they could use our plane to take an injured man to the hospital. I was suspicious, sensing they were searching for an excuse to get away from the war zone. The soldier on the stretcher in front of us was bleeding but was not in critical condition. It seemed he had gotten drunk and shot himself. I watched Eibner keep his gaze straight ahead as he said no. We had human rights work to do, and transporting this man to the hospital would take us away from that objective. There would later be times when I would see John acquiesce, but this was not one of them.

Gunnar, Eibner's right-hand man, nudged me and said, "This happens every time. We can't help everyone, but believe me when I tell you that we do whatever we can to save the most lives."

Before I had a chance to protest, one of the female villagers wearing a purple and red printed robe with a green head scarf had lifted my heavy backpack onto her head and joined the moving queue of citizens walking toward the village, which was a few kilometers away. Sharon and I locked eyes in amazement. "This is really something," she said, beaming. The few men that were not soldiers were wearing white turbans with *jalabiya*, long white robes traditionally worn by both Arab and African tribal people in Sudan and neighboring countries.

Following Marcus's instructions, we all got into a truck that would be taking us to our camping spot a few kilometers from the airstrip. Finally out of the noisy airplane and practically sitting on each other's laps, we took the chance to really introduce ourselves.

Dr. Luka Deng, impeccably dressed in a blue dress shirt, tie, and shiny black shoes, looked to be the oldest in the group. Out of respect, I asked him to go first. "Well now, what can I tell you about myself?" he began in a deep voice with a British inflection. "I think you can tell by my height that I am a Dinka, but by my shoes you can guess that I am a British citizen."

We all laughed.

He paused as if deciding what he might tell us next. Like many people who had suffered, I guessed that Dr. Luka understood how fragile life was. He also knew how to celebrate it. "You know," he told us, "we Dinka live not only in the Sudan, but in parts of Uganda, Kenya, and the Congo. And when we see each other, we don't call each other Dinka, but *Moinjaang*, which means 'people of the people.' So if you want to know more about my people of the people, please come and talk to me!" He finished with a smile, and then suddenly raised his finger to make a final point.

"Of course you want to know how old I am, right?" he said with a playful grin. "I think my wife told me recently I was fifty-five, or something like that, anyway . . ." We all laughed along with him, and he suddenly grew somber.

"I am coming back now to help my *Moinjaang*. Several of my family members were captured and held as slaves at the beginning of the second civil war," he said, "but we managed to get them out. My dream now is to set up a clinic here for the internally displaced people."

After Sharon, Lucian, and I had taken our turns, thirty-five-year-old Dominic Deng Kuoc spoke up. In immaculate English, the Dinka father of three young sons told us about the diversity of his work as CSI's field coordinator and main translator. "Anything you need done, I can handle it!" he said warmly, rubbing his big hands on his shaved head, which was shielded by a blue baseball cap. "Also, if you want to know about the snakes and insects you find in your tent—I mean, which ones you can eat and which ones want to eat you—don't hesitate to ask!"

I noticed the only people laughing were Dr. Luka, Dominic, and Dr. Eibner. Even from a seated position, Dominic towered over the Westerners. After the introductions, we joked about which of us was the best prepared for the arduous workload that lay ahead. By the time we pulled up to the campsite a few minutes later, I felt as though we had already formed a cohesive group.

True to his word, Dominic expertly slid a camouflaged cobra out of the thicket under the trees where we were about to pitch our tents.

"Oh God," Lucian said to no one in particular. "I don't even have a tent. I thought we were going to be sleeping in base camps like the one in Loki." Although Lucian was in his sixties and an intrepid Africa veteran who'd covered the Rwandan genocide, even he was unprepared for these primitive conditions.

Eibner reacted like a firecracker, his blue eyes blazing under a floppy sun hat. "Who's going to risk building something permanent here?" he asked. "The Antonovs [government-owned aircraft] only need to drop one bomb on this place and it's destroyed. Then they send the *murahaleen* in to finish off the rest." He disappeared into his tent. It was apparent how deeply protective he was of the tribes who were being victimized. And I could tell from what I had already seen that his love for the Dinka was reciprocal.

"You can share my tent, Lucian," I offered. He gratefully accepted.

Later on, Lucian and I talked Sudanese history in my tent. I had read everything I could on the subject and was happy to find that he was just as passionate about understanding the complexities of the conflict. "Eibner's definitely right on one thing," he said. "The NGOs and the mainstream media are missing the key issue here."

I urged him to go on. "Look," he said. "Not only is the Sudanese government behind the bombing campaigns, but where do you think it gets its Antonovs from? Russia. And those missiles and cluster bombs they're dropping? Also Russia, although China's purchase of oil futures helps finance those purchases." He stopped to gauge my reaction. "I've heard that, too," I said.

"As far as I know, the Chinese already get about seven percent of their oil from Sudan. The U.S., Europe, India . . . we all want to get in on the oil action," Lucian went on bitterly. "And our money is going directly to buy weapons that murder civilians. It's just sick."

I nodded again, and let him continue.

"It's also pretty clear to me that the government is instigating ethnic tensions between the *baggara* and African tribes. Although the Arab nomads here don't have any land, they've gotten along with African tribes for centuries, bartering for water and grazing rights. They've always resolved minor territorial disputes through their tribal chieftains." Lucian smashed a mosquito against the tent's flimsy wall and finally exhaled. I understood his frustration.

I knew, too, that the Sudanese People's Liberation Movement had a lot of willpower behind it. John Garang's ancestors had successfully resisted conversion to Islam and protected their land from the Ottoman Turks in the mid-1800s.[8] Before colonialism came to Sudan, the Dinka were nomads, living in clans of one hundred or so people and building villages designed to last about twenty years. When the grazing land was exhausted or swollen by flooding, they moved on. But with the arrival of the British and their administrative centers, Dinka began to stay put in the villages. This new mode of living would later make them more vulnerable to attack.

We went on to talk about how the Sudanese government had been arming and organizing *murahaleen* taken from among the ranks of the *baggara*, a collective term for the nomadic Arab herders who had long roamed peacefully with their animals from Sudan, Morocco, Egypt, and Tunisia to West Africa. The term comes from *baqquara*, from the Arabic for "cattle," although these people refer to themselves by their individual tribal name.[9] *Baggara* and southern tribes like Dinka and Nuer had long shared their resources and helped each other survive through periods of drought and famine. For more than two decades, the government had incited both sides to hatred, and more recently had been exploiting the *murahaleen* to serve its own narrow, maniacal agenda. Although the international community had still stopped short of calling it "genocide,"[10] even in 1999 it was apparent that Sudan's African tribes were in danger of extinction.

"The 1988 famine[11] alone killed almost a quarter of a million southern Sudanese, most of them Dinka," said Lucian. "Tell me this wasn't part of the government's master plan . . ."

My mind had become saturated by that point. "Hey, I know we could easily talk about this all night, but we've got a huge day ahead of us tomorrow and we both need some rest," I said at one point, although the full moon was making me feel restless. "Want to pick up where we left off in the morning?"

Before Lucian could answer, the sound of tribal drumming from the other side of camp drew me out for a look. And there was Eibner, wearing a headlamp—busy getting our gear ready for the morning. The man never rested. He didn't seem to notice the rhythmic beats and whoops, which were growing increasingly louder.

"Can I give you a hand?" I asked somewhat hesitantly.

"No," he answered without looking up from his tasks. "You need your sleep. We've got a sixteen-hour day tomorrow."

This response made it harder to form my next question, but Eibner was the field commander, and I wanted his approval.

"I've been hearing the drums," I started, "and you know how important music is to me. Would it be okay if I went over there to listen and maybe record a bit?" I wanted some tribal music to bring back to Perry.

"Do as you like," Eibner said, looking at me this time. "But don't stay too long. The guys will be smoking *khat* and drinking too much local moonshine. Hungover or not, we're going to be walking miles in the hot sun . . ." he paused, "all day." I nodded to assure my compliance.

Lucian had already told me about *khat*—the dried leaves of a local plant used for stimulant effect—as well as *siko,* a powerful alcoholic brew.

I was relieved to be doing something on my own. Grabbing a flashlight, I walked out into the blackness toward the drumming. As I passed the last tent, I was startled by something brushing my back, and whirled around to see a giggling Longar, the CSI translator who had joined us that afternoon. He was dressed with a real seventies flair, wearing a funky hat and sunglasses despite the darkness. "Hey, man . . . Give peace a chance!" he said. "What's your hurry?" Longar had been educated in Egypt and told me earlier that his biggest passions were reading and music.

"I want to check out the drumming," I said. "Wanna come with me?"

"Sounds like a party," Longar said.

And it was. A full-moon party, to be exact. A group of about twenty Dinka men and a few women stood in a circle, each banging a drum in a freeform style. I took in four or five string instruments and maybe thirty more people without drums, stomping their feet to the rhythm. As we walked up, many in the group gave us welcoming smiles and started singing at the top of their lungs. One man started a solo and the rest of the group surrounded him, becoming the chorus.

Longar and I joined the circle, clapping and stomping and singing as best we could. I felt caught up in a wave of sound, a music that was from so far away yet was still familiar. Its soulful melody made me think of black Baptist choirs I'd seen as a teenager in New York, and I got so caught up in the music that I almost forgot to go back to being an observer. I needed to record this for my friends back home. These "people of the people"—what music they made!

After about an hour of recording and politely refusing the *siko* and puffs of *khat*, I decided to say my good-byes. Since I was still unfamiliar with the Dinka language, my attempt at a farewell, a weak *"yin abi caath!"* directed at the group, was met with a good-natured round of laughter.

Longar was nowhere to be found, and some of the SPLA soldiers present were visibly drunk and starting to shoot their weapons in the air. Despite their offers of help, I wanted to make my own way back to the tent. The moon was so bright overhead that I didn't even need my flashlight. I dropped into the tent next to a slumbering Lucian and fell asleep with my boots on.

Which was a good thing, as it turned out, because the next morning I awoke to the sound of roosters crowing followed by Eibner's voice saying, "Come on, everybody, get your boots on, have your breakfast, pack your tent and we're on our way! We've got an important appointment today and we don't want to be late."

No one made a peep in response. "And, yes, in case you were wondering, we're *walking* the twelve miles to the redemption site," Eibner said, "so tie your boots tightly." He couldn't keep the glee out of his voice.

With that, Lucian and I were upright and moving swiftly. Lucian went to fetch water from the well, which we purified with our ceramic filters and then used to mix cold instant oatmeal. I had so few possessions with me that it only took a couple of minutes to pack up, and when that job was finished I felt an enormous sense of freedom overtake me. I was ready to go. All the essentials were on my back, and I felt as if I were starting a new life. Although we didn't know what was waiting for us on the other side of the Nile, I felt certain that something big was beginning.

As we set out, a CSI volunteer translator called Angelo Marac asked if he could walk with me. I told him I'd be glad to have his company. Eibner had already briefed me on Angelo's increasingly important role as a community leader. Like most of the people on this trip, the only compensation he'd be receiving for his work was the knowledge that he was doing something to help his decimated tribe.

Dinka are among the world's tallest people, but Angelo, about ten years my senior, was a rare exception. Unlike most of the gangly southern tribesmen I'd met, Angelo reminded me of a linebacker who'd put a few extra pounds around his middle. He shook my hand in greeting with a bearlike grip and adjusted his glasses as we started out over the dusty, rocky terrain. After we exchanged the basics, I gratefully noticed that Angelo had no use for frivolous talk. But our lack of conversation was not the least bit awkward. We were sharing the silence. As with Longar, one of the first things Angelo mentioned was a great love for books, which probably explained his contemplative nature. John Eibner had been supplying him with novels and nonfiction in English for years now. I pulled a Paulo Coelho novel out of my backpack and offered it to Angelo. "I finished it on the way over," I said. "Anyway, you'll be doing me a favor by lightening my pack . . ."

Angelo laughed and grabbed the paperback with one hand while reaching out to slap my other palm. "Excellent!" he said with another flash of the famous Dinka smile. We continued on in blessed silence.

THE TIME WHEN
THE WORLD WAS SPOILED

Poverty, ignorance, and spiritual darkness are all part of a complex set of social factors that exacerbate slaves' original vulnerability, but once enslaved, they need someone to rescue them from the brutal hand of their oppressor.

—Gary Haugen, International Justice Mission

THE MEDITATIVE HIKE WITH ANGELO WAS EXACTLY what I needed, because as we walked those miles across northern Bahr el Ghazal's lunar landscape, I had a lot to think about.

I felt like a struggling architect finally getting his crack at the grand cathedral he'd been sketching in his head all his life. Crunching my boots through Cush, the land of biblical plagues and locusts, I came to the realization that fleshing out the Jubilee dream was going to be my life's work. The missions I would devote myself to from here on out were going to be the pillars that built up that work. Drop the Debt had been my first pillar—learning how to build a grassroots human rights campaign with rock star activists. I could already tell that freeing slaves was about to become the second pillar.

As I trudged ahead in the heat across the clay and scrub, looking down at my boots to avoid stumbling, I sketched this Jubilee blueprint out in my mind. Drop the Debt had succeeded in reducing the crippling loans that essentially enslaved developing countries and their citizens to nations with deeper pockets. When we delivered those 24 million signatures to the G8, we had forced the Western powers to admit that there *was* something very simple we could do to reduce global poverty—cancel the debts that were keeping bankers rich and poor countries poor. As a result, policies were changed and some debt was indeed dropped. But we still had so far to go.

The second pillar was going to be more complicated. The imminent passage of the Trafficking Victims Protection Act meant that the U.S. government was doing about as much as a government could do: putting new laws on the books and enforcing them. Police officers, border guards, and task forces were being trained in anti-trafficking methods. With its new annual Trafficking in Persons Report, the State Department was about to pressure all the countries of the world to get tough on traffickers or face U.S. sanctions. The system wasn't perfect, but all these steps meant that the public was also becoming aware of the existence of modern-day slavery—a crucial first step to eradication. Now all we needed was a grass-roots movement to truly abolish it.

I thought of the world's trouble spots as enveloping each other in concentric circles. Each circle shared the same middle point—Israel, the center of our current global conflict. Here on the ground, crossing a different part of the same river my ancestors had waded through on their way out of slavery in Egypt, I knew that the scriptures I'd spent all these years studying were real. I was watching the teachings reveal their larger meanings, one by one.

Looking ahead at soft-spoken Angelo, lost in his own thoughts, it occurred to me that leaving the Venice scene of drugs and rock stars would be like forsaking my own Babylon. I was going to abandon the land of iniquity and head for Jerusalem, my homeland. Here—in a war zone—I found myself at peace. I felt my ego stripped away by the humility and grace of Eibner and his selfless colleagues. No one—not my father, older brother, sister, water polo coach, or even Perry—had ever been able to expose me like this, bringing me back to my natural state. With almost frightening certainty, I knew I was on the right path.

The arduous trek flew by in Angelo's calmative presence. Our group trickled into the slave redemption site just behind Eibner, Gunnar, and Marcus—all of whom were marathon-training partners back in Zurich. Young, healthy Dominic had no trouble keeping up with their steady pace. Sharon, Lucian, and a balding Protestant pastor called Tito, who had joined us in Malual Kon that morning, brought up the rear. Pastor Tito was smiling broadly and did not look to be feeling the 110-degree heat one bit, despite his clerical collar, black jacket, and pants.

"Pastor Tito and I have been talking prophecy," said Sharon, whose bush gear and unruffled appearance suddenly conjured up images of Marion, Indiana Jones's counterpart in *Raiders of the Lost Ark*—a woman who could easily leap across a cobra den without getting frazzled. She threw herself on the ground next to me and smoothed her hair back under her much more stylish safari hat. "You guys should sit down and talk sometime."

"I'm sure we will soon have that chance," said Tito. "I have heard you are a biblical scholar, too, Aaron—like me." He slapped me on the back and showed me two dog-eared copies of the Bible— one in English and the other in his native language. "By the end of your trip you'll be able to read this one," he said, tapping the cover of the Dinka translation.

"I hope we can walk back to camp together at the end of the day, Pastor Tito," I said, then directing his attention toward the impressive sight in front of us.

There, in the shade of the only tree around—a monolithic mango—sat a silent group of about a dozen Arab tribesmen, all dressed in long white *jalabiya*. Their faces were almost entirely covered by white turbans they had wound tightly around their heads, shielding everything but their eyes. Their flock of camels stood by, chewing on their tethers.

The Kalashnikovs the men were holding identified them as the dreaded *murahaleen*—the cattle raiders who had been grouped into proxy militias by the NIF, armed and instructed to plunder, rape, kidnap, and kill the African tribespeople of southern Sudan. Yet as we approached and I made eye contact with one of these men, I could tell I was not looking at a cold-blooded killer.

What I saw instead was something inscrutable in the hazel eyes of the Arab nomad who returned my gaze. It wasn't pure pain, or sadness, or frustration—but a mixture of all those sentiments. I think it was closest to weariness. The weariness of this war, not his own, that had dragged on for much of his life and threatened to stretch far beyond the desert horizon. In the same way that the "world had been spoiled"[1] for the Dinka by successive government oppression, so too had this man's freedom been taken from him.

Seated in the rough scraggly grass a few yards away from this group, under the area's only other tree, were the slaves—approximately six hundred Dinka people, mostly women and children, clustered together in smaller groups without so much as making a collective sound. They were probably too exhausted to speak to each other, after having walked several hundred miles to get here from the northern provinces of Kordofan or Darfur. In contrast to the Arabs, the heads of the Africans were bare. Many were coated in white dust that I took to be sand, and flies buzzed around and danced on the rims of the children's eyes.

Few of the children were wearing more than scraps of clothing, but of those who were, almost all had on dull blue shorts, all seemingly cut from the same cloth. None of their eyes rose to meet my gaze. Instead, these about-to-be-former slaves stared at the ground or at the horizon. They had not yet been told what was about to happen, and for all they knew, we had come to take them into a different kind of slavery. Some had been slaves for so long that they knew no other life. Many bore telltale scars on their backs, arms, or legs, and other signs of illnesses such as malaria or hepatitis. Neither sure of their status nor whether they could trust us, they were, simply and collectively—scared.

John Eibner approached the white-robed figures and exchanged a round of robust *asalamalekum*s with one man, who stood up and gripped both of Eibner's arms with his own. I wondered how Eibner could be on such good terms with a member of the *murahaleen*, but I struggled to temper my suspicions for the moment. I would find myself doing that again and again on this trip, since there was so much I had yet to understand. And Eibner was not one to waste his words giving a complex history lesson to an unproven assistant.

The rest of our group sidled up to the huge tree, sweaty but excited to begin the first day of work. Trees like the one we were crouching under had always been scarce in Bahr el Ghazal, but since the *murahaleen* started raiding and burning villages, single trees (and the valuable shade they provided) had become even more rare, and therefore valuable, to the local people. In villages that had been raided, destroyed homes could not be rebuilt without timber—so the PDF and *murahaleen* militias had been instructed to take the wood and burn whatever vegetation they could find. As a result, the people who survived had no option but to camp out under what few trees remained.

While Eibner was busy talking with the Dinka chieftains who had come to assist the slaves, Gunnar came back over to our team and urged us to sit in the shade to gather our strength. He bent over to set up the solar panels that would run his laptop, satellite phone, and the GPS unit that had guided us here.

"Get comfortable here for a few minutes; drink your water and have a snack if you like," Gunnar said. "Then we'll break into groups of two—one videographer and one translator—to do the interviews."

I guess he sensed that the Westerners were a bit confused by the presence of the *murahaleen* and their assault rifles.

"Ah," he said, "we should have told you earlier. Those aren't *murahaleen*—they are the Schindlers!" he said, allowing himself a slight smile.

Gunnar went on to explain that the man Eibner had just greeted was Nur Muhammad al-Hasan, a *baggara* tribesman who led one of four slave retrieval networks made up of Arab Muslims who knew that a return to peace with their darker-skinned neighbors was in their own best interest. By the early nineties, just before CSI first came to Sudan, Nur and men like him had already developed a kind of "underground railroad" that would reach across the historic border between North and South Sudan and grow alongside the local peace agreements that Arab and African chieftains had negotiated amongst themselves in the face of increasing chaos being orchestrated from Khartoum.

Taking into account the needs of both camps, the peace agreements allowed for Arab signatories, who did not have their own territory, to graze their cattle on Dinka land south of the Kiir River (a tributary of the Nile that marks the border of southern Darfur and Kordofan with the Bahr el Ghazal region) during the dry season and trade their goods at Dinka markets. In exchange for this right, the *baggara* working with Nur had agreed, at great personal risk, to resist the Sudanese regime's jihad of the sword against the Dinka and other African tribes. One way of doing that was by retrieving the persecuted from unjust bondage.

When Eibner and his colleagues arrived in the area in 1995, Dinka community groups solicited CSI's financial and organizational support for their struggling initiative. "And that's how," Eibner had told me at dinner the night before, "we found ourselves implementing and funding slave redemptions."

So although middlemen such as Nur were physically indistinguishable from the *murahaleen* and both shared the same ethnic and religious makeup, they were a breed apart. For lack of a better term, Eibner and Gunnar referred to Nur and his network as the "Schindlers" of Sudan—after Oskar Schindler, the German industrialist made famous by Steven Spielberg's film *Schindler's List*.

Just as Schindler stuck out his neck to protect one thousand Jewish employees from the Nazis, these brave Arab men risked their own lives to liberate Africans from the ancient bonds of modern-day slavery. For the past two months, Nur and his associates had been scouring the parched terrain of Kordofan and southern Darfur, paying visits to the farms and nomadic cattle camps of their fellow *baggara*—who hailed from several tribes, including the Missiriya and Rizeigat—in search of slaves.

Posing as slaveholders themselves, they found ways to buy or negotiate the freedom of as many African women and children as they were able to track down. This time Nur's network had brought almost six hundred individuals (hailing mostly from the Dinka, Nuer, and Nuba tribes) back to the south. Most slaves had borne witness to executions and endured other horrors at the hands of the PDF, the *murahaleen,* or both, since these units often conducted raids together. The list of crimes included (but was not limited to) kidnapping, death threats, rape, beatings, and genital and other kinds of mutilations. All this before they arrived at their new prisons in Sudan's central and northern provinces, where their names and ethnic identities were replaced with Islamic ones. Forcible conversion to Islam by their masters marked the customary start of their unpaid and brutal sentences as domestic, agricultural, and sexual servants.

Whenever possible, Nur brought a list of missing persons (obtained from Dinka and Nuer community leaders) to the Arab chieftains and asked permission to free the slaves. When that was not an option, he would pay off the master or, in rare cases, spirit the captives away under cover of night. Bringing black southerners across the front lines of a civil war was already extremely risky for men like Nur. Doing so in flagrant violation of the sharia law being imposed by their government was impossibly dangerous. Under Sudan's penal code, Nur faced punishment ranging from limb amputation (for theft, since slaves were considered property), to stoning to death, or crucifixion (assisting the infidel was akin to apostasy, a capital offense under the Bashir government).[2]

The money alone was clearly not worth their risk. At the time, *baggara* middlemen were paying anywhere from twenty to eighty dollars for each slave they managed to liberate. They were then in charge of protecting, feeding, and transporting their human cargo over treacherous terrain for hundreds of miles, and days or weeks on end. CSI had set its per-head limit at fifty dollars—it could and would not go any higher—to cover the *baggaras'* costs and sometimes leave them a modest sum for their efforts.[3] It was hardly enough to make the nomads rich—but it was enough to buy an occasional pair of sunglasses or rubber flip-flops (most of the Africans went barefoot) and move their families around from one hiding place to another. These men were heralded in the Dinka and Nuer villages as humanitarian heroes.

Since Eibner spoke no more than a few words of Arabic and Nur spoke virtually no English, there wasn't much they could say to each other, unless it was filtered through translators. But their mutual respect was palpable.

"This man has risked everything to free slaves," said Eibner, by way of introducing Nur to the rest of us. "He's been tortured, spent time in northern jails, and had his house burned down by government agents . . . His family is in hiding and he can only travel by night," Eibner said gravely. "He is an example to all of us."

Pastor Tito nodded and recited a line from Hebrews 13: "Remember the prisoners as if chained with them—those who are mistreated—since you yourselves are in the Body also."

John Eibner continued by reciting a short speech he customarily gave on these occasions: "Nobody should be afraid today, because this is a happy day. This is a day of freedom, and very soon many of you will go back to your villages and be reunited with your families and friends," he started.

With Angelo translating into both Dinka and Arabic (some of the slaves had been kidnapped so long ago that they no longer understood their native language), Eibner continued:

"As soon as you are interviewed and fingerprinted, you'll be free to go; so it's a good day, and if you just bear with the process, we can finish our work and help get you back to your loved ones."

He went on to explain to us that the money we were about to see exchanged should not be interpreted as a mark of these human beings' net worth—although it was tough not to compare the price per head with the cost of livestock at the Malual Kon market, where fifty dollars could buy you two goats. "Yeah, sure it's a gray area," he would say later, in response to an imagined critic. "But fifty bucks just happens to be the current price of freedom in a world turned upside down."

He turned back to the group.

Humanitarians—"Good people"—he interjected, had worked hard for the money he now had in his hands, and those people were overjoyed that it was being used to obtain liberty for their brothers and sisters in Sudan. The dazed and dehydrated crowd looked somewhat bewildered by this information once it was translated, and Eibner brought his hands together in a closing gesture. "May God be with you," he said. Then he wiped his brow with a bandana and stepped aside, looking relieved to be out of the spotlight.

Pastor Tito held up his hands and offered the group God's blessing. Many Dinka, I knew, had nominally adopted Christianity only after having endured forced conversion to Islam. A few sang out "*lau nhom!*"—freedom—and tried to stifle their musical impulses until the pastor had finished his prayer. As the newly freed slaves began to make sense of what had just occurred, big smiles started to spread across their haggard faces. Stirrings of emotion—laughter and tears—buzzed throughout the group. Some people leapt up and did an impromptu dance. Others jumped up and down in place, holding hands.

My jubilation at this sight did not last long. Among the rejoicers, there were dozens of people who remained still—simply dumbfounded, perhaps, or otherwise unable to imagine what they might do next. Through donations CSI had managed to scrape up the thirty thousand dollars needed to buy their liberty, but it could not guarantee their safety from this point on. Eibner had lobbied the World Food Program to donate sorghum and survival kits, which would help some, but not all, of these people get through the next few weeks, but that effort fell far short in terms of helping the returnees restart their lives in a war zone, where they could easily be recaptured by the marauding militias. The same militias who had killed their husbands and fathers, raided their livestock, and turned their world upside down.

Freed slaves might also have to walk for hours or even days to find their way home—if they still had a home to return to. Many of the children had been so successfully Islamicized they could not remember their Dinka identity or the name of their ancestral hamlet. If a returnee was fortunate enough to find surviving family members *and* an intact village, then his or her next battle would begin: staying alive in a province where the life expectancy was now hovering around fifty years of age. With most forms of humanitarian aid cut off to "rebel areas" by the government, villagers who survived the raids only too often succumbed to starvation or disease.

Scores of hopeful Dinka who were missing relatives had heard about CSI's visit and were waiting anxiously on the sidelines. A few of them were about to get lucky and be reunited with a missing child, sister, or mother. Most, unfortunately, would go home disappointed. But until the day the government's onslaught could be brought to an end, they would keep their hopes up for the next redemption.

Lucian had asked the expectant relatives if he could take their picture, and Sharon and I watched him approach each group with a smile and a deferential nod of his head. Already a friendly lot, the Dinka who had gathered here were happy to oblige—the fact that the *khawaja* photographer was in the same group as the redeemers vaulted him to superstar status. Like Eibner, I guessed that Lucian's work here and in other developing countries was largely successful because of the respect he bore for the local people.

Dominic and Angelo wandered over with clipboards bearing checklists of names and a list of suggested questions for our interviews. Angelo peered shyly at Sharon over his glasses, which were constantly slipping down his nose. "I think John wants us to work together today, Sharon, if that's all right with you."

Before she could answer, I took the chance to get a little teasing in. "Are you sure it's John that came up with that idea, Angelo?"

Dominic saved him. "No, it was I who suggested. I am married man, cannot work with beautiful woman all day in the hot sun!" We all laughed good-naturedly. But as Sharon turned to walk off with Angelo to another patch of grass, Eibner dashed up.

"Don't forget to keep drinking water, even if you don't feel thirsty," he said to Sharon and me. I thought it odd that I was barely sweating, even though I had never felt so hot in my life. Gunnar had been kind enough to give us the temperature in degrees Fahrenheit. ("One-nineteen in the shade," he had joked.) Even Sharon, Miss Indiana Jones, was starting to show signs of wilting.

"I need Angelo with me," said Eibner, who was doing his own interviewing under the mango tree. "Aaron, why don't you work the camera for Sharon and let her do the interviewing so you can see how it's done," he said. It was not a question.

"Great!" I responded, happy to have the chance to help Sharon do her thing for Senator Brownback's office. I was, after all, supposed to be here as an observer and field assistant. I also needed to go back with some good footage of my own if I was going to raise antislavery funds.

"So you two come with me over here." Dominic waved us over to another clump of high grass crackling in the midday sun. There was not enough shade to go around, and we needed privacy. "We will start with this girl here."

No matter how much research and soul-searching I had done up to that point, nothing could have prepared me to confront the sheer humility of an enslaved child.

Ayer, fourteen years old, sat across from us on the ground, her legs folded unnaturally off to the side as the sun beat down on her bare head and flies feasted on her bare feet, covered with sores. Her eyes were downcast and her fingers fidgeted with the holes in the torn brown sack that was her only garment. The scars on Ayer's legs, arms, and neck told me that the minor discomfort she was experiencing now meant nothing in comparison to what she'd already suffered.

Luckily Sharon was handling the questioning. I was so moved by Ayer's tragic appearance alone that I was grateful I could hide my eyes behind the camera.

9/11: NOT GOOD FOR BUSINESS

VENICE, CALIFORNIA

August 2001

It happens, man, you get older. Decisions . . . Sometimes, you run out of options. Like I can be 28, completely strung out and building Lollapalooza. But I gotta tell you honestly I can't be a 42-year-old, strung out, and building Jubilee. So I made my choice. Yeah, you can do Jubilee but you can't be a strung out [inaudible] on Jubilee. So I said, Okay. No problems. I'll do that. I'll hook up, I'll use all my vitality to building this time. Let's see something out there—not in my room, not in my head, not in my "future." Let's see something. Let's see something tangible. So. That's my choice.

—Perry Farrell, talking about how his life had changed with Jay Babcock for the *LA Weekly*, summer 2001

I WOKE UP EARLY AND WENT NEXT DOOR TO PERRY'S house to get the surfboards and pack up the truck for our quintessential ritual, an early morning Bible study and wave session. For the past few years, Perry and I had been studying the Torah, the Zohar, and singing King David psalms in Hebrew together. Before paddling out, we finished looking at the chapter in Genesis where Joseph is sold into slavery by his brothers. He goes to Egypt a slave, but winds up becoming a skilled interpreter of Pharaoh's dreams. After predicting that Egypt would experience seven years of abundance followed by a great famine, he is made the king's viceroy and oversees the stockpiling of grain. When the shortage comes, Egypt is prepared. Joseph's brothers then come to him seeking help, unaware of his identity.

"Only when Judah repents," I pointed out, "does Joseph reveal himself to his brothers and accept them as his own." To close the session, we lit incense and offered up our intentions for friends, family, and peace. Perry made special mention of Dave Navarro, whose drug problems were out of hand again and had been giving the concert organizers cause to worry. Perry and Dave had supported each other through some dark periods, and now it was Dave who needed Perry. Perry had stopped using hard drugs so he could focus on family and music. Being a father had changed his outlook, and he'd just released a solo album full of songs dealing with the Jubilee theme. The cover art depicted Perry blowing a trumpet similar to the one he was now cradling in his arms. He looked at me, and gave the ram's horn trumpet known as a shofar a long blast. Like a favorite song, the sound of the ancient trumpet was always at the back of my mind. Today, it signaled that it was time to look to the waves for revelation.

Just before leaving the house, we got a call from Red Hot Chili Peppers' bassist Flea, who had played with Jane's during the Relapse Tour and remained a close friend of the band. He was also heading north to surf. Summer was coming to an end, and a reunited Jane's was getting ready to head out on the Jubilee Tour, which had been four years in the making. Perry and I found Flea in the parking area and followed the cliff trail to the beach. We paddled out to the break known as Zeros, and hardly spoke as we waited for a set to roll in.

Perry paddled farther away and sat on his board praying for surf. He caught a few waves and then stretched out on the beach to meditate. I kept surfing with Flea for a while, thinking of how grateful I was. The Jubilee thesis was no longer just a stack of paper. It was about to become a living, breathing, musical tour with money going to free slaves in Sudan. Our Jubilee dream was coming true.

Later on, Perry and I drove to his manager Trudy Green's house in the Hollywood Hills to screen the video we were planning to show onstage during the Jubilee Tour, which so far included a reunited Jane's, Live, Femi Kuti, Stereo MC's, Hole, Goldie, and Foo Fighters. Trudy represented rock legends such as Mick Jagger and Steven Tyler, but reserved a special affection for Perry. She treated him like a superstar.

Perry and I staged a mock light-saber battle with Trudy's sons for a few minutes before sitting down to screen the video, which explained to fans why one dollar from every ticket sold was going to benefit the Jubilee Foundation and the American Anti-Slavery Group, an NGO working alongside John Eibner in Sudan. We had edited together video images that captured the essence of all we had been studying, a sort of "Jubilee 101" introducing the audience to the concept of a musical celebration for freedom and justice. The video was a mix of performance clips, tribal music, and footage I had shot of Sudanese slaves being interviewed and reunited with their families. At one point, we had crosscut an image of the Western Wall in Jerusalem with a clip of a tank rolling through the desert.

Trudy pressed pause and turned to me. "Oh, Aaron . . . Why have you put tanks in the Jubilee video?"

I explained that the arrival of the Jubilee year would coincide with a conflict in the Middle East and the failure of financial markets in the West. "It just means the stage is set," I said, echoing the point we had made in the video. Everybody seemed to love the 101 and 202 versions of the Jubilee, forgiving debts and freeing slaves. But they—Trudy included—preferred to present our Jubilee celebration as a feel-good music festival. Further explanations of Jubilee 303 with military conflicts and economic downturns would have to wait, at least for now, until people were ready to start connecting the dots themselves.

"Well, people are going to think you're forecasting a war. That part has to be edited out." Trudy turned to Perry. "You simply can't show that onstage." Trudy busied herself in the kitchen while the rest of the video rolled.

An uncomfortable silence fell over us. I understood then that it was simply not cool to mix biblical prophecy with a rock festival. To Trudy, I sounded like Chicken Little, predicting the imminent crashing down of the sky. Everything changed after that meeting.

"Well," Perry said in the car on the way home, "we tried."

I could see how disappointed he was. We had been so proud of our collaborative work on the Jubilee video. I didn't know at the time that it was going to be the last piece of media we would make together.

The tour started a week later, and so did the clear signs that the mission behind the Jubilee Tour was doomed. Although we'd founded the Jubilee Foundation and built up a core group of human rights activists to coordinate the charity side of things, they were getting the cold shoulder from the managers—the guys assigned to make sure that Perry's business was making money. First the new road manager indicated he had no interest in getting along with the activists and volunteers I'd brought on. Jesse Baker and Eric Lubitz had been coordinating our efforts with the American Anti-Slavery Group. When Jesse, one of our brightest people, was suddenly fired by the road manager for being fifteen minutes late to a staff meeting that didn't even require his presence, I knew it indicated bigger problems ahead. The veiled message was : *We don't like your vision for this Jubilee concept, Aaron, and you're either going to be reeled in or pushed out.* Two of the tour's dancers, Archie Bell and Etty Lau, had been working overtime overseeing the volunteers and doing the legwork to spread the word about the tour and raise money to free slaves in Sudan. But the tension between the activists and road managers only seemed to get worse.

About a week into the tour, in early September, I flew home to check on Papa, who was suffering from shingles. He was in terrible pain and had been begging me to come and spend time with him. I had been home for two days when I woke earlier than usual and headed to the gym to work out. On the way there, I tuned in to the car radio and heard that a plane had crashed into the World Trade Center. I knew that something was very wrong. A few minutes later I was on the treadmill, my eyes trained on the bank of televisions—all zeroed in on the same location. The other early morning runners and I watched in collective horror as the second plane smashed into the other tower and burst into flames.

I pushed the stop button on the treadmill so I could wipe the tears out of my eyes. I sank to the floor, staring at the television and the shock on the faces of everyone at the gym. Strangers grabbed on to each other as the reality of what was happening sank in. We were watching a mass murder on live television. How many people could there be in those towers at 8:30 on a Tuesday? What were their families thinking right now?

When I saw that people had started jumping from the windows, I ran out to my car and cried some more. Jubilee 303 was coming true. There would be more wars. But I knew from the way Trudy had reacted that if I said it out loud, people would be frightened or think I was crazy. I cried for what it all meant. I cried for the people who were suffering, and I cried for my own isolation, with the fear of G-d in my heart.

Manhattan was on lockdown, and the tour was stranded there. I felt fortunate to be by Papa's side in California, but also a bit lost at a moment like this. Part of me wanted to be in the thick of it all, surrounded by my tribe. And then the phone rang. Hoping it was Perry, whom I'd had a hard time getting a hold of, I pounced on it. But the line was silent. I hung up, and the phone rang again.

"Hello?" I said. "Hello?" Still no response.

This time I heard breathing. So I tried one more time. "Hello?"

"Jew dog," said a man's voice. "You die." And he hung up.

My heart started to race. I told myself it was just a prank, or a mistake. I tried to imagine why someone would be doing this, but couldn't find the answer. I had trouble sleeping the next few nights. After a few days of looking after Papa, I drove up to Venice to pack my bags so that I could rejoin the tour. I returned to my place on National to find it ransacked. My computer had been stolen and someone had taken a baseball bat to my truck.

Scrawled in the grime on the back windshield, they had left me a message: "Jew dog stay out of Sudan."

I felt strangely vacant. At first I was scared, and then I started to get angry. I called Charles Jacobs at the American Anti-Slavery

Group. He told me to call the police, and maybe even the FBI. "But don't worry, Aaron," he said. "This is how these things go."

Eibner was just as reassuring when we spoke. I stopped by the police precinct, and asked some of my friends there to look into it. But no one could give me the answers I was looking for.

By the time I boarded the virtually empty airplane back to New York a week and a half after 9/11, the world felt like a different place. The other passengers looked as uneasy as I felt.

But I couldn't stay home and hide out under the blankets. I had to get back to work.

When I arrived in New York, the city seemed unified in its grief and in its citizens' need to bond as a human family. But instead of bringing us together, the disaster had put the tour personnel on edge, and the rift between our activists and road managers had reached critical mass by the time I reappeared. The Jubilee concert date at Madison Square Garden had been put on hold until the authorities could address all their new security concerns. Bono and Paul McCartney had also decided to fly into town to do a separate benefit for 9/11 victims the night before the Jubilee show with Jane's Addiction. A rock tour being delayed by even one day unleashes a chain reaction of problems. Everyone loses money. So a tour that's delayed indefinitely becomes pure chaos.

As we waited for the city to pull itself back together, the road managers offhandedly broke the news that the concert monies for which I'd fought so hard were now going to be partially diverted to the 9/11 Fund instead of the American Anti-Slavery Group, which was understandable given what had just happened, but still devastating news for our cause. I felt as if my whole world was coming apart. They hadn't even consulted me before dismantling everything I'd worked so hard to pull together. This time I couldn't turn to Perry for support. He had fallen in love with star dancer Etty Lau, who had all of his attention. Once again I felt us moving in separate orbits.

Still, I tried to make the most of the remaining time with my colleagues, even though I knew that things would never be the same. At a bar that night, a few journalists came over and started asking the usual questions about Perry and the concert tour. One mentioned my trips to Sudan and said he'd heard something about Al Qaeda issuing a hit list featuring enemies of jihad. He knew that John Eibner had received death threats for the work he was doing in Sudan, and wondered if I, too, might be targeted for my involvement. He said he thought he'd seen my name on a list of infidels published on a website linked to Al Nida, a known portal for Islamic extremists. I'd seen it, too, but since 9/11 the site had been taken down.

I was already in such an emotional state that I barely thought about what I was saying. "How should I know if the death threats are real?" I asked him. "Maybe I should hunt down the terrorists in their caves to find out if they really want to kill us." *The death fatwa is not just directed at me, but at all of us.* I never imagined that the information would end up in the tabloids.

Sure enough, over the course of the next several days I fielded several more anonymous phone calls on my cell phone. The caller never said anything this time, but I could hear him breathing. When the calls started coming in at all hours, I took to turning my cell phone off when I went to bed. So I was startled to be awakened by the sound of the hotel phone ringing a few nights later.

"Yeah?"

"Jew, die!" the caller said.

Click. It was the same person who had called me in California, with the same Middle Eastern accent. I sat for a while staring at the carpet, listening to the dial tone. Whoever he was, this guy knew my location. I was scared.

Through my antislavery work, I'd made a couple of acquaintances at the Pentagon and FBI, and I called them for advice. They told me there wasn't much they could do unless the caller took a step further. They advised me to record the calls, or to change my number. The next morning I bought a new phone and tried to put the incident out of my mind. It turned out I had more immediate problems.

As we held our breath in New York to find out when we would actually do the show, a story titled "Terrorists Target Slavery Foe" was published on Page Six of the *New York Post*. The article claimed that Al Qaeda had issued a fatwa, an Islamic edict, imposing a death sentence on no other than Aaron Cohen. The story was sandwiched between pictures of Bono on one page and Perry on the next. Bono was quoted as saying he would never give up his struggle for human rights, even in the face of death threats.

We had been ushered into the post-9/11 era, and most people still weren't aware of it. I had already met the *murahaleen* firsthand and heard the testimony of *mujahideen* warriors, who believed wholeheartedly in the righteousness of their jihad by the sword. My experience told me that religious extremists were truly a threat to Western civilization, but given the anti-Islamic fervor the attacks had ignited in the United States, I knew a bigger enemy than the "terrorists" was the enemy within ourselves. Surely the response to terror was not to be found in another war.

We finally got a tour date in mid-October. I took a taxi down to Madison Square Garden from my midtown hotel. From fifty blocks away, I could smell the ash and feel the dust of Ground Zero in my lungs. A month after the tragedy, a look of mourning and disbelief still clung to most of the faces I passed. When I got backstage at the Garden before the show, everyone was still gossiping about the *Post* piece. The paper had since received an anthrax-laced letter that had sent three of their employees to the hospital. Everyone on the tour was looking at me as if I were a ghost. The road manager finally walked up to me and said, "Aaron, people are scared with you around. You're free to do what you want, but this stuff you're getting into just doesn't go with rock and roll." One of the other managers added, "You're in over your head, man. Not good for business."

The only one who didn't seem surprised by the outcome of 9/11 was Perry Farrell. We met for drinks that night after the show, and he was sanguine about it all. Naturally he was devastated by the loss of life but, like me, had been anticipating some radical changes. We'd both been telling people about the coming conflict. It was all part of the prophecies we'd been studying in the Jubilee. Even though we'd read the script and knew how the story went, the events still came as a shock. Perry had named his oldest son Yobel, which means "Jubilee" in Hebrew. I was his godfather. Now here we were observing the Hebrew high holidays—the time for revelation, renewal, and blowing the shofar. I knew we had reached the end of an era and were starting another, very different one.

We hugged good-bye. Only this time we didn't make any future plans together.

ALLEZ, ALLEZ, ALLEZ!

CRIED MY HEART OUT ON THE PLANE RIDE HOME, listening to Nirvana as the past decade came rushing back. The senseless deaths of 9/11 made me think about all our friends who had died needlessly. Colleen, my friend from college—dead of an overdose in her twenties. Hillel Slovak from the Chili Peppers, who, even after a four- or five-day binge, could lay down music that made your soul cry. He, too, had overdosed. Kurt Cobain had shot himself in the head with a shotgun after a week-long run on drugs. Later on, Elliott Smith stabbed himself in the heart after desperately trying to kick drugs.[1]

And now three thousand innocent people had been killed in a terrorist attack, our economy was faltering, and our president suggested we heal our pain by going shopping! I didn't want to live in a time or place where the pursuit of wealth was more valuable than bringing an end to human suffering. There no longer seemed to be a place in our society for new ideas, romantic dreamers, or prophets, and that's what hit me the hardest. I looked at the all-seeing eye on a dollar bill in my pocket. Would the 9/11 disaster really mean an end to the financial markets that were created to free us from kings and colonizers but had ended up enslaving us to the almighty dollar?

For the last four years I'd told myself that through the universal languages of love and music, peace on earth was within reach. That's how I'd been interpreting the Jubilee. But now I realized there was so much more to grasp.

My Jubilee dream was not lost, but I had to find a new direction in which to take it. Drop the Debt had been the first step. I remembered something Bono had said on that campaign, responding to the criticism some of the other musicians were leveling at politicians they deemed "uncool." He pointed out that we had to work with anyone who wanted to help us reduce poverty and suffering, no matter how uncool they might be.

We were getting closer to California, and as I went through all of this in my mind I prepared myself for the reality I was about to confront. I would have to set aside my spiritual mission for a while and tend to Papa—just another phase in my ongoing struggle to balance out my dreams and filial duties. By the time we touched down, I'd resigned myself to an immediate future as parental caregiver. Papa's condition was deteriorating and I needed to be there for him. But I was mentally prepared to start planning my next big assignment, one that would finally start bringing together all the elements I'd been striving to put to use. I'd already seen in Sudan that as a mere individual I could be a small part of the change we needed. I didn't need rock stars or Jubilee tours to make change happen. I merely had to help other people see what I saw—that we each had the power to act out against the very powerful forces that were corrupting our society and enslaving people.

I started to think of the struggle like the starfish parable. A man is walking along the beach one morning at low tide when he sees a woman picking up starfish that have washed up on the beach. She's throwing them back in the water, one at a time. He approaches and asks the woman what she's doing.

"I'm giving these starfish a chance," she says. "If I do nothing, they'll die."

"Yeah, but there are thousands of starfish washed up on this beach, and on every other beach," he says. "It happens every day. It's just the way it is. You can't possibly make a difference."

The woman throws another starfish back in the water, smiles at the man, and says: "Well, I made a difference to *that* one."

A few weeks after I came back from New York, Papa had a massive stroke and went into the hospital. Arthur and Ruthie flew in to help me see him through weeks of rehabilitation. We didn't know if he would walk or be able to talk again. The nurses looked at us and asked, "Which senior care facility will your father be going to after this?"

We looked at each other and discussed the options. Either I stayed with Papa to take care of him, or he would have to go into a nursing home—our last resort. Arthur had a wife, seven kids, and dozens of patients to take care of. Ruthie had a husband, five daughters, and a dog named Lucy at home. I'd just lost my job with Perry. I was available. I gave up my Venice apartment and moved my things back into my childhood bedroom in Costa Mesa.

Months went by. I didn't call Perry and he didn't call me. Every morning I would wake up early and make Papa his breakfast, change him, get him dressed and walk or wheel him to the kitchen table. I think Perry and I each felt abandoned by the other. He had released a solo album and was about to record another with a reunited Jane's. His name was everywhere again. And I was sitting at home in the suburbs, spoon feeding a father who'd abused me and yet whom I loved more than anyone in the world.

A journalist from a small magazine in Florida contacted me for an interview about combating slavery in Sudan, and after the feature appeared, an acquaintance at the American Anti-Slavery Group told me that Ricky Martin was interested in meeting me. Ricky had his own charity foundation, and had been active in rescuing Indian children from a lifetime in debt bondage.

Ricky's coordinator, Mireille Bravo, and I had an immediate connection, and within a few short weeks (while I worked on a laptop from Papa's bedside) we launched a new initiative under the Ricky Martin Foundation umbrella—People for Children, dedicated to protecting vulnerable kids from falling into traffickers' hands.

A few months later, Ricky asked if I would approach the Dalai Lama and ask him to star in a series of public service announcements (PSAs) warning children about the pitfalls of human trafficking. I had been languishing in the dark with Papa, dreaming of getting back to Sudan, and here was this big celebrity interested in doing more for enslaved children in India and in Latin America. Of course I was interested.

Juanita and Maxima had become like my surrogate mothers, and I knew I could trust them to take good care of Papa while I was away. He'd been responding well to therapy, and thrived under the glow of some female attention.

When I was invited to the Surfers Healing dinner to help kids with autism, I didn't expect to run into Perry. It was really strange to suddenly see this close friend with whom I hadn't exchanged a word in almost a year. We had both changed our cell phone numbers and fallen completely out of touch. Nevertheless, when I told him about the PSA project for Ricky Martin, I expected Perry to be happy for me. Instead I saw in his expression a sense of betrayal and contempt. Ricky Martin was a pop star, not the cutting-edge artist Perry was used to working with.

Still, I missed him, and told him so over a glass of wine. Once we started talking, I found myself pining for the days of surfing and studying together. "Hey Per," I said, looking him in the eye. "You've gotta come to Sudan and see for yourself. I think you could connect to these people with your music."

"It's going to be hard to get away," Perry said. "But I'll figure it out." We hugged good-bye again. I knew he was true to his word.

The next morning I was back to work on the People for Children task list. After months of lobbying Tibetan activists, intellectuals, and officials, I'd finally gotten the go-ahead from the Dalai Lama's special envoy, Lodi Gyari. His Holiness had agreed to participate in the PSA project. I was overjoyed. Ricky asked me to go ahead to India and set up the shoot. He and his team would arrive the following week.

I got to Delhi very early in the morning, and the first thing I noticed upon leaving the airport was the chaos outside the security gates. It was still dark. The stench of hopeless poverty permeated everything in India, even the darkness, in a way I had never before experienced. I covered my face with a scarf and began the journey that would take me up to the Himalayas where the Dalai Lama lived in exile. I had already traveled widely, but the series of hotels, taxis, and trains I experienced in India forced me to confront the kind of desperation I had only read about in books. Lepers begging in the streets, and armies of homeless, maimed, and destitute people for-gotten by humanity.

After nearly a week of traveling, I arrived in Dehradun, at the base of the Himalayan range near the Indian-Pakistani border. I immediately set out to hire a production company and get ready for Ricky's arrival. In my rare downtime, I read the Dalai Lama's book *The Way to Freedom* and befriended a monk at the Mind-rolling Monastery in Dehradun. Thin Ly showed me how human bones were sculpted into trumpets used in Tibetan Jubilee celebra-tions and taught me some meditation techniques. Ricky and his people were already a few days late, but I kept my mind in the pres-ent and learned to enjoy monastic life.

My thoughts drifted to Arthur, who was stationed with a med-ical unit far west of here in the mountains of Afghanistan. Right then my brother the army surgeon was probably setting up another field hospital and seeing all the worst things a war could visit upon an ER. I prayed for his safety.

Finally the phone rang, and I could barely make out Mireille Bravo's Puerto Rican accent through the static. "We're not com-ing!" she yelled, so that I could hear her. "We been denied airspace to come over there!"

In the midst of a war, it turned out, the Afghani authorities wouldn't grant Ricky's private jet permission to fly over Afghanistan to India. He and the whole team had to head back to Paris.

I'd just spent days learning to detach from worldly concerns, but my spirits fell at this news. For a moment I worried that the Dalai Lama wouldn't want to film the PSAs without Ricky. But I soon realized that of all people, this was a man who would understand.

Just as I'd hoped, His Holiness was still eager to go ahead. We would simply have to record Ricky's part separately when we got back to the United States. Lodi Gyari, the Dalai Lama's closest adviser, was not surprised to hear that Ricky had been refused air-space. "We're always denied the right to fly over Tibet," he chuck-led, "as well as over any other countries closely aligned with China." There was not a hint of bitterness in his voice, nor in his warm brown eyes.

"It means, perhaps," he said, with that same twinkle, "that our meeting today is very auspicious, Mr. Cohen."

We stopped the car at the base of a mountain, where a group of young Tibetan children had lined up to see the foreigners. I hoped they wouldn't be disappointed that they were getting me instead of Ricky Martin, but they were all smiles as I got out of the car.

One of the monks gave the kids a signal, and they started joyfully singing Ricky's big hit, "La Copa de la Vida" at the top of their lungs: "La, la, la ... *allez, allez, allez!*" They'd clearly been practicing. What a moment! Their sweet innocence melted all the worries that had been knocking around in my brain: Papa at home calling out for me in the night, my brother in the midst of a war zone, Ricky Martin stranded in Paris, Perry in California moving on without me. Right there I felt myself snap out of it. These adorable kids sang and cheered and held my hands with their own—rock star or not, they were just happy to have me there.

Then it was time to meet the man himself.

Tenzin Geche, the Dalai Lama's private secretary, and I walked along a cliffside path, surrounded by snowcapped peaks. It was a clear afternoon and everything I experienced from then on—from the wind on my face to the colors of the landscape—felt ancient. Wind chimes sent us their tune from every direction. We passed a few checkpoints until I could see a small wooden temple on the rise above us. It was like a small palace on a cliff offset by sky. Another monk approached, bowed, and said with a quick smile, "His Holiness will be here eminently." He may have meant "imminently," but either way the word seemed to fit.

I stood there, suddenly nervous, arms folded in prayer across my chest. I began to sweat a bit in my suit and tie, touching the multicolored badgelike prayer wheel Geche had pinned on my lapel. The badge was like a VIP pass that granted me access all over the compound.

In a moment, out came an older man dressed in a simple crimson monk's shift just like the others. I had no trouble picking Tenzin Gyatso, the fourteenth Dalai Lama, out by his incomparable smile and square glasses. The two monks flanking him carried umbrellas to shield His Holiness from the sun, followed by a retinue of a half dozen monks and advisers.

His Holiness ambled toward me on the Himalayan trail until we were face-to-face. One of the monks with a parasol extended it up high enough to ensure that I was also in the shade. The Dalai Lama reached out his hand and held mine with a peaceful expression.

"You are the man who frees slaves?" he said, without releasing his gentle grip.

"Your Holiness," I said. "I am the one who moves children from point A to point B." I had never felt so humbled by the presence of anyone in my life.

He had been briefed about some of the work I had done in Sudan and with the Drop the Debt campaign. But he also knew about Jubilee, and told me that the lamas had their own version of it in Tibetan Buddhism.

"What motivates you to free slaves?" he suddenly asked me, never losing the sparkle in his eyes. I thought about his question and gave the simplest answer I could.

"Your Holiness, I am a man of faith."

"Ah yes, you have a Hebrew name," he said. He was still holding on to my right hand, and he could see I was a bit perplexed. He tugged impishly on my hand, laughed, and teased me about my height. But he continued to hold my hand. The Dalai Lama had suffered greatly, yet bore no signs of that suffering. He radiated sincerity, humility, and happiness.

We moved on to discuss how Israel, deprived of its land, language, and national heritage, had maintained an identity and resurrected a nation after nearly two thousand years—an event predicted by the biblical prophets.

"There were many wise men, Your Holiness, in those days, who saw that Israel would become a nation again." The Dalai Lama raised one eyebrow. Here was a man who had lost his country but kept his nation alive through teachings that inspired people from every culture.

"After the exile of the prophets of Israel, the word spread to all people, so that the curse of Israel's destruction turned into a blessing," I said. "The world wars and the Holocaust changed people's perceptions. They began to return to the land."

I thought at first that maybe I had hit too close to home, because here the Dalai Lama responded with a long "Mmmm," before explaining his conception of detachment, which he cautioned was "not the same as indifference." He continued to look me directly in the eyes, seemingly without blinking, still calmly holding my hand. "I would like for you to help the Chinese children as well," he suggested. I sputtered out a reply, surprised that Chinese kids would be one of his first concerns after the treatment he had received from their government.

But that was what was so incredible about this man. He defied all expectation.

For the next few minutes, I tried to find the answers to a host of questions he and his lamas posed about biblical history, particularly in terms of the reestablishment of a conquered nation. I think he felt comfortable speaking with me about it because he could tell that my only agenda was to share *havruso* with him.

"Your Holiness," I said, "I'd like to tell you about the concept of *havruso* in Hebrew. It comes from *ahavah,* a Hebrew word that means 'love,' but not in a romantic sense."

He smiled, indicating I should continue.

"*Havruso* alludes to 'lovers,' but again, not in the traditional sense. It is usually applied to one who seeks wisdom with another learner and becomes one with that person in truth. Which is another way of giving love."

The Dalai Lama paused to consider all this, then pronounced the word himself.

"*Havruso*s give us hope for national redemption," I said. "So I hope your country will be reborn again someday, Your Holiness, and thank you for being a global *havruso* for so many people of high consciousness."

The Dalai Lama smiled again, graciously, and tied a white silk scarf around my neck. As I bowed to receive it, he mischievously pinched my arm and made a joke about how I made him look short.

Assuming how busy he must be, I kept waiting for him to excuse himself, but he continued to keep me engaged. He carried himself with a regal modesty that was infectious, and I found myself holding my head up higher as our conversation stretched on.

We finally spoke about slavery and the work of finding and assisting human trafficking victims. I mentioned that Abraham, Isaac, and Jacob's G-d had been the Bible's first slave retrievers, when He led the Israelites out of chains in Egypt.

His Holiness released the grip on my hand ever so slightly and told me he looked forward to seeing the results of our actions. It was time to shoot the PSA, and he excused himself with another affectionate smile and little fanfare. We would have time to say our farewells after lunch. The Dalai Lama expressed concern that I might be hungry or tired, and directed Tenzin Geche to make sure I was taken care of.

Even though this audience had been reserved for Ricky Martin, the Dalai Lama made me feel as though I were his most important guest. I noted that he treated everyone—from the cook to the top lamas—with the same love and respect. I could see the lightning bolts behind his dancing eyes and was delighted by his level of engagement in our work.

After a delicious lunch with Tenzin Geche and the lamas, we recorded the Dalai Lama's short speech warning children about human trafficking. Several hours later, after we had shot the second segment, His Holiness walked over to me to say good-bye. Crew members prostrated themselves at his feet, and he stopped to bless each one of them. He had come to offer another warm handshake, divine smile, and one more white scarf for the road. As he walked slowly up the hill to his temple, he turned, beamed, and proclaimed, "Free the slaves!"

THE FREEDOM PARTY

COSTA MESA, CALIFORNIA

Fall 2002

MEETING THE DALAI LAMA HAD HELPED RESTORE confidence in the Jubilee dream. Through the Ricky Martin Foundation I'd been meeting more activists and could feel a real momentum building within the growing antislavery movement. But I was still being torn between my professional aspirations and personal obligations.

Papa was struggling with the role reversal we had undergone. Although he'd had a year and a half of rehabilitation after his stroke and could walk again with some assistance, he was often confused and depressed. The idea of me disappearing for more than a week upset him both emotionally and physically.

Juanita had more or less moved into our extra bedroom, and while I still handled getting Papa up and dressed, she took over the job of making his pancakes—one of the few things he still liked to eat. After breakfast, Papa would settle into the shabby old couch he loved. That meant it was time for me to turn on the Western channel—*Barney* for seniors. He had gone from being my father to being my baby.

I passed the time writing, singing, playing songs on the guitar, and surfing, but my mind was always on getting back to antislavery work. Even though some of the Jubilee Tour monies had been diverted to other charities, Jane's Addiction had managed to raise enough from one concert to free 2,300 slaves through the American Anti-Slavery Group, which was pooling its funds with CSI. One afternoon, John Eibner called to thank me and asked if Perry and I were interested in coming on a trip together during the winter dry season. Of course we were. It was exactly what Perry and I had talked about doing the last time we'd seen each other. Perry had helped create the foundation, given the concerts, and raised the funds—now he would get to see what was being done with them.

Six weeks later, I went over to Perry's to help him pack for the trip. But instead of concentrating on supplies, I spent most of my time reassuring Etty that everything would be okay. Etty had worked hard to raise money and inspire the charity workers behind the Jubilee Tour. But now she was pregnant with Perry's baby, and concerned for his safety in a war zone.

Ruthie came out to spend some time with Papa, and Perry and I flew to Zurich to meet up with Eibner. On the plane, we finally got the chance to talk about everything that had happened since I was pushed off the Jubilee Tour. It turned out we each felt we'd been taken for granted by the other.

"Look, man," he said. "I heard some things on the tour, and I want you to know that I gave you the benefit of the doubt."

I didn't want to go down that trail. The rumors, gossip, and backstabbing that went on in the music world no longer concerned me. So what if someone had said bad things behind my back? "You know none of it's true, Per," I said.

"Well, better to know what people are saying then get side-swiped," he replied. It was going to be hard for both of us to shake off people's past perceptions.

"Look . . . I relapsed after Papa's stroke," I confessed, "but I'm clean now." He nodded. So was he.

We both wanted to change the subject. So we ended up talking about how the study of Jubilee had changed both of our lives. After being on drugs full-time for more than a decade, rediscovering his spirituality and finding the way into fatherhood were like miracles of divine proportion for Peretz Bernstein. He had learned to surround himself with healthy people who loved him, and now he had a family. The Jubilee dream and the antislavery work had already taken me to some fearful places. But I believed

in the dream enough to know that I'd eventually break through
to find deeper meaning.

The seat belt light was on, and we could see the ground now.

"Jambo!" I said, excited, using a common Swahili word for
Hello.

"It's amazing, Aaron," Perry said. "We're actually going to
Sudan."

It was great to smell the African earth and stand beneath a big sky
again. We flew first from Nairobi to Loki, and jumped in Heather
Stewart's plane to northern Bahr el Ghazal, where Dr. Luka's clinic
in Wanjuk was finally open for business. The regular crew had gathered to greet us: Pastor Tito, Dominic, Angelo, and Longar. We all
hugged, and I felt as if I were introducing a long-lost relative to the
rest of my tribe. Perry fell into the rhythm of the group and the
fieldwork immediately.

This trip was shorter and less strenuous than the previous two.
Africa's longest and deadliest civil war was showing signs of slowing down, and I heard the word *cease-fire* being whispered around
the evening campfire. Eibner's work with the Arab-Dinka peace
committees was helping to replace discord with dialogue. Government negotiators from north and south had also been meeting to
discuss terms for a possible treaty. Over the last few months, slave
raids had been decreasing in severity and number.

That meant there were fewer redemptions to be made and less
mileage to clock between each site. I told Perry we had it easy, and
joked that I missed the days of Gunnar and Eibner's grueling ten-
mile hikes through the desert. Our tiny group spent the first two
days in the vicinity of the big mango tree, interviewing, fingerprint-
ing, and handing out survival kits to the three hundred women and
children that Nur's redemption team had brought back from Kordofan and Darfur.

Groups of scraggly, smiling kids clustered around Perry, making
him giggle back. His sensitive nature made him approachable, and I
watched him relate easily to everyone in the camp—particularly the

former slaves. Perry's charisma attracted all kinds of people, no matter what language they spoke. His face simply shone. Even though they had no idea he was a celebrity, the Dinka elders treated Perry with reverence.

When the temperature one afternoon had become unbearable, Dominic came over to see if Perry needed anything.

"Hey, Dominic, remember when you used to check on *me*?" I laughed. Dominic was listening to a portable CD player, and I pulled the headset off his ears. The sound of Perry's album *Song Yet to Be Sung* reverberated through the tent. So the word was out! Perry had never had trouble finding new fans in the strangest places, and a Sudanese war zone was no exception. But at least his new groupies left him alone at night.

Until, that is, Perry organized the Freedom Party.

Before leaving L.A., he had bought a huge boom box he could use with a digital interface to record, remix, and amplify sound. He'd pull up a beat, program in the drum lines and some additional parts . . . *et voilà*! DJ Peretz was completely mobile. The night the first group of slaves was reunited with their families, he set up his lightweight equipment on a folding table near the mango tree.

We watched as a pair of long-lost adolescent brothers found each other in the crowd. They gasped in excitement as they grabbed at each other's heads, one finally settling on an embrace that was closer to a headlock. Angelo would later explain that the boys' parents had been killed in a village raid, their children whisked off to separate fates with new masters in the north. It had been six years since they'd seen each other.

Perry raised the boom box over his head and grinned.

No advance warning or explanation was needed. *Click!* Perry pressed the play button, and right away people started to dance and sway their hips in unison. Perry joined them in a chant that became a cheer, and eventually a song. He handed me the boom box, pulled out his attachable microphone, and sang.

"Hallelujah!" Hallelujah!" they shouted. *"Lau nhom!"* Freedom! Other tribal members came out of their *tukul*s, and Perry sang louder as the group's dancing kicked up a dust cloud. "Put on your mask!" Perry yelled to me as I joined in the pandemonium. But I was too caught up in the moment to worry about a little asthma. I felt a familiar joy come rushing back to my heart. The belief in Jubilee—in redemption for the slaves, and for us all. "I'm free!" I cried with the group of slaves as they surged around me, getting bigger and more frenzied by the minute. It wasn't quite as insane as the mosh pits at one of Jane's Addiction's first Scream shows. But there was that same feeling, that mystical connection Perry had always been able to make with his audience.

"What else should I do?" he mouthed.

"Just keep doing what you're doing!" I shouted back. "Keep playing!"

As the party wore on, the whole village turned out to dance, sing, or just stare at the wild American who had pulled together an impromptu music festival in the midst of the African bush. The dust rose higher, and my wheezing became so severe that I had to step out of the mob to get some air and wash my face. Moving away from the crowd, I passed a ring of SPLA soldiers on the lookout for raiding militias. And off to the side, under the mango tree, was the cluster of *murahaleen* Schindlers, the Arab tribesmen who had negotiated the slaves' release. A half-dozen men in white *jalabiya* sat in a semicircle on the ground, sipping tea and watching the spectacle bemusedly. I was surprised not to find Nur, their leader and Eibner's friend, among them.

I walked closer to see if something was wrong, and found Nur lying down on a blanket, not looking well. When I tried to greet him, Nur made an attempt to stand up. In so doing, he knocked over the teapot, spilling it everywhere and causing him to lose his balance. His men moved to see if he was hurt, but he shooed them away. Nur was the strong, fearless man who had overseen Eibner's intertribal slave retrieval program in three provinces—now he looked positively ill.

As soon as Eibner got word of Nur's condition, he gave the order to pack up the Freedom Party, which was in full swing. I watched him speak quietly with Dr. Luka, who was shaking his head and touching Eibner on the arm. I had never seen Eibner look so concerned.

"Nur is probably in the advanced stages of malaria, and possibly liver failure," Eibner said, walking over to me. "We need to get him to a hospital. Pack everything up now. We leave at dawn."

The next day, we said good-bye to the local crew and boarded the plane. Nur was coming with us to Nairobi, no matter how much red tape Eibner was going to have to deal with to get him there. One of the SPLA soldiers guarding the plane demurred, reminding Eibner that Nur could not be treated in a Kenyan hospital without a passport. The nomadic tribesman did not even have a Sudanese identity card.

"If you think I'm going to leave behind the man responsible for freeing fifty-thousand slaves to die here in the bush . . . ," Eibner responded, his emotions starting to take hold.

We were cleared for takeoff.

A few hours later, in Loki, we transferred Nur on a collapsible wheelchair to the plane waiting for us on the airstrip, setting him up in the two back rows so he'd be more comfortable. He slumped down to hide himself from the Kenyan customs officer in the tiny airport office where the rest of us went to have our passports stamped. The universe smiled on us that morning, and the inspectors decided not to check the new aircraft for stowaways.

With all the focus on Nur, I'd completely disregarded my old responsibility—making sure Perry was doing all right. I looked over at him, buckling himself into the seat next to me. He had a faraway look on his face. He missed Etty.

I asked him about it as we took off. Just thinking about her made him perk up. "Etty and I are going to make music together," he started to say, just as the plane—which had reached its altitude—started to fall fast, wing down. It sounded like one of the engines had gone out. One of the pilots screamed and for a few seconds I thought that was the end of it. But when I looked over at Perry and saw the look of serenity on his face, I knew this wasn't our time. He was about to be a father again. I had seen that same look on his face the split second before he walked onstage in front of twenty thousand fans. He knew then that nothing could touch him, and his confidence in that moment gave me hope. We exchanged a long look and held on to the armrests. In a few moments, the plane pulled out of its wing dive and headed away from the ground.

"Oh, my God!" yelled one of the copilots. "It started, it started! We're okay."

We were still congratulating each other on the crisis averted when Eibner yelled from the back, where he was tending to Nur, "Where do you think you're going?"

He noticed that the pilot had changed course—heading for the closest airport, where he could have the plane checked out. That would have been fine in normal circumstances, but these were far from normal circumstances.

"You can't change course without consulting us!" Eibner protested.

"But sir—" the copilot tried to interject.

"If you take us to the other airport, then you're in violation of our agreement, and we don't have to compensate you," Eibner snapped.

You didn't argue with John Eibner when he was angry.

The pilots hadn't realized we were trying to smuggle a dying man into the hospital. They also couldn't have known that Dr. Luka and Dr. Justin, his Nairobi counterpart, had arranged for an ambulance to pick Nur up at the original airstrip. At any rate, they quickly changed course, obeying their directive.

The cold blast of Nairobi air was a shock to the system after our week spent in the sweltering Nile lowlands. I swaddled Nur in my field jacket, and Perry helped him into a wheelchair. We all knew that Nur was going to die, because there is a face to death, and if you've seen it, you know what to look for. Nur wasn't looking at us. He was resigned—he already belonged to another world.

Dr. Justin was waiting on the tarmac with a wheelchair, ready to hook Nur up to an IV bag. Perry cradled Nur's crumpled body and placed him gingerly in Dr. Justin's arms. The doctor wheeled his charge through the terminal's front gate to an ambulance waiting on the other side. Those who would suggest that the slave redeemers did their work for the money had only to look at the three possessions the old man had accumulated during his illustrious career: one graying *jalabiya*, one pair of sandals, and a walking stick.

Eibner's face was stoic as he watched them take away his friend and colleague. He and Nur had worked together to achieve the peace accord that was on the horizon, but that peace had terms and limitations. The pending cease-fire would likely bring an end to militia raids in South Sudan, and allow millions of captives to return home. Within a year or two, the Sudan Peace Agreement would be signed and the north-south civil war would officially come to an end. But even if all the slaves were freed, Eibner could never have enough humanitarian resources at his disposal. Promised international aid would show up late, or not at all. Freed slaves became refugees who would later die of hunger. He also knew that Bashir government–sponsored militias were being given the assignment to clear new territory. The militias would move on to other provinces. There was rumored to be oil in the northwestern part of the country, in a desolate region the West had yet to hear much about: Darfur.

Our last lonely night in Nairobi, I walked out to the guesthouse garden and prayed for Nur, the Sudanese Arab Muslim who believed that enslaving his black countrymen as a weapon of war was wrong. His life had been a testament to courage, freedom, and humanity. Of taking great risks for strangers of a different faith and ethnic origin.

Back in the Zurich airport, Perry and I had a few minutes to go through the duty-free area, and he stopped to buy an expensive watch for Etty.

"You really love this woman," I said.

Perry grinned. "What should I do, Aaron?"

"Marry her, Peretz," I said. My voice was steady. I knew our friendship was about to become distant. We could no longer be in each other's lives on a daily basis. He had obligations to his wife and children, and I had Papa to look after. Perry and I had been partners in the Jubilee, a quest that had taken him deeper into his music and spirituality and put me on a challenging path to redemption that was still unfolding.

On the second flight, we were both lost in our thoughts until the lights of L.A. came into view.

"Well, man," Perry said, "we did it." And he held out his hand for me to shake. It felt like a real farewell this time.

We waited for our luggage to come off the conveyor belt together. The bags arrived and we looked at each other for a second, until Etty came running up and embraced her husband-to-be. "Take care, Aaron," Perry said, stiffening up to give me a light pat on the back and an awkward hug.

What beautiful music the silence makes, I thought, and walked away to find a taxi home.

Unpacking survival kits for Darfur refugees with Dr. John Eibner, Sudan 2007

This Sudanese slave baby was redeemed for fifty dollars.

Negotiating slave redemptions with the *murahaleen* "Schindlers," Northern Bahr el Ghazal, Sudan

Eibner handing out sorghum rations to IDPs

Slave boys from Darfur waiting under a tree

Dr. Luka treating a young
victim of the Darfur conflict

Freed slaves reunited in Sudan

Perry singing for freed slaves

We found Malwal dying of starvation.
His family had fled the fighting in Darfur.

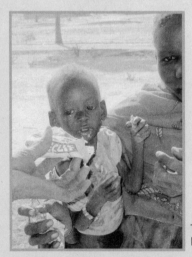

The next day he decided he
liked my apricot Clif bar.

A father is reunited with his sons after six years of enslavement, in Darfur, Sudan.

Perry holding up a boom box as former slaves celebrate freedom

With Perry during slave redemption missions in Sudan, 2002

Visiting with His Holiness the Dalai Lama

PART IV:
LATIN AMERICA

SI DIOS QUIERE

WASHINGTON, D.C.

Winter 2003

THERE'S NO SOUND WORSE THAN A RINGING CELL phone, particularly when it's your own and you have the sense that the call will bear news you are not ready to handle. Before I even looked down at the screen, I sensed that Juanita was on the other end of the line. And I could hear her words before she even spoke them:

"Aa-Rone, Aa-Rone! *Tienes que volver immediatemente . . .*"

I closed my eyes and clenched my fist against my heart as if to stop it from pounding. Papa.

I'd just flown from the Dominican Republic to D.C. and was sitting in Michele Clark's office. Michele was the codirector of the Protection Project, a human rights think tank based at the Johns Hopkins University School of Advanced International Studies. Since 2000, the Protection Project had been doing groundbreaking work in documenting and disseminating information about the scope of human trafficking all over the world. As a consultant for the Ricky Martin Foundation, I wanted to partner with them.

The previous spring, Sharon Payt had made an email introduction after which I attempted to contact Michele to ask how we might get involved in her research—and failed miserably. Michele had left me a voice mail essentially saying, "Thanks, but no thanks," to teaming up with us on a public awareness campaign. I think she initially assumed our effort was merely another lightweight offer from a pop star eager to join the cause célèbre of the moment.

Serendipity had brought us together anyway—at a June 2003 program in Managua, Nicaragua, to help their police officers develop prevention programs for schoolkids. Michele was there as a trainer, and I had been asked[1] to present the research I'd been doing into the growing role of the Internet in the exploitation of minors. The Ricky Martin Foundation had been producing PSAs that were being aired in Nicaragua and other parts of Latin America—the same PSAs for which the Dalai Lama had so graciously filmed a segment.

Although I had already been a part of John Eibner's slave redemption team in Sudan, the Nicaragua trip was the first time I had seen so many people from all facets of the antitrafficking movement come together. It was exhilarating. The conference was held at a training center for Nicaraguan police—a mansion former dictator Somoza had once kept for his mistress. After hearing from a range of experts about everything from legislative issues to the kind of outreach available for rescued women and children (not enough), I finally made my presentation, first elaborating on how traffickers were exploiting online communities to recruit unsuspecting victims, and then suggesting that a modern-day Jubilee observance might be one effective, albeit unorthodox, approach to combating the darkest side of the technology explosion.

A charismatic former actress who started her human rights work as an inner-city public school teacher, Michele Clark was born to a Polish mother and a Russian father who was also a foreign service officer. As a result, she had grown up in the Middle East, Europe, and Africa, and spoke several languages. She moved to Israel in 1996 to teach at the University of Haifa, and quickly found her way into the activist community, along with a bunch of brave women and a few men at the forefront of an emerging movement against a new brand of slavery that had yet to be given a name. Michele has since become a major behind-the-scenes crusader against forced labor, chattel, and sex slavery worldwide.

In the course of an average workday, Michele might have breakfast with government officials, do lunch with think-tank intellectuals, and sit down that night to talk nail polish with a young prostituted girl. She would later move to Vienna to serve as the first head of the Organization for Security and Co-operation in Europe's (OSCE, the world's largest regional security agency) new antitrafficking assistance unit. It had taken some time, but once she warmed up to me I knew Michele was someone I wanted as a friend.

On the Managua trip, Michele and I had discovered a shared passion for history and literature, but perhaps more important, learned that we both saw a victim-centered approach as essential to antitrafficking work. She quickly became a mentor and surrogate big sister, and we talked late into the night over watered-down beers about our dreams of eradicating modern-day slavery. As a diplomat, Michele had a thick rulebook to play by. I didn't. In order to break into the undercover world, I knew I had to be a chameleon, constantly adapting myself to a new set of rules and codes.

Which was how, in much the same way that I had found my way backstage at the Scream club, out on the savannas of Sudan, and up to the hilltop refuge of the Dalai Lama, I wound up accompanying a State Department official called Tom on his evening assessment of Managua.

We had just finished a long day at the training conference, and most of the participants installed themselves at the hotel bar for a safe night in with their colleagues. I decided to get a feel for what was going on in the streets and bars, and ended up out front competing for a taxi with Tom, whom I'd noticed at the conference. I think he must have decided that by the way I looked, it couldn't hurt to have me along. He asked if I wanted to share the taxi and see if we could find out a few things together. "Sure," I said, intrigued.

At the first club, we met a sparkling young woman, about eighteen years old, who clearly didn't want to be having sex and giving massages to men three times her age. I took a liking to Rosie and started up a conversation. Within five minutes I'd already started cooking up a plan to get her out of there, but Tom seemed uncomfortable and said it was time to go.

I was a bit baffled by his Man-in-Black technique, which seemed to consist of striding into each place conspicuously, briefly looking around, and then leaving without talking to anyone or even having a drink. It was apparent to me that his approach was too abrupt—that we were missing an enormous opportunity to dig up some dirt. But Tom was engaged in a bureaucracy and had no script or example to follow. During the war on drugs of the seventies and eighties, field agents had figured out their procedures by trial and error. Even though he was a straight arrow, Tom was still a trailblazer and could see that my detachment made me perfectly suited for this kind of work. We talked about it on our way back to the hotel, as the first rays of sunlight dawned on the horizon.

After two hours of sleep, I had breakfast with a few other conference presenters including Michele Clark. They were all well rested and jokingly referring to me as the "party boy." I remember helping Michele communicate with the waiter, which I found a bit intimidating at first, since she's something of a linguist. I think those moments brought us closer, since we both shared a desire to connect and communicate with the locals that many of the other participants seemed to lack. Michele possessed a true passion for life, and we had a great time discovering Managua together.

So when she was invited back to Managua to consult and help lay the foundation for a national task force, I went along to deliver my own presentation. A few months after that we teamed up on a very successful public education and awareness-raising seminar in the Dominican Republic, cosponsored by the Protection Project, the U.S. State Department, and former congresswoman Linda Smith of Shared Hope International.

Freshly back in D.C., Michele and I now sat in her office talking with Protection Project codirector Mohamed Mattar about what they'd already learned on the Latin American trips—and how much more they still needed to know. Anecdotal evidence cited in the State Department's Trafficking in Persons Report had indicated the Dominican Republic was a huge source of human trafficking victims and that Haiti was primarily a transit country. My firsthand experience of the nightlife in those countries backed up that evidence.

The Protection Project was preparing to launch a study into countries of origin—with Peru first on that list. During the Persian Gulf War, I'd spent about eighteen months living near Lima, playing water polo for the National Federation and doing charity work with orphanages helping street children. The Maoist group Sendero Luminoso (Shining Path) was then in the midst of a long guerilla war against the Peruvian government, in which an estimated sixty thousand people were killed or "disappeared" during the eighties and nineties.[2] While hanging out with a rag-tag army of shoeshine boys I'd befriended, I had heard sordid stories of traffickers who profited from the chaos by yanking children out of the jungle to work in the streets and brothels of the capital.

It was in Peru that I first learned how organized crime units trafficking drugs and arms had shifted some of their energies into the human flesh trade, a huge moneymaker. Colombian drug cartels supplied guerrillas with guns in exchange for bodies that could be exchanged for cold cash—which kept flowing until the individual bodies were used up. Unlike arms or drugs, human beings could be sold again and again.

Growing up with a Spanish-speaking father paired with the years of water polo and travel in Argentina, Chile, and Peru had made me fluent not only in the language but the culture of the region, which made me an ideal field agent to accompany Michele on her next trip.

As we talked in her office, Michele let on that she'd already bought our tickets. "We're leaving in two weeks." She smiled as she waved the receipt in my direction. Like many women I know, Michele often surprised me by knowing long before I did what was good for me. I nodded happily, sure that our skill sets played well off one another—my fieldwork on the previous trips had been a nice complement to her diplomacy.

But my dreams of chasing the Jubilee in the wilds of Peru quickly evaporated like so much jungle mist with that one cell phone call from Juanita, which tore me away from my future and back to the present.

"*Papa está en hospital de nuevo*," she said, sounding upset. "*Hay mucho sangre. Está vomitando sangre*." Papa had just recovered from his last intestinal episode. And now he was vomiting blood. A lot of blood.

"You need to come home now," Juanita said.

I stepped away from Michele and Mohamed, and assured Juanita I'd be on the next plane out.

"*Mañana—seguro*," I said, putting more strength in my voice than I truly had.

"*Si Dios quiere, si Dios quiere*," Abuelita Juanita responded. If G-d wills it. She was not a churchgoing woman, but her strong sense of faith comforted me now.

Michele and Mohamed overheard the conversation and tried to make the situation easier. "Your father needs you," Mohamed said. "Go home. You can join us later." He patted me on the shoulder, and then Michele led me out by the arm.

I knew they were just trying to make me feel better, because it was clearly going to be one or the other. If I didn't go back home right away, Papa could die alone. I couldn't let that happen. But leaving D.C. now meant that Mohamed and Michele would have to plan their next round of assessments without me. That meant no Peru. And more little girls trapped in their impossible situations with no one to help them.

Michele tried to comfort me by taking me down a notch. "You're not the only one who can find the victims," she reminded me. But I didn't know anyone else who would do the work I did for so little money or recognition—and neither did she.

Even though retrievals were not yet a part of my official objective, finding underage victims and getting them to safety had already become my own private barometer of success. And although I knew that the intelligence we gathered during the assessments alone would eventually wind its way into the hands of the people working hard to protect victims, the retrievals gave me a higher sense of purpose. No matter how harrowing, they had an immediate and tangible result. I could go to sleep that night knowing that a few more girls were out of their tormentors' clutches. For me, encountering a child in those circumstances and then leaving her behind—even for only one more day—was unbearable.

When the mission was over, I tended to deal with the grief by sleeping too much, blocking it out, and refusing to discuss things for a while. Which didn't leave much room for a woman in my life. As I moved deeper into my work, it became even clearer that the cumulative anguish I'd absorbed had left scars on my psyche. Although it had never been diagnosed, the symptoms were similar to those exhibited by someone with post-traumatic stress disorder. I initially dealt with the pain by relapsing into drug use, diving into meaningless affairs or one-night stands. But now even those behaviors had taken their toll, and I had begun to resign myself to the idea of a monastic existence. Either way, being detached and emotionally unavailable to the women who passed through my life was the perfect attribute for getting the undercover work done.

As we got to know each other better, Michele tried to turn me into more of a realist and less of a dreamer—and although she didn't entirely succeed, I did come to accept that politics and diplomacy are all about compromise. Our professional relationship rested on a genuine respect for each other's position, but it would be tested more than once. While Michele stayed in her safety zone, I kept being drawn more deeply into the darkness.

We walked back to Michele's Capitol Hill town house in contemplative silence. Early the next morning I was on a plane to LAX. When I arrived at the hospital hours later, I was told that Papa was in serious but stable condition. He was still undergoing tests.

Despite his visible weakness, Papa flushed with excitement when he saw me. "There's my Aaron!" he said proudly, showing me off to his nurses. "Where have you been?"

I indulged Papa with a few stories from the Dominican Republic while he underwent a blood transfusion. As soon as he fell asleep, the nurses filled me in on his condition. Papa was bleeding internally, but they hadn't yet been able to pinpoint the precise location. For the next five days I slept about two hours a night on a bamboo mat next to his bed while the doctors poked, probed, and scanned him endlessly, still unable to determine the source of his bleeding. The tests were extremely uncomfortable, and with no end in sight, Papa was becoming increasingly upset. I called my brother Arthur and put him on the phone with the doctor, who seemed taken aback that another M.D. was encroaching on his territory. After a few minutes, I finally heard the doctor say, "All right, I'll try that. Okay, I understand."

When the doctor handed me back the phone, Arthur said, "Aaron, this guy might be a great doctor, but he's lost here. He doesn't know what to do with Papa." I nodded and stepped out into the hallway as my brother continued. "He should have done a red cell tag. That will give us the answer."

I didn't know what a red cell tag was, but as soon as it was done, the doctor was able to isolate the bleeding to Papa's upper intestine. He blamed it on the blood pressure medication Papa had been taking and suggested we try a different one to see what happened.

I spent a few more sleepless nights in Papa's room, holding his hand and calming him down while the doctors monitored his progress on the new blood pressure drug. When he no longer needed a blood transfusion, they let him go home. Juanita and I now had to monitor his blood pressure constantly, and for ten days I barely left the house.

Since there was no generic available for Papa's new medication, which cost a mystifying three hundred dollars a bottle, I suddenly found myself spending an additional six to nine hundred dollars a month on Papa's health care, since the drugs were not covered by Medicare.

I wanted to get back on the road to regain my sanity and break away from the monotony of my hermit's life with Papa. Washing him, feeding him, taking him outside, putting him to bed, and keeping him there was consuming all of my energy. But I knew I couldn't leave him. At this point he went into a tailspin if I left his bedside for more than a few minutes at a time. I finally called Michele to formally turn down the Peru assignment. She'd have to find another agent. When I hung up the phone, I felt utterly trapped. It was as though I was submitting to slowly dying along with my father.

The doctors had figured out that Papa had an even larger stomach ulcer, and they were debating whether or not to operate. I called Arthur right away and got him involved from the outset. Ruthie flew in to help, because she could see I was depressed and starting to get sick myself. This time Arthur asked that the ultrasound results be sent directly to him. After having a look, he told me, "If they operate, Papa could die on the table. This is such invasive surgery that it might be better to just treat the thing out."

The doctors in Irvine decided to follow my brother's instructions. They took Papa off his blood pressure medicines and started him on a new one to treat the ulcer. There was no generic version of that drug, either, and as the bottles were emptied and the months passed, I found myself digging deeper and deeper into my savings.

I had barely been making any money on the trafficking assessments. More than a month of grueling work—two weeks of travel, at least two weeks of research, and writing a thirty-page report— didn't even earn me enough to pay the mortgage on Papa's house. While on assignment, motels and meals were part of my per diem, but the additional expenses from my extracurricular night frighting usually added up to more than my earnings. "Lady drinks" and buying girls out by the hour or evening in order to glean information on the traffickers were not part of my discretionary fund. At best I was breaking even—but more often than not I was losing money.

Here's how the math worked when I was in Haiti and the Dominican Republic. I'd go into a high-end club where drinks could be anywhere from ten to fifteen dollars each. I'd choose a girl, pay the mamasan $120 for an hour and tip the girl another twenty. I'd do this five or six times a night, ending up spending $500 in a night, or about $3,500–4,000 a trip. Kindhearted donors helped me raise the extra money to cover these research costs.

Unless they understood how I had incorporated Jubilee into my life, it was hard for the average person to comprehend what motivated me. I had no salary or government agency backing to facilitate my work, most of which went unrecognized. But my belief in the divine Jubilee, freeing slaves, and forgiving debts—in finding redemption for us all—is what kept me going.

After a few months of trips and buying Papa's medications, my savings were exhausted. I started to go into debt just as his condition began to deteriorate even further. He was completely incontinent by this time, and on the nights that Juanita went home to her family I would feed him, comfort him, and change his sheets and diapers. But often he'd wake up during the night, become confused about where he was, and scream for me.

One night he burst into my room while I was sleeping. His arms and hands were smeared with feces from the diaper he was holding, and he had no idea where he was or what he was doing. Horrified, I led Papa to the bathroom so I could wash him off and get him comfortable again. When he was really out of his mind like this, I'd pray out loud in Hebrew, which seemed to comfort him. He had no idea what had happened, and sat slumped in the bathtub with sad and confused eyes. I had never seen him look so small. And I had never felt so old and broken.

After that episode, and a sequence of similar ones, I let myself sink into the depression that had been waiting for me in the shadows all these months. Taking care of Papa was an excellent excuse for not leaving the house at all. I couldn't see a way out, and if it weren't for a few close friends, I don't know that I would have made it.

My family friend Julie Weiss would stop by occasionally to see if we needed anything, and my friend Darrel Adams never gave up on me, either. He'd come over and say, "Man, you've gotta come out tonight. My brother's band is playing; it will be fun. You need to get out." But from where I was on my downward spiral, just getting dressed was a momentous feat.

"I can't leave Papa, Darrel," I'd say. "He'll wake up and I won't be here."

My body had finally allowed itself to revolt against the abuse I'd been heaping on it over a two-year period. I lost my appetite and started to shed a lot of weight. Sleep deprivation, malnutrition, and constant emotional and physical stress compounded by complications from back problems I'd been ignoring had turned me into a recluse who resembled his infirm patient more and more. While Papa was in the hospital for a blood infection, I went to a nearby clinic for tests. They gave me antibiotics to treat a staph infection that may have come from taking care of Papa and changing his diapers.

But somehow I think I had internalized my poor father's ailments. Despite his dementia, he knew he was terminally ill and had essentially given up on the idea of ever getting out of bed. I was so closely bound to him by that point that his pain became my own. I'd sit and stroke his head and tell him everything was going to be all right. But there was no one to stroke my head and tell me not to worry. I was broke and alone, and knew that soon Papa would leave me.

A few months into my self-imposed exile, Michele called and invited me to come out to a seminar in Arizona where she and Mohamed were going to speak on human trafficking. She asked if I would present my findings on how traffickers used the Internet as a recruitment tool. The offer to work again was the first spark of light that had come into the house in months.

Nonetheless, I made excuses, citing Papa's need for me, and my own deteriorating condition. Michele went into her no-nonsense mode.

"You get on that airplane, Aaron, and come to the conference," she said. "If your dad goes into the hospital again, you'll have to deal with it. But you can't live your whole life at his bedside. It's been four months since Peru, and you've got to get back out there. There's more to your life than just taking care of your father. If you have to go back to take care of him again, then so be it. But at least get out of there for a few days."

Her speech prevented me from slipping further into the abyss.

Besides, I knew she was right. I wanted and needed to go to Arizona. I started reviewing my presentation notes and preparing for the trip. But one day before I was scheduled to leave, I woke up unable to eat and found myself battling a bout of diarrhea. Thinking I needed more antibiotics, I drove to the hospital. The nurses immediately hooked me up to an IV, saying I was extremely dehydrated and had lost too much weight. They suggested I rest while they did blood tests to figure out what was wrong with me.

I called Michele and begrudgingly told her I wouldn't be coming to Arizona after all. She promised to come and visit me after the conference.

The next morning I awoke in my hospital bed, felt a pang of regret, and told my nurse I was checking out. She looked worried. "I wouldn't do that, honey. You're not well."

I promised her I'd come back for more tests in a few days, and called Michele again as I walked out to the hospital parking lot after removing my own IV.

"I'll be on the next plane," I said, feeling weak but sure of myself for the first time in months.

When I walked into the terminal a few hours later, Michele was there waiting for me. We hugged and I noticed tears in her eyes. I wondered if she had simply missed me, and soon got my answer.

"You look terrible," she told me in the way that only good friends and honor-bound Southeast Asians can get away with. I hadn't even thought to consider my appearance in the months that had passed since we'd last seen each other.

Michele marched me to a full-length mirror outside the restrooms, where I took in the sight that had so upset her: a gaunt, sallow-skinned depressed man who reminded me of the drug user I had once been—or was it my dying father I saw manifesting in me?

She grabbed my hands, shook them, and said, "You've got to get out of that house, Aaron. We need to get you back on the road looking for children." I nodded, submitting to her authority.

"You also need more help with your father," she continued. Arthur and Ruthie had been telling me this for years, but I couldn't imagine putting Papa in a home. Michele suggested I ask Juanita and Maxima for more help. She was right—but it wasn't so simple. Since L.C. had died, it was as though Papa's slate had been wiped clean. All the love I had reserved for my mother had been funneled toward him. There were no words to explain how intertwined Papa's life now was with my own. If I left his care up to anyone else, he would lose his will to live.

But by just getting me out of the house, Michele had helped me see that I had hit rock bottom. That night in my hotel bed, I made a list of everything that was torturing me. I worried that I was failing to take care of my father properly, and was sure I'd let Michele down by skipping the assessment to Peru, the country where my background would have added the most value. My physical condition was an obvious manifestation of my taking on other people's pain.

I was still reflecting on all of this the following morning at the hotel restaurant when Michele and Mohamed walked over with T. March Bell, senior counsel for trafficking issues with the Department of Justice.

The ensuing conversation was transformative. They each told me that I needed to get back in the game—that I offered something special. "There are guys in the law enforcement agencies doing assessments and retrievals, too, but no one gets the kind of information you do," said Michele. March and Mohamed nodded in encouragement. Here were three greats of the antislavery movement telling me the cause needed me—that they needed me. For the first time in months, I stopped feeling like a failure.

That afternoon, I found my groove and gave my presentation just after March, who tackled trafficking from a prosecution standpoint. The other seminar participants included NGO workers, members of law enforcement, educators, counselors, and social workers. I was buoyed by their collective energy, intellect, and enthusiasm and felt honored to be included in the group.

Afterward I told March I was hoping to go to Ecuador and see what I could do there. He wished me luck, and then started telling me about some things he'd been thinking and hearing about in Southeast Asia.

"There's a tremendous slavery problem going on there in the Mekong region of Cambodia and Vietnam," he said. "The Vietnamese mafia is running drugs out of Burma, down the Mekong through Laos . . ."

For March this might have been an offhand remark, but for me it felt like a wake-up call. He made me start thinking that afternoon about patterns I had begun mulling over in Latin America but hadn't yet fully developed. Patterns I suddenly knew would take me into even darker and more faraway places in search of the light on the other side.

SOUR LAKE

COSTA MESA, CALIFORNIA

2004

> The Government of Ecuador does not fully comply with the minimum standards for the elimination of trafficking and is not making significant efforts to do so. Because there has been very limited information on trafficking until the release of an ILO report in late 2003, the government is only beginning to grapple with this challenge, including a serious problem with the commercial sexual exploitation of minors.

—From the State Department's 2004 Trafficking in Persons Report

WHEN I GET HOME FROM THE ARIZONA CONference in early September, a contract from the American Bar Association is waiting for me. I've been asked to serve as a field operative and consultant to the ABA for its research into human trafficking in Ecuador. Since the Trafficking Victims Protection Act was passed in 2001, the State Department has been issuing a government report card measuring other countries' efforts to combat human trafficking within their own borders—the Trafficking in Persons (TIP) Report. It has taken three years to accumulate enough data on Ecuador, and more is needed.

The country's first appearance in the 2004 TIP Report was damning, placing it on tier three—the lowest rung—along with some of the world's worst environments for human trafficking. Tier Three countries are expected to clean up their act or face U.S. sanctions that would cut off nonhumanitarian, non-trade-related aid, and U.S. support for IMF and World Bank assistance.[1] Even though Ecuador was among the first countries, in 2001, to ratify the U.N.'s Palermo Protocol,[2] which laid out the first modern-day definition of international trafficking, it had made few concrete steps in the years since. Human trafficking had yet to be identified as a prosecutable offense there.

My fieldwork is intended to shed more light on trafficking patterns as well as provide insight into the victims' perspective. The ABA wants to know who's involved in the game in various regions of the country, especially near the Peruvian, Venezuelan, and Columbian borders. Then I'll be discussing the results of my investigations with the assessment team, providing input on the team's final report, writing my own mini-report on my findings, and making suggestions for what to do next. Although I'm not sure I'm ready for what awaits me, it's also clear that all my years learning Spanish are about to culminate in another meaningful adventure.

As reluctant as I am to admit it, it is a relief to focus on something besides Papa's illness. After looking in on him, I take the contract out to the backyard and look it over more carefully. This kind of work occasionally requires me to delve into the gray areas where diplomats don't dare tread. My faith in following my instincts and using nonconventional methods is about to bring me into conflict with Michele Clark, whose political position means she always has to go by the book. The reality is this: I get close to the women I meet on the job. This might mean that they end up sitting on my lap or hanging on my neck while we're talking in a karaoke bar. Some of them have even stayed overnight in my hotel room—which definitely goes against official rules. I have cuddled and even kissed a few of these women. As a single man who meets an endless amount of attractive young women, I'm not going to say it is easy to play the monk—particularly when some of them would like nothing better but to be "saved" by becoming an American's girlfriend. It's a struggle to remain detached. I try and conjure up the image of Ulysses, begging to be tied to the mast in order to resist the Sirens' calls and keep his ship clear from the rocks.

As for all the johns I meet when I'm out in the bars and brothels, none could guess that I'm having anything other than the time of my life. We appear to be partners in crime, these guys and I—out for a good time.

"We're men, we have money, and we're here to gorge ourselves on booze, girls, and cocaine!" their dancing eyes and local-beer breath convey. And *I'm* one of them—with the desire for sex, drugs, and a guilt-free good time in my heart. The trapdoors back to a life of vice are still there, just waiting for me to fall through them.

I use the social skills I learned partying with rock stars to appear comfortable even in the tensest of situations. By being my normal self, I give these women space to get comfortable with me and build up enough trust so they can talk freely. I use the laws of attraction to my advantage—engaging the girls in talking about their lives and dreams. If I sense natural chemistry between a potential informant and me, I know how to harness it so that she will voluntarily divulge more of the information we need.

When I first take a girl upstairs and tell her that I just want to talk, she may look relieved, while another will start looking for the catch, or wonder if her pimp will find out that she's not really working. Many become starry-eyed. For older sex trafficking victims, the *Pretty Woman* fantasy is sometimes the only thing that keeps their hope of a real life alive. Some seem to think, "If he doesn't want to sleep with me right away, maybe he loves me?"

If only I could take each of them away from all of this . . . but the numbers are staggeringly against us. The good guys are losing, big-time. I may not always be able to save the girl I'm talking to today, but I *can* harness others' compassion to help future potential victims stay free. The rest is all about love, peace, and honesty. If a woman trusts me, her complete testimony will inevitably prevent even more young girls from being brought into the trade.

I'll have to negotiate out the clause forbidding the use of alcohol. I pick up the phone and call Michele Clark for advice.

"Playing it totally straight means no access," I tell her. "They can't expect a field agent in a dangerous environment to act like a guy with a tapered haircut. If I end up in a drug dealer's den where there are trafficking victims and it comes down to me having to party with them to find out how they operate, then I can do it. I'm not there for the sex or drugs. But if they really want to get the information, they've got to leave me some room to move."

Michele agrees. I also put in a call to Mohamed Mattar, who has encouraged me in the past and whose work I greatly admire. He patiently points out that since this type of assessment is still relatively new, there ought to be some flexibility in the contractual language.

The ABA's legal representative is receptive to my concerns about the restrictive language. He delves a bit deeper into my past field experience, and by that afternoon, the clauses have come out. I have no predecessors in this job, and we are figuring out what works and what doesn't as we go along. In the outsourcing era, governments often use a subcontractor like the ABA to limit their liability. I am not considered a State Department employee and cannot be traced to the U.S. government. So if I get hurt while on assignment, I can't turn around and look to Uncle Sam for help—and, more daunting, I have no special privileges if something goes wrong.

I hate leaving Papa in such a fragile state, so Arthur and Ruthie have both timed their visits to coincide with my departure, to lessen its impact. I also feel confident in the care that Juanita—who is practically family at this point—has been providing. The good news is that Papa's been responding well to the costly new blood pressure and ulcer medications. But I've got to keep working.

It's the day after George W. Bush has won his second presidential election, and I'm on my way to meet Michele Clark in South America to begin the work in Ecuador, which the president recently bumped up to the TIP Report's Tier Two Watch List in recognition of the "significant efforts" it's made to combat trafficking in the last few months. This order effectively waives any threat of U.S. sanctions or efforts to block the country's other sources of international aid—pending further study. The move looks to me like a poorly disguised quid pro quo, but I try to remember that backroom diplomacy is not my concern. The State Department has urged Ecuador to "develop, implement, and publicize a comprehensive anti-trafficking policy" and learn how to work more effectively with NGOs. The next step will be updating its laws, doing a better job of enforcing them, and prosecuting traffickers who lure minors into the trade.

Michele has already conducted a training program in Ecuador and will be in charge of the ABA assessment. I sleep on the plane and wake to a breaking dawn as we begin our descent through the clouds over Quito. The rainy season has already begun here. Soon I can make out the city's towers, jutting upward like ragged teeth from a volcanic basin. We debark directly onto the tarmac. A rush of cool air speaks simultaneously with the pungency of Latin America and the purity of the snowcapped Andes.

Although we're just a few miles from the equator, Ecuador's capital city—the second-highest in the world at 9,300 feet—gives off a sparkling and evergreen first impression. I let everyone else hustle past me with their belongings as I gratefully breathe in the air just a second longer. I know this will be the last time I'll be able to see the city's beauty with the same innocent eyes, and I want to make the moment last. Soon I'll be digging up its underbelly, just as I've already done in so many other cities. Just this once, I'd love to be able to flick a delay switch, temporarily turning off the part of me that feels compelled to find and expose the violence and lust for power that drives this economy and so many others. Just long enough to enjoy a night on the town or a day of sightseeing like a normal tourist.

But that's not to be.

The next morning at breakfast, Michele briefs me on the contract and fills me in on some background. Ecuador's poor rating on the last TIP Report resulted from what the State Department considered a failure to "fully comply with the minimum standards" to eliminate trafficking. A 2002 International Labor Organization study figured that at least 5,200 minors had been exploited for commercial sex in Ecuador,[3] while also suggesting that the government was not doing much to prevent or prosecute such crimes.

In the same way that dirty restaurants get slapped with the L.A. Health Department's "C" rating, a country that lands on the TIP Report's Tier Three or Tier Two Watch List has a lot of cleaning up to do. Michele reminds me of our mission: analyze the scope of the problem on the ground, find out what's already been done to establish a framework, and help local officials develop a national anti-trafficking strategy. In short—call it as we see it. Our work alone will not make or break anything, but we can certainly hope that it will be made available to Ambassador John Miller, director of the State Department's Office to Monitor and Combat Trafficking in Persons and senior adviser to Secretary of State Condoleezza Rice on human trafficking. Miller has only been at the State Department for two months, but has already proven himself a champion of human rights victims everywhere.

As we order coffee, the two Ecuadoreans who will be helping us conduct the assessment come over and sit down at our table. Their big smiles and genuine natures win us over from the outset. Carlos is an attorney and consultant for the American Bar Association—baby-faced and handsome. I immediately peg Ernesto—with circular glasses and thinning hair hidden under a baseball cap—as a compassionate intellectual. He's a social worker with the agency that will be helping us with logistics, and the first local man I've met who, at six feet two, even comes close to my height. Both men are in their mid-thirties, married with young children. I can tell immediately that these guys care deeply about human rights and will do everything they can to help us.

"First thing to know," starts Ernesto, "is that this country is a center for document fraud." He explains that obtaining fake documents is so simple here that waves of illegal migrants take advantage of lax border controls to transit through Ecuador. "We're not yet sure what percentage of these people come through here against their will," says Carlos, "but it's safe to say that the traffickers are well aware how easy it is to pass through Ecuador unnoticed."

Even larger numbers of the human trafficking victims in Ecuador have reputedly been coming from Colombian cities where the drug cartels are based. Cocaine from Cali, Bogotá, and Medellín, along with the chemicals to process it, is transited through Ecuador on its way to the United States, Japan, and other destinations. In the last few years, drug and precious-gem traffickers have learned they can double or triple their income by moving women and children along the same routes.

And they've been doing it here with virtual impunity.

While I will be gathering firsthand evidence in the brothels by night, Michele will be spending her days talking to the relevant authorities in Ecuador's big cities—NGO workers, judges, prosecutors, chiefs of police, social workers, and even members of the clergy—to identify, as she calls it, "the gap between the walk and the talk."

When we meet again later that day, she has just come from a round of meetings with U.S. Embassy officials, Interpol, and the Narcotics Affairs Section (NAS), a division of the State Department's Bureau of International Narcotics and Law Enforcement Affairs, which works in conjunction with the government of Colombia to combat trafficking. All of the organizations have agreed to pool their information on human trafficking trends in the region in order to best serve the victims. As a subcontractor, I'm not directly involved in the political and emotional turmoil surrounding Ecuador's poor showing on the most recent TIP Report. But I can tell the local agencies are feeling the pressure—they seem more than willing to cooperate with us.

"Lago Agrio kept coming up today," Michele says suddenly.

It's the first time I've heard of the place.

"A lot of girls are being transited through there," she continues. "We might want to do some digging up that way."

Carlos is nodding.

"Lago is the transit city for everything going in and out of Colombia," he says.

After dinner, I use the Internet to look into the basics on Lago Agrio. Officially known as Nueva Loja (after the first colonizers, from the southern city of Loja), the town was carved out of the jungle in the late sixties, after oil was discovered nearby. Located way up in the northeastern jungle province of Sucumbíos near the Colombian border, it sounds like the end of the earth—so naturally I'm intrigued.

By ten o'clock I turn off my laptop and look out the window, ready to start the night fright. Quito is about to show its ugly face. The first cab ride feels portentous, and I begin to breathe and focus on seeing the interconnected nature of us all—taxi drivers, johns, traffickers, and innocent children. As I engage the driver in the usual dialogue—I'm just here for a night, and yes, I'm looking for a good time—in the back of my mind I'm praying for guidance through the wide-open darkness of these muddy streets.

I'm surprised by what I find in the city's strip bars. Many of the girls there are Colombians, reputed for their beauty, intelligence, and racial purity—the latter a quality prized by many of the men looking to buy sex. My last stop for the night is a high-end place called Club Cinco on a busy street downtown. I immediately start chatting with a girl in her twenties called Jacinta. I buy her a drink and she points to an exotic-looking teenager sitting alone near the bar. "That's Gina," Jacinta says. "She's sick, and the boss is mad at her because she can't work. Maybe you can talk to her instead, and give her a big tip?"

I am touched by Jacinta's gesture. The older girls in these places often look out for the youngest ones. I hand over $150 to the pimp for an hour with Gina and say good-bye to Jacinta.

We walk up a plush staircase and down a well-appointed hall-way. It's such a contrast to the shantytown brothels of Cambodia—almost like a hotel. Once upstairs, I find out that this fragile girl's real name is Yinabei. She is wearing too much makeup, and her arms are covered with bruises. Like many girls in her situation, her pimp has even taken away her name, her last vestige of identity and home. No matter that she's from Colombia, Venezuela, or Peru and being held against her will . . . the johns will have their thrills and be gone before giving any of it a second thought.

Yinabei has just turned nineteen, but looks much younger. She shows me her public health card, which is issued to every girl in a strip club or brothel as proof she is Ecuadorean and disease free. It's clearly a forgery, because the next minute Yinabei tells me her mother is Colombian and that her father was Japanese. She boasts her mother's passionate temperament alongside her father's delicate facial features and diminutive stature. She is distant and somewhat jaded, and after I hear her story I understand why.

"My father died when I was thirteen, and my uncle took care of my mother and me for a while. But it wasn't long before he and my cousins started raping me," she says matter-of-factly.

Looking at this tiny, delicate girl, my stomach turns over at the thought of what this must have been like.

"Then when I was sixteen, my uncle sold me to one of the big drug cartels in Cali to pay off his gambling debts." I start to react, but she continues. "I expected this," she says. "In my country, prostitution is legal. Plenty of girls I knew did it, and I needed to help my family."

The cartel eventually trafficked Yinabei to Ecuador, where she was forced to become a sex worker in a Quito massage parlor. After a few months, she was purchased by a Japanese businessman who brought her back to Tokyo to work as a high-end prostitute, probably for the Yakuza, a gang notorious for its brutality and tendency to tattoo its "merchandise" across their breasts.

Yinabei's exotic hybrid looks boosted her into the top echelon of working girls, and she saw thousands of dollars exchange hands, night after night, over a few hours' worth of her time. Her Japanese pimp saw to it that she was outfitted in designer clothes, and she was eventually escorting her clients to the city's best restaurants. After two years of this life, one of her regular clients (who had fallen in love with her) paid off her debt and arranged for her to go back home.

But after a few weeks there, she was recaptured by the Cali cartel and forced to work in Quito again. These pimps had since manufactured a new "debt" for her, and she'd been at Club Cinco for almost a year. Now she is two months pregnant, by a boyfriend who has abandoned her. She blushes at this point in her story, but carries on.

"And the boss tells me I still owe him money for my plane tickets," Yinabei says with a snort. "But I've paid my debt over many times." I'm amazed at the light in this girl's eyes, even as she speaks about the terrible hand she's been dealt.

"I'm not as much of a lamb as they think," she continues, almost haughtily now. "Now that I'm pregnant, I'll soon be too ugly to work. They'll have to let me go. This is my way out."

"I don't think it's safe for you to stay here any longer," I respond.

"I know!" she says, laughing off my obvious statement. But the laugh is forced and nervous, and I can sense the fragility beneath her tough exterior. She's terrified.

"Soon you'll be showing," I say, trying to find the words. "Do they . . ."

She picks up my question. "Do they know I'm pregnant? Yes. They want me to have an abortion. Usually they force the girls to do that—but I'll be gone before that happens."

"How much is your debt?"

Yinabei looks down and picks at a loose thread on her skirt. "I don't know," she says. "It's not that much. But it never seems to get any smaller, no matter how much I work."

Autopilot takes over for me at this point. "Are you free to leave during the daytime?"

"Yes," says Yinabei. "In the afternoons I sometimes go to the mall for Colombian food, since they barely give us any food here."

Without really knowing what I'm going to do, I make an appointment with Yinabei for the day after next at a nearby bus stop. I'll need that extra day to find someplace to take her. I hug her good-bye. It's hard to imagine there's a baby inside this tiny frame.

"You take care of yourself until I see you again," I say.

My body moves downstairs, nodding my thank-yous to the bartender, madam, and bouncers, but my mind has raced ahead somewhere else. My only consolation in leaving Yinabei now is that these will hopefully be her last two nights in this place.

A few hours later, I'm on the phone with Michele, who's already working from Carlos and Ernesto's overcrowded office. I tell her about Yinabei, and she tells me what I already know—that there are few options in Ecuador for women in Yinabei's situation.

"But we'll find a solution," she says, with signature confidence. Carlos and Ernesto are on top of it.

At dinner that night, Michele is exuberant. "We've found a place for Yinabei." She smiles, clinking her glass to mine. She explains that Ernesto called in all of his connections in the small social worker community, and found a home for pregnant girls run by Catholic nuns. "It's in the suburbs," Michele says, "and it's usually only for Ecuadorean girls—victims of sexual abuse—but they're willing to take Yinabei."

Michelle raises an eyebrow at the thought of a girl with Yinabei's experience living within the rigid confines of a convent, especially given her own intense experience at a Catholic boarding school. "But after what I heard this morning," she says, "I'm sure it's the best chance she's got."

Michele goes on to tell me about her earlier meetings with the legal adviser at the foreign ministry and the head of a national coalition to fight the commercial sexual exploitation of children. "I asked everyone what we could do for a hypothetical young woman like Yinabei," she says. "And everyone kept talking about following international conventions and respecting human rights. But no one could tell me where this woman was going to sleep while we were so busy defending her rights."

I just hope that Yinabei is willing to give the convent a try. Even though the brothel is her personal hell on earth, at least it's familiar. It will take a lot of courage to walk away from it all tomorrow.

Just after noon the next day, we take a taxi to Club Cinco, which in the light of day looks like an ordinary warehouse on a block of run-down buildings. Yinabei spots us from the bus stop down the street and runs over to the car. She hugs me and offers Michele a shy smile and her delicate outstretched hand. "Yinabei, this is Michele Clark. Michele, meet Yinabei." Out here on the street, she looks even smaller than the night before. Her black hair is covering most of her heavily made-up face, and her clothes are hanging off her still-adolescent frame. But her eyes are lit up with excitement.

She jumps back in the taxi with us and directs the driver to a nearby mall. "We can eat Colombian food, yes?" she asks as we make our way around a crowded food court.

I can tell that Yinabei likes and trusts Michele; she's already linked their arms together. After eating and talking a bit more about Yinabei's past, we walk around the mall—shopping like a normal family on an afternoon outing. I stop and buy her some jeans and perfume; simple things that can usually put a smile on any teenager's face. We giggle and chitchat while picking out a cute stuffed animal for Yinabei's baby. For a few blessed minutes we lose ourselves in the moment.

Sitting down on a bench, Michele tells Yinabei about the offer to stay at the convent. "I know it's not ideal," she says, "but it's the best we have for now. We'll go with you, and wait there until you decide whether or not you want to stay. We can take you there tomorrow."

Yinabei nods slowly, but she's made up her mind. "Okay, I'll try," she says in a small voice.

"Now, what about your debt?" I ask.

"I will talk to the boss about it tonight," she says. "But because I'm pregnant, I know he wants to be rid of me. I think if I give him the amount I can make in a night or two, he will be happy to see me go."

I press five folded hundred-dollar bills into her hand. "Give him this," I say. Neither Michele nor I like the idea of putting a price on Yinabei's head—or putting more money in the traffickers' pockets— but there is no other safe alternative if we are to get her out of there tomorrow. We alone are not going to bring an end to prostitution, to brothels, or to the mafias that rely on human trafficking. But we are giving her a chance at life—maybe the first one she's had in a while.

Yinabei holds my hand to her heart and her eyes fill up with tears. "You are my angel," she says, touching my shoulder as I climb into a taxi. We drive back to the brothel in contemplative silence.

Early the next morning Michele and I pull up in another taxi down the block from Club Cinco, where Yinabei is waiting at the bus stop as before, without a suitcase. My heart sinks. Something went wrong, or she decided not to do it.

Yinabei approaches the car with a sunny *"Buenos dias!"* and explains she's going to have to ask one of the bouncers to help her carry her bag down. Michele jumps out of the car, and walks up to the gate behind Yinabei. I watch one of the bouncers let them in, and then ask the taxi driver to take us around the corner. If they're not down in a few minutes, I'll go after them.

Yinabei's told us that the girls are housed in cramped living quarters on the building's top level, above the lavishly decorated sex rooms. I just hope that no one gives her any trouble. Michele has plenty of cash in her wallet, and is ready to pay off whatever new debt might suddenly be declared.

The cab driver looks at me questioningly, but I assure him he'll be paid for his time and say nothing more. I'm sure he doesn't get many customers coming to this club at this time of day.

A few minutes later, Michele emerges from the building followed by Yinabei and one of the bouncers lugging a cheap oversized suitcase, which he puts down unceremoniously at the curb before turning back without so much as a good-bye.

"I'll tell you about what went on in there later" is all Michele will say for the moment. Yinabei is sweating slightly and tries to give me her best smile. After stopping to pick up Ernesto and Carlos, we make our way to the quiet suburb where the convent is located, about twenty minutes outside the city. The nuns are very welcoming and show Yinabei to her private room. There's a window overlooking the garden, a flowered bedspread, and matching curtains. A nun explains that there are ten other pregnant girls here, each under the age of eighteen. Every girl has her own room, for what may be the first time in her life.

The mother superior is jovial and warm as she explains their daily schedule. "The girls wake up early, go to Mass, and help with a few light chores," she says, looking at all of us as though to gauge our reaction. "In the afternoon they can study or do whatever they like. We do, of course," she laughs, "go to bed early."

Yinabei looks at me, rolls her eyes, and sighs audibly. Michele catches this and looks worried. She leans in and whispers to me in English, "Here we are putting a young woman who's worked in high-end Tokyo bars in a provincial convent with Ecuadorean country bumpkins. It's like trying to mix oil and water," she says, dismayed.

"I don't know, I could take her back to the hotel with me," I start to say, as Michele, Carlos, and Ernesto shake their heads simultaneously.

The mother superior reads our thoughts and says, "I need to be frank with you. This is a shelter for young Ecuadoreans who have primarily been abused by their uncles or fathers. Incest is a taboo in our culture, and their mothers don't want them at home because of the shame. Colombian big-city girls like this don't do well here." She looks at Yinabei and gently smoothes her hair back off her face. "But we will certainly try and help you adjust, *querida*."

Yinabei manages a weak smile, and we all hug her good-bye, promising to come and visit before we return to the States in a few days.

On the ride back, Michele explains that no additional money exchanged hands at the brothel over Yinabei. Michele got the sense they were relieved to be rid of her. But it had been hard for Yinabei to leave behind the other girls, who had become like sisters.

Now we are leaving her in an alternate universe. But until the Ecuadorean government recognizes trafficked women as victims of crime, and provides them with services and shelter, girls like Yinabei will keep falling through the cracks.

Back in the hotel room that night, I pack a tiny tactical bag with enough supplies for a couple of days and head to the airport, where I board a dual-engine prop plane bound for Lago Agrio near the border of Colombia. Out my window, it's hard not to miss the gaping scars of deforestation in what used to be dense Amazonian jungle. The oil companies that dominate the regional economy build the roads, the settlers take out the trees and replace them with livestock, and what's left becomes desolate grassland. Before I've even set foot in Lago Agrio, I feel depressed and tune my iPod to a Joy Division playlist.

We exit the plane directly on the tarmac into a torrential downpour. Now I'm really in the jungle, and the humidity hits me like a tidal wave. The two NAS agents that have been assigned to work with me, Ignacio and Pablo, smile politely when we meet and pat me on the back while joking about my height. They appear to be in their late twenties, are wearing military fatigues and carrying M-16s.

They ask to see my passport, and after verifying my identity, it's all smiles and respect. "Nice to see you, sir," Pablo says in Spanish while Ignacio shoulders my bag and walks it toward their car. "Please don't call me sir," I chide them gently, reaching out to shake both of their hands. "We're working together. Call me Aaron."

We drive directly to the police station to meet their commander, who fills me in on the battle they've been waging against not only the drug cartels, but also with FARC, the Revolutionary Armed Forces of Colombia, who have been conducting an armed struggle against their government since the sixties. The United States, European Union, and Canada consider FARC a terrorist organization, while Cuba and Venezuela call these Marxist-Leninist guerrillas ideological "insurgents," representing the rural poor in a class struggle against the U.S.-backed elite. Meanwhile, a Human Rights Watch report estimates that 20 to 30 percent of FARC's forces are conscripted children under eighteen. Other media reports have identified FARC's main funding sources as kidnapping, illegal drugs, and extortion.[4]

Between the cartels and FARC, the commander explains, lie the petroleum companies—who enjoy a symbiotic relationship with both sides.[5] The synergy of these factors has made Lago Agrio a boomtown for all kinds of undesirable people—especially traffickers.

I check into a hotel on the main drag, noting a couple of strip bars and nightclubs operating out in the open. The roads are rutted and muddy, and everyone seems to be looking at me with suspicion. Many of them are wearing tall white rubber boots. It feels like I've stepped into a tropical version of the Old West.

After a rest, I set out to find the "sour lake" that gives the town its unofficial name. Depending on whom you ask, the name Lago Agrio can be traced either to the Texas town of Sour Lake, the former home of Texaco, from which many of the first homesick settlers here hailed, or to the bitter taste that life here left in their mouths.

Now home to about thirty-five thousand people, Lago started to boom just after Texaco's first regional well started pumping here in 1964. It later became the field headquarters for other companies exploring for crude in the jungle the locals call Oriente.

Those explorations have virtually destroyed the natural habitat, not to mention the traditional lifestyle of the native Cofán, Secoya, and Siona people, who are endangered with cultural extinction.[6] The first pipeline, all 315 miles of which runs from the oil fields across the Andes and down to the Pacific, cuts directly through their tribal hunting lands. Along with state-owned Petroecuador, Texaco managed to squeeze out 5.3 billion liters of oil here in only three decades. Although it withdrew from the area in 1992, the company left behind an area of contaminated rain forest roughly the size of Rhode Island.[7] A class-action suit was filed in 1993 against ChevronTexaco on behalf of thirty thousand Ecuadoreans, charging that the corporation "intentionally dumped toxic waste water and raw crude into swamps and streams, decimated indigenous populations, and created a toxic environment leading to elevated cancer rates." The suit is still pending.[8]

The French, Brazilian, Canadian, and Argentinean oil companies still operating here continue to dump oil and wastewater into the ecosystem. An August 2006 spill contaminated about thirty thousand hectares of the Cuyabeno Reserve, and another in June 2008 affected four thousand square meters of marsh zone in Dayuma parish.[9]

On my way to the lake I pass some shady-looking characters—probably pimps or cartel thugs. Many of them are getting into shiny SUVs, which seem a ridiculous choice for these filthy streets. One aggressive vendor tries to sell me everything from designer sunglasses to a baby crocodile on a leash. A couple of soldiers—looking bored and vaguely surly—watch me walk past. Amidst all this, contented children play in the mud, blissfully unaware of their surroundings.

As darkness falls, people sit down to eat *ceviche de boa* at a sidewalk restaurant outside the main market. The sound of thunder rumbles in the distance, so I start to look for a place to escape the coming storm. Hungry for something outside of the serpent family, I stop and order *maitos*, steamed fish wrapped in a banana leaf with fried plantains and rice. Watching fluorescent flashes in the sky, I smile for the first time all day, savoring the food and realizing I've never found the sour lake. I'll later discover there is no lake in Lago Agrio.

Now I've got to clear my mind and steel myself for the long night fright ahead. Back in my room, I listen to the rain and read from Job:

Are not my few days almost over? Turn away from me so I can
have a moment's joy before I go to the place of no return, to the
land of gloom and deep shadow, to the land of deepest night, of
deep shadow and disorder, where even the light is like darkness.

Two hours later, I wake from a nap to a clear sky and fresh, cool
air blowing through the window. I change into a clean pair of jeans
and collared shirt and set out along Avenida Quito with Ignacio and
Pablo. The first karaoke place we hit is called Cumbios, named after
the county. The three of us walk in and sit down at the bar in a large
but almost empty room. Ceiling fans whir and shake the bottles of
beer and glasses of whiskey on the few occupied tables. A plump
white parrot in a corner cage is chattering away in Spanish. It's hard
to make out much else in the cloudy light coming from a few dim
fluorescent bulbs. "*¡Hola! ¿Qué tal?*" the bird calls out over and
over again.

Unlike in Asia, where karaoke is part of the communal culture,
in Latin America it is a spectator sport. Girls get up onstage to perform in the main room, with numbers pinned to their dresses. A
prospective client simply notes the number of the girl he likes and
then pays to take her to a back room. But here I don't notice any
johns, even though it's 11 P.M.—usually prime party time. The men
sitting at the tables look like drug lords, and they are not happy to
see us. Even the bartender gives us the cold shoulder. We ignore
him, order beers, and try to look interested in the "merchandise."
I motion to the bartender to select a girl, and she begins to walk
over to me. But I feel eyes on me, and look up to see one of the
mafia types from a nearby table motioning to her instead. She
obeys and goes over to him. The guy looks at me as if to say, "Get
the hell out of here."

"It's not safe here," says Ignacio pointedly. "We should leave."
I give in without a second thought. The man's look says it all. Back
on the street, Pablo and Ignacio confirm my suspicion that this is
another wholesale warehouse for girls. Ecuador is merely a transit
point for Colombian girls on their way to Spain, France, Portugal,
Japan, or the United States.

There are only five or six brothels and karaokes on the strip, and we visit them all. Lago is a small town, and the nightspots are dirtier and more drably decorated than the clubs I've seen in Quito. At the next place, we take our time over drinks before making a move. This time when I try to take a girl to the back room, she says no and tells me she's going with someone else. I watch Pablo and Ignacio tense up, gauging my reaction. Catching their vibe, I smile and wave good-bye to the girl. She must be the "property" of a big boss. It is heartbreaking to leave her there, but we can't do anything yet. We move on to the next place.

At one of the last brothels of the night, I manage to interview a girl and get her solicitation on tape. She is probably about fourteen years old. Back in the car, I hand the evidence to the men and tell them to take it to their commander. I hope he'll be able to do something with it.

That night is yet another when sleep refuses to come. Mosquitoes are buzzing around my troubled thoughts. So many women and children suffering.

The next morning the agents take me to a refugee camp run by the U.N. Office of the High Commissioner for Refugees, up near the Colombian border and surrounded by twelve-foot-high chain-link fencing topped by barbed wire. The occupants include infants, old men and women, and everything in between. Although they are being fed and well treated, it's hard not to compare the place to a prison.

The director, a helpful yet harried Frenchman called Yann, explains why.

"You know," he says, "main reason people come here is violence . . . You have the cartels, you have les FARC, you have paramilitary, and it is simply not safe for women and children along this border." The paramilitary units, he tells me, roam the jungles looking to kidnap people and hijack oil trucks, cocaine, and chemical shipments. They're constantly battling each other for assets, resources, and territory. The sheer amount of wealth flowing across the border from Colombia's Putumayo Province puts anyone in the vicinity in grave danger. Some camp occupants have been living here since 2000.[10]

The camp is full. And even if it were empty, UNHCR is only authorized to take in "refugees." Trafficked women are not deemed worthy of that status. If we are able to make a rescue, we'll have nowhere to take the victims. There are no trafficking victim shelters in Ecuador yet, as we discovered while looking for a place for Yinabei.

"If you want to see where the girls come in," Yann says, "follow the road to the river and cross the San Miguel Bridge, which the locals are calling La Puerta Dorada, the golden door. Then you understand very well." He urges me to be careful and wishes me luck.

Although Ignacio and Pablo have been assigned to assist me, their authorization does not extend across the border or into the no-man's-land between Ecuador and Colombia, where all kinds of illegal business takes place. We drive a few miles to the checkpoint. I jump out and urge them not to worry.

"I'm going to do a little research. I'll meet you back in Lago tomorrow. *Te voy a llamar.*" I'll call you. The guys nod respectfully and wish me luck.

I'm a bit shaken up by what Yann has told me. I hadn't realized how hot this border was. The reality of my predicament is setting in. It will soon be dark, and I'm going into the unknown—without backup and no idea what I might find. On my own again, I take a deep breath and consider my surroundings.

I show my passport to a half-asleep border guard, walk a short distance down the road, and enter Colombia. After finding a taxi and driving the winding roads, I reach the first location. Just as I expect, it's not exactly a brothel—but another depository for women about to be sold to traffickers and cartel buyers. It's not unlike a barn, packed with girls, but few clients. Twenty-five or thirty young women are standing on a stage performing a perverse version of a talent show or beauty contest. The girls are halfheartedly singing karaoke and gazing blankly into the distance. Some looked drugged while the others are simply terrified.

After buying a beer at the bar, I go back to a table and scan the stage. Remembering the suspicious looks I've been getting back in

Lago Agrio, I kick into full-blown party boy mode. I sway to the music and smile at everyone like the naïve, happy-go-lucky American surfer I really am.

I sense a connection with one of the younger girls, who's staring fixedly at me, and pay the full fee to take her to one of the back bungalows. Her name is Carolina, and she's young, maybe fifteen years old. "I'm a musician with a girlfriend and I just want to talk," I say to her. She massages my shoulders with her tiny hands and begins to tell me her story. I tape her story on my phone.

Carolina's from Medellín, and was recently sold to the mafia by a cousin needing to pay off his drug debt. After a long, winding bus ride to this hellhole, she's about to be moved to Lago Agrio and then to who knows where.

"Are you ever allowed to leave this place?" I ask her.

"No," she responds. "But I want to go with you. Take me with you, please!" she begs, with tears in her eyes. "I am afraid."

Carolina has no documentation. If she tries to run away and is caught, she'll be severely beaten, or worse.

I make a split-second decision. "We have to get to the other side of the border," I say. "If you think it's possible," I say in Spanish, "tomorrow morning meet me by the boat crossing near the San Miguel Bridge. I'll go across with you and take you to Lago Agrio. From there we'll put you on a bus to Guayaquil. ¿Está bien? Okay?"

Carolina nods, reading my thoughts. "If I go back to Medellín," she says, "they'll just find me again and take me back here. In Guayaquil we can blend in, maybe find real jobs. ¿Hasta mañana?"

"Absolutely," I assure her. In reality, I know she will probably end up struggling to earn money, looking for a break that may or may not come. But at least she'll be out of here.

Carolina keeps talking excitedly about how great it will be to start over, and I begin to realize how insane this is. What am I doing? Maybe this one time I can do something more than just collect the evidence.

At dawn the next morning, after having slept a couple of hours in a cockroach-infested hotel room, I wait behind some trees near the ferry landing. A frightened Carolina strides up briskly with five other adolescent girls who have summoned up the courage to run for it. Their eyes are downcast as they approach me, and I'm surprised to see so many of them.

I make contact with each pair of eyes and say, "I'm just going to try and get you across this river and on that bus."

This time, however, I can't cross the border at the official checkpoint. We follow a narrow dirt path down to the Putumayo River, where I've already made a deal with a guy who owns a small wooden skiff. Although it's only one hundred yards across to Ecuador, this man is putting himself at considerable risk, so I am more than happy to pay him a hundred dollars for the passage as well as his silence. The average wage in this part of the world is about nine dollars a day.[11]

By taking the girls into Ecuador, on one count we have already outwitted the traffickers—who expect fleeing victims to run the other way, toward home. The mafias have the roads out of San Marcellino heavily guarded for this purpose. In comparison, there are only a handful of Ecuadorean Army officers guarding the forty-mile-long border with Colombia.

Once we've crossed the river, we walk up the bank and cross a field until we get to the Lago Agrio road. As I'm wondering what to do next, a flatbed truck coming back from the border region passes by, and I flag it down. I offer the driver some money to take us to the bus station in Lago near the airport. He nods, and the girls and I pile in the back.

Two hours later, Carolina and her five friends board the bus for Guayaquil after hugging me tightly. I've given them all the money I have in my pocket—enough to pay for their tickets, an apartment, and some food when they get there. On the envelope with the money, I've written down the phone number of a social worker in Guayaquil. The girls are still terrified, but at least they now have a good chance of making it. It's not exactly a textbook ending. But it's a start.

TIE YOURSELF TO THE MAST

TWO WEEKS LATER, I'M BACK ON THE TARMAC AT Guayaquil Airport. Ecuador's largest city is more spread out and industrial feeling than Quito, the capital. Unlike evergreen Quito, this port city reveals its sleaze immediately, and I have no illusions about looking for beauty here. I want to work. After dumping my bags in my room and having a quick plate of rice and beans in a canteen near the hotel, I jump into the first taxi that stops.

"*Hola,*" I say while sliding across the backseat. The driver nods and smiles over his shoulder. I note a set of rosary beads hanging from the rearview mirror, and pictures of his young children stuck to the dashboard.

"*¿Como estas? Es mi primer día aquí, y quisiera ir a un* 'nightclub,'" I say, making eye contact with him in the mirror. "*Me entiendes? Las discotecas . . .*"

"*Listo,*" he nods. We understand each other.

"*¿Cuanto tiempo tienes manejando el taxi?* (So how long have you been driving a taxi?)" I ask.

"*Siete anos,*" he says noncommittally, unsurprised by the fact that I'm speaking Spanish. Lots of gringos come through here looking for sex. Some of them even stay long enough to master the colloquialisms.

"Wow . . . *es mucho tiempo—conoces muy bien la ciudad, entonces.* (That's a long time—so you must know the city really well . . .)"

He knows Guayaquil well enough to introduce me to some lovely young girls, he says, smiling at me over his shoulder. I don't even have to ask. He's pegged me as a sex tourist. We introduce ourselves by first name.

I smile appreciatively and enthusiastically, just to get him talking. "Since you know this city so well," I say, "can you tell me if it's true that Guayaquil is home to the most beautiful women in South America?"

In response, Javier hands me a brochure depicting a massage parlor, with pictures of beautiful girls in sexy outfits, a bar, and private rooms. "*Las Colombianas son conocidas por ser las chicas mas lindas del mundo,*" he says. Colombian women are considered the most beautiful women in the world.

My silence while pondering this thought is taken as a tacit approval; in a few minutes we are pulling up in front of a glitzy nightclub in a business district.

The evening is unremarkable in the sense that the girls I see in the high-end clubs all seem to be of age. But almost all of them are Colombian.

After getting an overview of the nightclub scene, I make it into bed by 6 A.M. and then sleep all day. After a quick powwow with Michele around sunset, I decide to take it easy on my second night in town. I check in with Juanita, who tells me Papa's responding well to his new blood pressure and ulcer medications. Relieved, I decide to get into bed with a book, even though it's barely ten o'clock. But just as I'm falling asleep, there's a knock on the door. Ernesto is standing there, baseball cap in hand, with a man he introduces as a police officer from the Narcotics Affairs Section of the U.S. Embassy. "Sorry to bother you, Aaron," he says. "But we have some information we want to share with you."

I stand back to let them pass, pulling the room's one chair over to the bed before motioning for them to sit down. The officer starts in first. "We have someone we want you to meet," he says. "An informant called Tigreton."

Tigreton. The huge tiger.

I look at Ernesto, who nods. "Tigreton is our direct link to the taxi mafia," he says. "He's a driver who takes kickbacks from the big strip clubs for delivering customers to their door. Since most of the clubs are owned by the drug cartels, he sees and overhears a lot of things in his taxi."

I try to hide my skepticism about a source like this. "So he's an informant, then?"

"You could say that," says the officer. "Or you could say he's our best chance at finding the connection between Raoul Gutierrez's Cali drug cartel and his businesses that use trafficked women."

I nod, waiting for more. *I'm a human rights worker, not a drug cop.*

Ernesto picks up where the cop left off. "Gutierrez owns Showgirls, a fancy club here in town that we believe he uses as a front to move drugs and women. But he's smart. He senses every time a local cop or an Interpol guy goes anywhere near his place. We've been watching him for more than a year, but we haven't been able to get any hard evidence on him."

"So you're thinking that I—"

"You go and meet Tigreton tonight," the cop says, cutting me off. "He'll take you to Showgirls so you can see for yourself. Meet the women there—talk to them. Find out what you can about Gutierrez," he says, smiling for the first time since he walked into the room. "And there's no doubt you'll get the other information you need much more quickly by going through Tigreton."

He pauses to gauge my reaction to this comment.

"I mean, faster than you would by just jumping into any taxi that stops for you."

They were watching me last night.

"I'd like to help you," I say. "But I work alone, and I don't trust informants. They have no loyalty."

I could get smoked by this Tigreton guy. I don't want to risk getting exposed by an informant.

"*Sí, yo lo sé, Aaron,*" says Ernesto, switching to familiar Spanish. "But Tigreton is your best bet for getting the inside track here. It takes years to build up the kind of contacts he has. Besides, Michele wants us to look into the clubs with probable links to the mafias doing the trafficking. Showgirls is where it's happening, Aaron."

It occurs to me that they want to use this guy to keep an eye on me. But I don't say that. Instead, I agree to do a ride-along with Tigreton—just once. "But that means you and Carlos are coming, too," I tell Ernesto.

Ernesto immediately starts shaking his head. "Cannot do that," he says. "They might already know my face."

"Then I go into the club alone," I insist. "This guy can take me there, but that's it. I don't want an introduction, and I definitely don't want him by my side the whole night."

The cop raises an eyebrow, but shakes my hand in agreement and wishes me *buena suerte.*

Forty-five minutes later, we're standing in front of Tigreton's taxi shaking hands with the guy. He's wearing jeans and a baseball hat pulled down over his eyes and sucking on a cigarette so smoky he has to squint under the cap. I take an immediate dislike to him, even more so after he starts patting my arm and repeating "*Todo tranquilo, no te procupas, todo tranquilo.*" The minute someone starts telling me not to worry, I start to worry.

Nevertheless, I get into the car with Carlos and Ernesto, who suggest again that Tigreton walk us into the club and introduce us to the hostess. Our dear driver suddenly cranks up the salsa music to a painful level, and I take the opportunity to air my thoughts.

"No!" I snap. "He can drive us there, but I am not letting this guy take credit for having brought us in."

Carlos and Ernesto nod grimly. They understand that I don't want to risk being identified with an informant. But it's only later that I will understand their insistence on this step. At the next red light, Carlos says he thinks it's better if I go to the club without them. Tigreton will take them home as soon as they drop me off. I nod my agreement—somewhat confused, but also relieved I don't have to worry about anyone except myself for the next few hours. Although invaluable companions, short-haired, conservative-looking guys like Carlos and Ernesto are not necessarily an asset in situations like the one I'm headed into.

We pull up in front of the brightly lit Showgirls, and I jump out before Tigreton has the chance to open my door. There's a gauntlet of taxis lined up here, their drivers having congregated in front of the lead car. A dozen men are sitting or leaning on the hood, talking intensely. Their body language tells me they know each other very well.

As we shake good-bye, Ernesto leans in close and whispers "*Cuidate*, Aaron. Let Tigreton walk you to the front door. That's it."

The urgency in his voice makes me concede. "Okay," I say, nodding to Tigreton, who walks around his car with a slippery smile and motions for me to follow him past the bouncers to the VIP entrance, where a guy at a counter is stamping vouchers. I suddenly realize my earlier mistake. Taxi drivers get credit for having brought customers like me in for the evening. One john is worth a tank of gas—the cost of which can run a taxi driver about half of what he pulls in for a day of driving. I almost prevented Tigreton from getting his cut. It seems like I get into trouble every time I step between the oil money and the slave runners.

While he's chatting with the gas coupon guy, a tall, striking woman with long dark hair strides up to me, touches me lightly on the arm and addresses me in English. "Welcome to Showgirls— I am Naomi," she says, with barely the trace of an accent. We walk together into the huge space, which is packed with upward of two hundred people shouting to be heard over the pumping rhythmic music. The clients look to be mostly Ecuadorean businessmen, their shirts unbuttoned to show off their chest hair and gold necklaces.

Slowly adjusting to the circus-like atmosphere, I take in the mirrored walls, smoke machine, and dozens of alluring women strutting up and down the elevated catwalks and bobbing on poles for the wonderstruck men sitting below them. On the surface, everything is on the up-and-up here, since prostitution is legal and, just like in Quito, all of the youngest ones probably have fake papers saying they're eighteen.

Every one of them is gorgeous.

But I am completely smitten by Naomi. She's a sexy Colombian beauty—chiseled features and brimming with self-confidence. "Where would you like to sit?" she asks.

When I respond in Spanish, Naomi looks amused, but her smile turns to interest when I start flirting and cracking jokes with her. She leads me over to an exclusive section near the hostess stand, where she works. "I am the manager here," she explains, "but it's crazy tonight so I'm also hosting." Smiling again, she looks into my eyes intensely.

For the rest of the night I sit in Naomi's corner, watching her work and talking whenever she gets a moment. I have learned that she's twenty-four.

"You know, my aunt was named Naomi," I tell her at one point, feeling the alcohol on my breath.

"¿*Claro*?" she says dryly, flipping her hair and fixing me with her big brown eyes. "So you are telling me you feel the same things for me you might feel for your aunt?"

"Yes," I should respond, but I find myself unable to tell her that. I only manage to laugh nervously, like I've been caught at something.

"Okay," she says. "So you like girls, but I'm guessing you want someone younger than me." This couldn't be further from the truth, but I remind myself I am working, and allow her to keep talking. "So I'll send some beauties your way," she winks.

Over the next few hours, Naomi brings over a series of younger girls—ranging in age from "seventeen" to "nineteen"—to meet me. They're each wearing a bikini covered by a slinky wraparound outfit, all color-coordinated. Each one is more beautiful than the last, and most of them are from Medellín and say they have come through Lago Agrio. I follow protocol, smiling and buying each girl a drink before tipping her. But I make it clear to Naomi that I am not interested in them.

As tiny slivers of light from the street make their way into the room, she comes back over and slides into the booth next to me. "I send you only my best girls and still you find no one you'd like to take home?" she says flirtatiously.

"I would rather go home with you," I finally say, hoping my honesty will give me some credibility with her later. I'm sure this woman can lead me to the people I'm looking for.

"So why don't you?" she replies with a half smile, half pout before abruptly standing up and striding toward the exit. I am not presented with a bill, although I'm sure to tip the other manager and the bouncer on the way out. We jump into a taxi, and Naomi's hands are all over me. We kiss briefly, and there is enough fire there to tell me that it is going to be very, very difficult to tie myself to the mast tonight.

Walking down the hotel hallway hand in hand, I dread running into Michele, who would not be pleased if she saw Naomi here with me.

I think back to the time when I began honing my night frighting skills—on our first trip together in the Dominican Republic—where my techniques led to my first real argument with Michele. At that point I had just realized that letting my guard down and simply being myself with everyone from victims to madams to traffickers was the key to success.

One night in the casino, Michele walked in to see one of my sources sitting on my lap, playing with my hair and caressing my chest. Another was nearby, laughing with me and flirting openly. Michele did not look happy—in fact I got the sense that she was utterly disgusted. She muttered something under her breath and strode out of the casino after issuing me an enraged look. The scene might have ended there, except that in her haste Michele tripped over a carpet edge and fell flat on her face. I trotted over to pick her up, but she refused my help. That was the first time we disagreed on what we would come to know as "the line."

"You're too far over the line," she said.

"Where the line is depends on my ability to resist temptations certain men would find impossible," I remember telling her. "But you already know I'm not like those guys. And if you want results, you've got to let *me* decide where to put that line."

That night Michele sighed in frustration and walked away. I understood her protective feelings toward these women, and her sincere desire to prevent any of them from being further exploited. But I knew how to function effectively in the dysfunctional world of vice work, where the boundaries are never clear-cut. From then on we agreed I would be the keeper of my own "line."

On this trip we've agreed to take rooms on different floors. And if anyone asks, Michele is my cousin and partner. We work together for a children's charity and are here on business.

Once in my room, Naomi quickly strips down to her bra and

panties while I try to explain why I can't be intimate with her. "You're really attractive," I tell her, "and I really like you, but I have a girlfriend back home." As the words come out I realize how ridiculous they sound. Not only because the line is a cliché, but because my most recent girlfriend has just left me for someone else, saying she couldn't handle the thought of me doing this kind of work.

The truth is I am single, and very attracted to this woman.

She purses her lips and looks me hard in the eyes. "Your girlfriend is not here," she says matter-of-factly as she starts to unbutton my shirt.

I try to block out the sight of her flawless skin, curly brown hair, and perfectly formed legs, and focus on how to get her to trust me without giving myself away. I let her strip me down to boxer briefs.

"Naomi," I try again. "I *do* really like you. But I'm confused. I don't know what to do. So let's please just hold each other and fall asleep."

She gets that amused look on her face again. "Okay, Aaron. But tomorrow you gonna party with me."

"Deal."

We climb into bed and wrap ourselves around each other. She starts telling me the story of her life. About how she was trafficked from Colombia at fourteen, paid off her debt, and rose up through the ranks to a managerial position. "Since then I've had a million lovers," she says, staring at me again. "No good guys, though."

She leans in to kiss me again, and I immediately feel myself getting carried away. Naomi wriggles herself closer to me. I hold her firmly by the shoulders, put my hand to her lips, and tell her to calm down. And then I spoon her, forcing her body to be still. She keeps trying to back up against me, but I just hold her tight and then feign sleep. Soon she's breathing evenly.

I try to simply enjoy the closeness of this fragile, intriguing female, but my body is fighting my mind—tortured by this exquisite woman I can't have. By the children here who need our help. By the vision of Michele busting in, taking in the scene, and misinterpreting everything. At least, I think as I finally nod off, I've bought myself one more day . . . I thank G-d and say a prayer for Papa before falling asleep.

A few hours later we're awakened by a faint knock at the door. Through the peephole I tell Michele I was out late and that I'll catch up with her later. We fall back asleep until 2 P.M., and I awake ravenously hungry. Naomi reaches for me, but I'm already up and dressed before she can make a move. We decide to walk down the street to a shack where we drink guanabana juice and order rice and beans to be brought over from a streetside café. Naomi has to go and get ready for work, and we kiss good-bye.

"Remember, tonight, you party with me!" she says mischievously. "My boss, Raoul, is having a big *fiesta* later."

"Okay, but first, you let me take you out for a nice dinner," I say. "Candles, atmosphere—you pick the place."

I put Naomi in a taxi and walk back to the hotel. After a shower and some acrid room service coffee, I call Michele and arrange to meet downstairs to recap things for Carlos and Ernesto. I don't go into detail about Naomi, and thankfully no one asks.

A few hours later I walk through the waterlogged streets to Naomi's chosen restaurant on a quiet plaza overlooking a fountain. We order wine, laugh, and eat Italian food while sharing the intimate details of our lives. It's not difficult for me to put aside what she does for a living and relate to her as a human being. Under her tough exterior, Naomi is a victim, too.

After dinner we take a taxi to a bourgeois residential neighborhood. At first I think we're going to Gutierrez's house, but instead we walk up to a club stealthily operating inside a private home. The street is lined with Ferraris, BMWs, and Mercedeses. Inside, the place resembles a mafia McMansion, complete with laser lights, spiral staircase, white shag carpets, and tacky statuary. The women are clearly working girls on their night off—most likely mafia mistresses.

Some of the men (most of whom know Naomi) look at me with curiosity. Naomi introduces me as a musician friend doing work for a children's charity. Her friends nod noncommittally as they take in every detail of my appearance—without making eye contact. These are mob people, drug dealers, and addicts, and I start to feel uncomfortable when Naomi happens to mention the name of my hotel. At the same time, I feel my head becoming lighter and the colors around me becoming more intense. I watch Naomi do coke with a few of her "friends" and start to wonder if she's dosed me with something. I stop drinking and pull her aside the first chance I get.

"Did you put something in my drink?" I say, looking at her glassy eyes. She refuses to look at me, and now it's my turn to get mad. "This is not cool," I protest. "Understand?"

I can't let myself lose control here. There are too many dangerous people around.

"All I know now is I can't trust you," I continue, before she touches her finger to my lips.

"A-ron, A-ron . . . I just wanted you to be free with me, be happy," she says sadly. "*Lo siento mucho.*" I'm really sorry. "*Aaroncito . . .*" She leans in to kiss me.

I feel the drug coming on strong, and struggle to keep my head together without floating off into the ether. I've been in this situation before. Perry and the other guys were always counting on me to be the sane one—the friend who could party all night but manage to get out of bed in the morning and make everything all right again. I learned how to do the drugs while keeping my head above water, and that's what I've got to do now.

The drug has transported Naomi to another world, and she starts grabbing at me earnestly. "Come back inside and dance with me—let's party!" she says. Sensing her vulnerability, I decide to withdraw a bit. I'm still angry with her for dosing my drink, but I can't miss the chance to visit Raoul's house.

"Naomi, you know I'm here to help children," I begin.

"Yes, and I love that about you."

"Well, how old is a child to you?" I ask.

"*Yo no sé*, smaller than fourteen?" She looks at me quizzically.

"I don't know, either, but it makes me really sad to see those young girls working at Showgirls," I say. "I don't think they want to be there."

"*Claro qué no*," she says. "They are forced to work, just like I was."

Hearing her say this straight out, I get emotional. "Then why don't you help them?"

The look on her face tells me I've given too much away. "I'm sorry," I say. "The ecstasy is making me freak out. Let's get out of here."

"Okay," she says. "We'll go to the after party."

After our fourth taxi ride of the evening, we pull up in front of another million-dollar home. I recognize some of the same cars from the previous party. There's a waterfall in the living room and a huge tank of exotic fish. The clock says 4 A.M., and the party is just getting started. People are snorting lines of coke off the coffee table and others are dancing to Latin pop music, cocktails in hand. I sense the same kept-woman dynamic as the other party—festivity without joy. The men are predators, still looking at me mistrustfully.

I recognize an older, well-dressed man as one of the bosses at Showgirls. He walks over and puts his hand out. I take the gesture as more of a challenge than a warm welcome, but decide to shake his hand and try to put him at ease. He introduces himself as Raoul Gutierrez.

Naomi tells him I'm a musician and friend. I mention the charity work, just in case anyone's cross-referencing. Gutierrez walks us to the bar and tells us to order whatever we'd like, then disappears. In a few minutes Naomi leads me up the stairs to a quiet loft with a couch and a few chairs. She starts trying to kiss me when Raoul and a few friends walk in with a guitar. I gently push her away.

"Here you go, my musician friend," Raoul says, passing me the guitar with a wink. This, too, is a challenge, and probably not a friendly one. I accept with a nod.

"Have you been partying tonight with Naomi?" he asks, a smile dancing on his lips.

"Yeah, we've been partying," I manage to smile back, and show him I'm not nervous. Again, I'm grateful for the rock and roll credentials. I take the guitar.

I know just what to play, and start strumming the opening bars to the same tune I played for Perry years earlier, Silvio Rodriguez's *"Oleo de Mujer con Sombrero,"* that sad and romantic favorite of the Latin American Left. I pour myself into it, thinking about my own lost love and my addictions as I connect with the music in my heart.

I'm so into the song that I almost forget I'm playing for a collection of drug kingpins and their mistresses. So when I finish, I'm startled to hear them break into a rousing round of applause and cheers.

Gutierrez makes eye contact and nods approval. I laugh, feeling totally at ease now. I've proven my awareness of his people's struggle with this metaphor of two lovers — a small, fragile female representing Cuba and a dominant, overreaching male symbolizing my own country.

He and I talk a bit about American exploitation of tin in Bolivia and of oil and timber from the Amazon. My experience in Peru and Argentina serves me well during our conversation. "When you come in and rape a group of women, it's difficult for them to follow your advice on human rights," I say at one point, without even thinking about the ravages that Gutierrez's business is unleashing upon an entire generation of Colombian females. He nods in agreement, catching only my main metaphor.

One of Gutierrez's friends asks for a Beatles song, and so I play John Lennon's "In My Life" and a few others before passing the guitar on to someone else. People start coming up to pat me on the back and chat about the music, and even politics. Yes, these people may be drug dealers or traffickers or broken women, but first they are human beings — and music has brought us together. Jubilee.

"Otro!" "Otro!"

The group asks for an encore, so I close the set with David Bowie's "The Man Who Sold the World":

> *We passed upon the stair, we spoke of was and when*
> *Although I wasn't there, he said I was his friend . . .*

I sing my heart out, feeling like my life could change in a heartbeat. But at least I've got these last few bars of music.

After the song, a group of us head downstairs to the dance floor. I've been accepted.

Over the next few hours, as Naomi catches up with girlfriends and talks business with Gutierrez, I talk to a few of his men. With the barriers down, I find out a lot about their operation—which is very sophisticated. Most of the girls are recruited online in Medellín or Cali after answering advertisements for models posted on networking sites. "Too bad," they're told. "You're not quite right to be a model, but we can give you another opportunity to make a lot of money . . ." Most of the girls recruited are over sixteen, with the freedom to come and go as they please. But then there are the shadow children—grammar-school-aged girls and boys kept in secret locations, with their services sold at a premium. No one wants to talk about them. I tread carefully, not wanting to give myself away.

I leave Gutierrez's mansion with a stronger sense of the link between drugs and human trafficking and the immense power of the cocaine mafia. As well as a firm awareness that we are all part of the problem, as well as the solution.

Naomi and I are back in my hotel room by breakfast time. The drinking and dancing have built up her desire, and she is longing for intimacy. She pouts, letting herself go, touching her hair and pressing against me. I have to work so hard to keep her away that we are practically wrestling. A beautiful, strong-willed woman like this is not used to being rejected. I maintain my story from the previous night, but my defenses are still down from the partying and all the drinks. We kiss and squirm around on the bed. The drugs have taken their effect on Naomi as well, and her frustration comes out in a burst of physical energy. The sexual heat between us continues to build. I pull away, convinced Michele will knock on the door any moment.

"What is wrong with you?" Naomi says. "You tell me you have girlfriend, but you bring me back here again and then you don't want me? Maybe you not a real man, hah?" She strikes out at me clumsily, missing her target.

I want her so badly, and try to calm myself down. We share a passionate kiss. "Listen, Naomi, I'm just getting to know you.

Things aren't going well for me at home, and I just need more time to figure out how I feel," I say. The truth is that I value the closeness we've developed, despite the fact that I've withheld information from her about myself.

I grab her, pick her up, and take her to the bed, to repeat our near-chaste routine from the previous night. This time she gives in to sleep without a struggle.

Awakened by a light rap on the door, I open it to see Michele standing there. It's after 1 P.M. and she's planned a professional lunch with Carlos and Ernesto to thank them for their work. She peers around the door and takes in the scene: me in my Calvins and a sleeping Naomi sprawled on the bed.

"I'll meet you downstairs," she says curtly.

I quickly shake Naomi awake and tell her to get dressed and come downstairs. "Michele's upset with me," I offer. "But don't worry. She'll love you," I add.

I'm annoyed I have to bring Michele into it at all.

A few minutes later, we find Michele, Ernesto, and Carlos having lunch in the hotel restaurant. The men seem hypnotized by Naomi's beauty, and are at a loss for words. I can tell Michele is furious, because she refuses to look me in the eye. When Naomi excuses herself to go to the bathroom, Michele turns to me.

"How could you?" she says accusingly.

"I know what it looks like—" I start, but she interrupts me.

"I told you I'd let you use your quote-unquote 'nontraditional methods,'" she says. "But this is taking it too far." She's practically spitting as she lays into me.

"I'm not having sex with her," I retort. "And I'm on the verge of a breakthrough here. You have to back off."

Michele sighs in response and focuses on the near-distance beyond my head. Carlos and Ernesto are looking down at their plates. I suggest perhaps the three of them should change hotels so I can get on with my work without interruption. I'm tired of Michele's bureaucratic approach, and I don't have time to defend myself. But at the same time, I see why Michele is angry. I've brought an informant into a professional context.

At that moment Naomi comes back to the table and Michele turns on the charm again, complimenting her on her outfit. She's got a background in acting, after all.

Back upstairs, I ask Naomi to stay with me again that night. We're both exhausted, but with our defenses down the conversation flows easily. I can tell she's going to help me.

"I just want to make sure these children find a safe place to live," I say. "I don't even know where they are, but you do, Naomi."

"If anyone knew I told you where they keep these children, they'd kill me."

"I'm not a cop," I remind her. "I'll get Social Services to help these kids."

Naomi smiles wistfully. "The Social Services people are kind, but naïve," she says. "They always call the police—and most times the cop they call is already being paid by Raoul."

As we talk, I realize that the situation for trafficked children in Ecuador is worse than I thought. Even if I am able to find a group of young girls and get them away from the cartel, where will they go? There is no shelter system ready to receive them. But at least I can report what I find through the ABA and hope that Interpol or the State Department will take action.

Despite her initial reluctance, Naomi has decided to trust me. She starts reciting the names of a few brothels where she knows underage girls are kept. I jot them down in a notebook, and she looks at my face, as though confirming I'm not an undercover cop. She smiles uneasily before falling asleep in my arms. Tomorrow she has to go back to work.

While Naomi returns to her long nights at Showgirls, I spend the next few days following up on the leads she's given me. I night fright the brothels and get the testimony of as many underage girls as I can find. Each one of these interviews leaves an indelible mark on my conscience, since for the moment I can do nothing more but listen and record. I tell myself that I must remember their faces and bear witness to their stories. But the reality is that nothing can be restored until there are no more clients—a prospect that seems far-fetched, if not insane.

Alone in my hotel room, I fall into a troubled sleep and dream about all the taboos I've been trying to block out with Naomi. In the dream, we are surrounded by the faces of the little girls I've interviewed—the children whose childhoods have been stolen by a series of sick men and their perverse fantasies. Men not unlike me, I think, as I wake and try to shake off the images of Naomi's long legs.

The next day Carlos takes me around to visit a few orphanages—the only potential lodging option for rescued children at this time. The prevailing attitude among the workers there seems to be that prostitutes of any kind are dirty and even beyond help. More than one NGO worker uses the term "lost cause."

My nightmares continue, both while asleep and awake.

Now that I've become a "special customer" at Showgirls and have passed the party test with Gutierrez, I've earned my entrée into the second tier of sex clubs—those for men looking for S&M, or underage boys and girls. All I have to do is mention Raoul Gutierrez at the door, and I'm ushered right in.

One night the driver brings me to a mansion at the end of a cul-de-sac—one of the addresses Naomi has mentioned. There is no sign and there are only a couple of cars sitting out front.

Inside I'm frisked lightly before shaking hands with the bartender and a couple of guys in uniform—white shirts, black pants, and shiny shoes. I'm the only customer. While sipping my beer, I casually mention that I love pretty girls, and the bartender smiles understandingly. "The girls will be down in a minute," he tells me reassuringly. One of the uniformed guys nods and places the order on a walkie-talkie. The mood is relaxed. No one here is worried about a police raid.

I've only had half my beer when ten or so girls parade into the room one by one and stand in a line behind the bar tables, about twenty feet from where I'm sitting. They're all wearing lingerie or see-through dresses barely long enough to cover their buttocks. Everything is on display. These girls are very, very young—no more than thirteen or fourteen. I get that wretched feeling in the pit of my stomach again, and fight back the urge to cry out or vomit.

Ordering a shot of tequila—Patrón Silver—for myself and one for the bartender, I try to make eye contact with a few of the girls, but they are all looking at the ground in humility and despair. Unlike the confident gazes of the girls at Showgirls, who compete for male attention, here their body language screams out, "Oh G-d, please don't choose me!"

A third man in uniform walks into the room and shakes my hand.

"We're special," he says. "You're going to love our girls." Then he asks me to pay in advance. I hand over about $500 before tipping the bartender and the doorman.

I struggle to swallow my shot and finish the rest of my beer, but keep a smile on for the bartender, who has proposed a toast to the good times I'm about to have. "Can I chat with a few of the girls before choosing one?" I ask.

I select the girl closest to me, then ask her to invite a couple of the youngest girls over. I offer them a drink, recognizing in their faces the dull sheen often seen on methamphetamine users. One of the three asks for a drink, and the others follow suit. We sit down at a table and I try to engage them in conversation, but they all wear deadpan expressions and respond in monosyllables.

I choose little Maria, whose face shows no emotion when I say her name, and follow her upstairs to the hotel-like room. There's a queen-sized bed, condoms on the table, extra sheets and towels stacked on a dresser. So tidy and efficient.

"Please take a shower first," she asks, and I obey. I come out wearing my underwear and a robe. We go to the room and lie down on the bed.

"You're really pretty, Maria. But I have a girlfriend in the U.S. I'm here because I'm lonely. I'm going to pay you and give you a good tip. But I don't want to have sex . . . Can you give me a nice massage? It hurts right here," I say, indicating my neck.

Maria looks confused, but she pulls down her skirt and goes to remove her top. I ask her to keep her clothes on. She yields and starts to massage my shoulders halfheartedly before protesting: "I don't know how to massage well, señor. If you don't want me, you can pick someone else."

"How old are you, Maria?"

"Eighteen."

"What year were you born?"

There's a pause while she does the math in her head. She's clearly following instructions, and is scared. I start to record her with my videophone, explaining that I've got to make a phone call but have been having problems with it. Maria's face is impassive, as though she hasn't even noticed the phone at all. Although I've already paid for an hour with her, I need the solicitation on tape, so I ask her for a breakdown of costs and services.

"You can pay me for suck you, which costs hundred," she says. "Sex is two hundred, and the room fee is fifty."

Once I've got the solicitation, I pop out the memory disk and slip it into a pocket sewn into my pants, just in case. I put in a new disk and ask Maria to tell me her story. She's from Cali and came here via Lago Agrio by bus. There's no question she's been trafficked and is being held here against her will. She is so heavily drugged, though, that it is almost impossible to get a sense for the child she once was, and somewhere still is. Nonetheless, I am able to see hope in her eyes.

I let her rub my shoulders until enough time has passed for us to have presumably had sex. "Please don't tell them we didn't do it," she says to me with a panicked look as she walks out the door. In many brothels like these, sex acts are ranked on a point system, with intercourse earning more points toward paying off a girl's debt than oral sex.

I walk over to the sink and wash my face, trying to make sense out of the image I see in the mirror.

On my way out, the bartender and his colleagues smile and ask me how everything was. "*Todo hecho; todo tranquilo*," I've learned to say, so no one suspects I'm anything other than a satisfied customer.

I hail a taxi and force myself to hit the next place on my list. My last stop of the night is Showgirls, where Naomi is thrilled to see me. By this point she's more than a bit confused. She knows I've been out "partying" with younger girls, and yet I've still refused to sleep with her. From her point of view, it's starting to look suspicious. I've got to leave before my cover is compromised.

I explain I've got to go home to take care of my father, but that my charity work will bring me back to Ecuador in a month. I try to be noncommittal. "I guess I better hit the road then . . ."

Naomi turns cold and fixes a spot on the ground, like a child trying not to cry. She's taken more rejection from me than she can handle.

"Being with you these last few days has been amazing," I say, trying to get her to look at me. "But drugs and addiction are a problem for me, Naomi. I can't go back to that life." I kiss her briefly on the cheek. I can't find a way to explain to her that I've flipped my drug curse around—that my party experience grants me entry into these underworlds, and protects me while I'm navigating the oppressive territory of pimps and drug lords. The party skills keep me alive, but I'm always grateful when I get to set them aside again.

Although I'm relieved to be leaving Ecuador, I couldn't feel worse as I step into the taxi waiting to take me to the airport. The feelings Naomi and I have for each other are real, even though I can't act on them. Learning to say no to my desires has been like kicking an addiction. It's been a lonely, painful ride. But the upside is that I've found a sort of serenity in the celibate life. Still, the experience with Naomi has awakened my desire for a mate—a true love.

I pack my bags and fly home.

"Look who it is!" Papa exclaims when I finally walk into his bedroom and bend down to hug him. He seems to have shrunken again in the short time I've been away, and I try to hide my surprise at his faded appearance. He wants to hear every detail of my trip—what did the airplane look like, and what about the airstrip? Although I'm heartbroken about what I've just seen, I try to pick out the happy details for him. Now that he is completely bedridden, my stories are what keep him going. Those and his dream life—in which he is flying his plane way up in the sky, far away from the suffering of his earthly body. He dozes off a few times while I'm talking, but I don't dare leave the room. Whenever he wakes up, he cries out for me.

I bring a cot into Papa's room so I can catch him when he is most lucid. In the middle of the night, he sits up and starts talking about flying missions out of Casablanca during World War II. His eyes sparkle as he talks about the danger of smuggling ivory, gold, and people out of the war zone and into the liberated areas.

A month later, Michele, Carlos, Ernesto, and I begin our final Ecuador assessment together, right after Christmas. The rainy season has just started, and this time it's a relief to land in Quito's perpetual spring instead of Guayaquil's swelter. Now that we've got a good idea of how things work in the big cities, we've planned a whirlwind tour of the rest of the country to fill in the missing pieces of the trafficking puzzle. From Quito we pass through the states of Napo, Pastaza, and Morona-Santiago, where I go through my usual routine in several other provincial cities. The others take appointments with all the official agencies, gather information and resources, and work on a shelter plan for victims.

By 6 P.M. Michele, Carlos, and Ernesto are ready to unwind after their day. After having been out until 5 A.M., mine is just beginning. So I share a quick dinner with them, sketch out my plan for the evening, and then hail a taxi to start my rounds. Our experience in the rest of the country indicates the clear pattern we noticed in the big cities: thousands of girls are run in groups from Medellín and Cali, Colombia's second and third largest cities, by mafias linked to the drug cartels and taxi gangs.

We spend only one night in Guayaquil this time, and when I spontaneously stop by Showgirls, Naomi is upset I haven't called or emailed her. I search my brain for a way to explain my feelings without hurting her or giving anything away. But as our dinner stretches on, she relaxes and unexpectedly turns the conversation to shopping. "I know that we will never be anything more than kissing cousins," she says with a mischievous smile, reminding me of the conversation we had the first night we met. "*Pero todo está bien,* Aaron." I hug her tightly good-bye, knowing it will probably be the last time we'll ever see each other. She and I are headed back to our respective worlds, to serve different masters. But I'm leaving a part of me with her. It's not easy to walk away from this woman—who may be just one human connection short of being set free from her confusion and sadness.

Five minutes after we arrive in Esmeraldas, a resort town with beautiful Pacific beaches, a scream from the room next door pierces my melancholic mood. I run over and knock on the door.

Michele is standing in the corner of the room brandishing a shoe. "I can't stay here," she says. She's just seen a giant cockroach scuttle across her bed. We leave and try another hotel, but the rooms are small, dirty, and without air-conditioning. The trip budget won't cover the cost of a luxury hotel, but Michele offers to pay the difference so that we can all stay in a nice beachfront place near the market.

We manage to frolic in the waves for an hour after checking in, and I try to focus on the beauty of the present instead of the upcoming night fright. Preliminary reports have told us that Esmeraldas is a trafficking hot spot. It also happens to be the terminus of the pipeline that crosses northern Ecuador, all the way from the oil fields near Lago Agrio. It's not the first time I've noticed that an abundance of oil goes hand in hand with the presence of slaves.

I dive to the sea floor and stay there awhile, tuning in to the underwater landscape. Floating on my back watching the clouds, I suddenly get the inspiration to run on the beach the way I used to, back and forth over the ice plants of Newport Beach until my asthmatic lungs burned. I emerge and take flight, barefoot but barely noticing the pebbles and shells underfoot. My whole body responds to this freedom, and I push ahead, my desire for Naomi—for anything in the physical realm—receding with each step. This ocean has always been able to heal me.

Michele is smiling playfully when I get back to where she is relaxing, stretched out on a towel. "You're back in the game, aren't you?" she asks.

I nod sheepishly. She can read me so easily.

The first taxi driver takes me to a nightclub and finally to a strip club after I tell him I like beautiful Colombian girls. With its Pacific backdrop, at first glance Esmeraldas reminds me of Costa Mesa. The clubs are not as glitzy as the ones in the big cities, and I don't make a connection with anyone at first. I cut the driver loose and keep walking until another one stops to pick me up.

He introduces himself as "El Niño" and smiles at me through silver teeth. "Why do they call you that?" I ask in Spanish.

"Because of my baby face," he says, stroking his cheeks and chin with his fingers. "You want what, cocaine . . . girls?" El Niño gets straight to the point. I ask for the latter first. "Pretty girls."

"Hey amigo—I *only* know beautiful girls," he flashes me another smile in the rearview mirror. "Good-looking guy like you, *no problemo.* I have a friend you gotta meet. You're going to love her. *Es una mina, una embra* . . . (She's a hot chick)."

El Niño offers to take me to his friend's house to pick up *la mina.* He tells me stories as though we've been friends forever. We stop on the way to buy some beer.

"I own nine cars, you know," he says proudly. "I've only been driving six years, but I got a lot of people working for me."

I can see that's the case, because when we pull up at the house, a bunch of other taxis pull in and surround the car in a flower-petal formation. I count eight of them.

El Niño tells me to wait in the car while he goes in. I assume he's re-upping—getting more drugs to deliver to his customers. A minute later he walks out with two women—one of whom is his girlfriend. The other woman is gorgeous and comes to sit in the back with me. "*Soy Elizabeth,*" she says, kissing me on both cheeks. She is clearly not a trafficked woman, dressed in designer clothes and happy to be here. She touches my arm while talking animatedly.

El Niño keeps telling me how happy he is to have met me and what an honor it is to have an American musician in his taxi. I feel a genuine connection to these people, and even though I'm slightly worried that I'm getting sidetracked from my original mission, I'm pretty sure this guy knows everything there is to know about the scene here. We walk into a dance club and are allowed to bypass the long line at the front door with barely a nod. The four of us head to the dance floor and Elizabeth immediately puts her arms around me and starts swaying her hips to the music. Slightly uncomfortable with this scenario, I decide to invite Michele down to dance with us. She's a social creature and may be able to defuse this budding romance for me.

When she shows up, I buy us all a round of tequila shots and introduce Michele as my cousin. We all dance together a bit longer before Michele pulls me aside. "I'm not sure how this all ties in with our research," she says. "I understand if you need a night off, but it's late and I'm going home."

She's right—but I don't want a night off. I need to get back to the night fright. I thank El Niño, say good-bye to the women, and head out with Michele. After putting her in a taxi, I walk for a little while and think about where to go next. A taxi pulls up and asks me where I'd like to go. "Wherever the young beautiful girls are," I say, but before I can close the door, another guy slides into the backseat next to me. I feel the unmistakable chill of a gun pressed to my temple.

"I hope you don't mind sharing the cab with me," he says coldly. "Now we're going to see what you get for fucking around with my girlfriend."

As the car starts to roll, I think quickly. Once they get it to full speed I'll have no chance of getting out. I take some cash from my wallet, throw it in the gunman's direction, then push open the other door and jump out. I'm vaguely aware of rolling on the pavement, then being up on my feet again, running flat out. I charge through a restaurant and an open-air mall, aware of the sound of my legs on open throttle, muffled by the sound of my own breathing—surrounded by paranoia. I move around the side of a house and have to scale another fence near a pack of dogs, which immediately start barking. But adrenaline gets me over the fence and through another with no problem. *I've lost them,* I'm thinking as I turn reluctantly up the street and double-time it to the next corner. I can hear ambulance sirens in the distance. That's when I see them again—one block ahead—and they spot me in their rearview and pull a one-eighty.

My heart practically explodes in my chest, and I have the sense of being outside of my body, watching myself from above, as my feet open up again in flight. They're shooting at me from the car, and now I can see that I had better go for another round of backyard dodge-and-dash. I've been through this before, and this time I recognize the sound of bullets sizzling by me.

I dart out from my hiding spot and make it across the street and into a small yard with chickens and a pen full of guinea pigs. Over the fence, and through another garden . . . but I hear a car screech around the corner and so stay where I am. I can see the chase car through the fence boards. Luckily there's not a lot of ambient light, and I finally have a chance to think about what's happening. Has El Niño set me up? Or was he just using me to disrespect his rival?

The car finally drives on, and I hightail it down to the highway and manage to hail a cab almost immediately. The driver identifies himself as Pedro, a friend of El Niño's I met earlier in the night.

"I've just been robbed and these guys are shooting at me," I say, out of breath.

"I know," he says. "It's El Padre." Pedro explains that El Padre is the head of a rival taxi gang at war with El Niño's guys. The car behind us speeds up, and I hear shots being fired. Pedro floors it down the coastal highway. "Don't worry, we've got our guys here," he tells me after yelling into a walkie-talkie for help. In a minute we're flanked by two other cars—our protection. The chase car, outranked, peels off. Both sets of cars exchange rounds of gunfire.

El Niño is waiting for us on the street in front of Pedro's house: "*Pendejos!*" Fuckers!

"Come on inside, Aaron. We'll figure out how to get those *pendejos* for what they did to you," he says, looking down at my ripped pants and skinned elbows I earned jumping out of the moving car.

"Let's all stay calm," I say, gradually piecing together what's happened by listening to the other drivers' conversation. Elizabeth, of course, is, or was, El Padre's girlfriend, and El Niño has just used me to humiliate his nemesis.

"I'm sorry," he says, handing me a beer and offering me a line of cocaine. "The best!" he says proudly, as though it can make up for putting me in the middle of a gang war.

"It's all right," I say. "I'm just tired. Can someone please take me home?"

A young driver named Tomas offers to take me to the hotel, and I ask him to wait until I get through the front door. After midnight, guests have to ring the front doorbell and wait for the night receptionist to let them in. My heart is still pounding as the groggy attendant opens the door and fixes me with an annoyed look. Another American party boy out sampling the nightlife.

From my room, I call Michele and tell her briefly what's happened. In a second, she's on the phone with the attendant downstairs asking him for a guard. He tells her he'll get back to her.

Now Michele is back over to my room and checking on me to see if everything is okay. She sits me down on the chair and begins to clean my cuts with disinfectant. I tell her about El Niño's rivalry with El Padre for girls and drugs. "Do you think we should get out of here?" she asks.

"No," I say confidently. "It'll be all right. They've probably forgotten about it by now."

I hear the buzzer go off downstairs and look out my window. El Niño's car gang has pulled up in formation, music blasting. Eight faithful drivers get out of their taxis simultaneously, and I can see they've all got guns.

El Niño waves up at me. "Let's go, Aaron," he says, holding out a pistol for me. "Those guys are gonna pay!" he screams. His men are ready to back me up and track down my two hundred dollars. I slowly back away from the window.

Michele has come into my room by now, and is on the phone with the manager ordering him to call the police *ahora*! Her Spanish has really improved in the last few weeks.

The police arrive in a matter of minutes, and El Niño's boys have disappeared. The cops get down the basics, but are not interested in a long explanation. By this point everyone wants to call it a night. It's clear this city has a vibrant gang culture dealing in girls, guns, and cocaine. Although we've only gotten one or two underage solicitations in Esmeraldas, there's no way we can stay any longer. Our presence here has been compromised, and I'll have to get out of town if I don't want to end up in a coffin. The police have little control over El Padre's war with El Niño.

I say a prayer for Elizabeth as we wait for the signal to depart. My prayers are not only for the lost children of these Ecuadorean cities, but for the gang members' girlfriends, who, despite their designer clothes and picture-perfect mansions, are also prisoners. We are all, in a way, enslaved to our material desires.

Driving out of Esmeraldas back into the mountains early the next morning under police escort, I think about El Niño and his twisted sense of loyalty. He may have used me to improve his status and dishonor his rival, but I think in his own way he was respecting his own moral codes. He's grown up in a culture of violence, where being a man means proving your courage and fighting to the death. Today when he comes by and finds his *amigo* gone, I have a feeling he's going to be surprised.

When I look at a pimp or a drug dealer like El Niño, I can no longer see a "bad" guy. Instead I see an extension of myself, a person caught up in a system. Mamasans, traffickers, pimps, mafiosi, kidnappers, corrupt cops, dishonest judges, parents who sell their kids . . . all mixed in with the "regular" people who see themselves apart from it all. But the regular people are both the cause and the cure. They all need compassion, because they are suffering just like me. That's the way to stay afloat in all this—meditating on the oneness of us all. I can't judge El Niño. He could have gotten me killed and probably would have, if I had been off my game; yet I forgive him, and I forgive myself, and I know that that is the only chance we have as a human race. There should be no discrimination, no more labels, no judgment.

Fleeing at dawn packed into a tiny car with Michele, Carlos, and Ernesto, the fear and tension of the last twelve hours culminate in a group laughing fit. Having narrowly escaped being caught in the crosshairs of a gang war, we're carried away by a sense of camaraderie and adventure that these "civilian" colleagues have probably never experienced. And although I keep telling myself that all I crave is the simple life, deep down I know I'll keep getting myself into situations like this. Just like Papa's illness, the plight of the Colombian girls in Ecuador has already became an extension of myself.

EIN SOF

COSTA MESA, CALIFORNIA

Spring 2006

EVER SINCE MY ECUADOR TRIP, PAPA'S CONDI-tion had deteriorated to the point where I stopped accepting overseas assignments. In the decade since we had lost my mother, he had suffered through shingles, strokes, and ulcers. As he approached his ninetieth year, he had started to show signs of dementia.

I'd been assisting a local NGO that worked to free human trafficking victims in Southeast Asia, which led me to Thailand after the 2004 tsunami to help an Italian father search for his autistic half-Japanese daughter, Lea Torelli, who had survived the natural disaster but likely fallen prey to human traffickers. Once there, I became aware of the plight of other Southeast Asian children and made contact with human rights groups in Vietnam, Cambodia, Laos, and Myanmar (formerly Burma).

During that period, I stayed home and watched Papa suffer as we checked him in and out of the hospital. Even with the kind attention of his nurses, the hospital experience itself was killing him. After another series of strokes, he had partially lost his ability to speak. Papa was confused by his surroundings and frustrated by his inability to move or do anything for himself. Several times I walked into the room to find he'd fallen to the floor. I'd pick him up like a baby and put him back in bed.

Over the next few months I watched him decline even further. A rage stirred within me. I was powerless. But I knew he didn't have

much time left, and called Arthur and Ruthie to tell them the end was near. They dropped everything to be by his side. Soon the three of us were at his hospital bed, consoling each other. Papa was slipping away.

"Honey . . ." Papa called for me.

"Yes, Papa, I'm here." He opened his eyes to find focus.

"I want to go home to my own bed," he said. "Can you make sure you take care of that?"

"Yes, Papa," I assured him.

"Aaron, I want you to promise me now!" He was agitated despite his weakness.

"I promise, Papa. We'll go home together." I brushed his hair back off his face the way he liked. Ruthie seemed so heartbroken it hurt my heart to look at her. Arthur was trying to be strong and took charge of the situation, requesting a hospice nurse so we could care for Papa at home. Arthur had always been the head of our family, and he proved it that day. He made sure everything was done right, and as soon as the paperwork was signed we were bundling Papa into the car.

"God bless you, Aaron," he said. "My golden boy."

Our late afternoon drive home took us past Newport Beach, where my brother, sister, and I had spent our sun-kissed childhood summers—the blissful days of my mother's remission, when for a brief time we lived like the model family. I was driving while Ruthie and Arthur sat in the backseat, their arms around Papa wrapped in his blankets, looking as small and bony as a malnourished child. I lost myself in memories, watching the sun dip over the water as we slid past. My soul was groaning, knowing that this would be our last sunset as a family. Papa's hallelujah day was near.

I slept on my bamboo mat in Papa's room for two nights. On the third night, I fell asleep in a chair next to his bed, our hands interlocked. Papa just held my hand and squeezed whenever he could to let me know we were still hanging on.

Just after 4 A.M., Arthur, who had come in to check on us, let us know that Papa had stopped breathing. He checked his pulse and told Ruthie and me that it wouldn't be long now. Then Papa's heart stopped beating.

"It's okay to let go, Papa. We love you," Ruthie said.

I wept the last rites in Hebrew. Arthur embraced me, and I grabbed on to Ruthie. It was finished.

Arthur and Ruthie pulled me away from the cold body, but my arm was numb from holding on to Papa's hand for so long. "I love you, Papa, and I'll always be with you," I cried. "We're a team, you and I, and we'll always be together. I'll never leave you." I echoed the words Papa had always had for me when I called him from the road: "Don't forget about me."

I couldn't believe this moment had arrived. *This can't be it.*

I was alone, once and for all.

For five of the ten years I'd been taking care of Papa, he'd been an invalid—my baby. Now I was the last ghost standing; empty and gliding down the hallway.

I listened to the Rolling Stones' "Moonlight Mile" to get me through that first morning on my own. I tried to sing, but couldn't find my voice, so I simply let the melody wash over me. I lay in bed, trying to find the will to stand up.

> *When the wind blows and the rain feels cold . . .*
> *Don't the nights pass slow . . .*

I invited G-d into my loneliness. There was nothing I could do. *Ein Sof*, No End.

At Papa's funeral, Rabbi Dauermann spoke of how Papa's children had opened his skeptical, agnostic heart. "Late in his journey," the rabbi said, "this man found himself surrounded by children and grandchildren who adored him and inspired him to faith." He led us in traditional Hebrew prayers including the Kaddish, and we buried Papa that afternoon next to our mother's grave.

Arthur and Ruthie stayed as long as they could after the funeral. Juanita, Julie, and Darrel came by every so often to check on me.

But eventually they all had to get back to their families, and I was alone again in the house where I grew up. No one from the Jane's days called, not even Perry. I was hurt. Even though I had always been there for the people I loved, it felt like no one was there for me. I was bitterly alone, and suddenly afraid for the future. To stave off the fear, I walked around the house switching lights off and singing Hebrew dirges in the dark. Periodically a noise would puncture the silence.

"Hello?" I listened, but it was only the Santa Ana wind at the door. I contemplated going to score some meds and checking out indefinitely. But that was a fleeting moment of weakness. I wanted to honor my mother's memory by getting back to freeing slaves. On her deathbed, Papa had promised L.C. he would do whatever it took to help me realize that dream. He had bought me that first plane ticket to Sudan. Now there was no one to help me. I had to get myself back out there.

But I couldn't think straight. The lights were out. I had stopped answering the phone, and turned on the air-conditioning as a buffer against the outside—even though it was early spring. I didn't want to be disturbed by a world I no longer felt attached to. Sleeping pills helped me do that, and I slipped back into the old habit all too easily. I slept by day with the shades drawn. Nights were for nightmares and catnapping. One evening I was watching the shadows on the wall when there was a knock at the door. It was 4 A.M. Anyone else would have been frightened, but in my grief-stricken state I welcomed the idea of company. Anything to ease my loneliness.

A police officer was standing there. He had his flashlight out and was shining it in my face.

"Someone called 911?" he asked, looking nervous as he took in my ghostly appearance. I told him there must have been some mistake. "Everything is okay," I reassured him. He came in, took one look at the empty house, thanked me, and went away.

Two hours later a different officer appeared at the door, saying the same thing. When I explained that I had not called 911, and that all was well, he said he'd check with his dispatcher. "There must be some kind of error," he said, looking perplexed. Later that same day, a supervisor came by. "Listen, Mr. Cohen . . . ," he said delicately, talking to me like I might be just a little bit crazy. "The dispatcher played me a recording of the calls that came in, and they're definitely coming from a landline in your house. Do you mind if I come in and check it out?"

I invited him in, and stood while he played me a tape the dispatcher had given him. It would be the last time I would hear my father's voice. It was the message Papa had recorded for his voice mail box: "You have reached 646-7536. Your call is very important to us. Please leave a message with your name and telephone number, and we will be sure to get back to you promptly. Thank you." Then we heard the voice of the dispatcher, answering the call: "Hello? Hello? Are you okay, sir? Is anyone there?"

It sounded to me as though Papa's voice was calling me from the other side. But I didn't tell the officer that. I showed him that Papa's phone had been disconnected. "My father died almost three weeks ago," I said. The officer's face drained of color, and he got up to leave. "This is really strange," he stated. "I'll be in touch."

Over the next few weeks, more police officers came and went, all asking the same questions. The calls to 911 kept coming in, all from the same voice mail message and almost always in the middle of the night. It gave me something to focus on besides my grief and loneliness. I started looking forward to their visits. One morning just before dawn, a female officer knocked on the door, waking me. CNN was blaring something about the Middle East peace process. I knew I hadn't been watching TV when I went to bed; in fact I hadn't turned it on for weeks. So it was not surprising when the officer told me that more calls had come in that night. I switched off the TV and invited her in so I could explain the strange set of circumstances.

When I'd finished talking, she too turned pale. Here she was standing in a dark house with a skinny, unshaven, long-haired phantom who seemed to be imagining things. Or maybe the 911 calls were coming from beyond? She asked me a follow-up question her male colleagues had not: "Do you believe in G-d, Mr. Cohen?"

"I do," I said without offering anything else. Visibly nervous, she made an excuse and left.

That woman helped me realize something. Whatever was happening belonged to the mysterious realm. Papa might have been trying to send me a message, but I couldn't try to decipher what it was any longer. Maybe someone was simply playing a cruel joke, or maybe all this was the result of a technical malfunction. If not, I was going insane. I decided to take this lady officer's visit as a sign I should stop trying to understand it all. I was scaring people away. I needed to snap out of my depression and get back to living.

Waiting for a plane with Carlos and Ernesto in Quito, Ecuador

Preparing to cross the San Miguel Bridge from Ecuador into Colombia

With military squad and NAS agents in Lago Agrio

With military personnel in Ecuador

With Michele, Ernesto, and Yinabei, just after we bought her freedom from the brothel

With Michele Clark back in Washington, D.C., after the mission

Driving away from the brothel with Yinabei

PART V: MYANMAR

A SIMPLE TWIST OF FATE

BANGKOK, THAILAND

Emancipate yourself from mental slavery
None but ourselves can free our minds

—Bob Marley, "Redemption Song"

MARCH 17, 2007. I KNOW THE DATE BECAUSE there's still a St. Patrick's Day party going on across the street.

Today I wish I'd awakened as a regular guy, in New York, or Dublin, or anywhere else they celebrate St. Patrick's Day—a guy with a nine-to-five job, a monthly commuter rail pass, and a lawn mower. I'd stop in the pub on the way home from work and have a beer with the guys, and then go home. A bit red in the face maybe, but happy. Because home would mean my wife and kids, who might even have baked me a cake for my birthday. Which is tomorrow.

Instead, I'm sprawled on the bed of an anonymous hotel room in Patpong, Bangkok's red-light district, drinking myself numb. Just another night of my life on the run. Every time I get back to the "real world," people say things like:

"It must be amazing to do all the traveling you do."
"You're really making a difference!"
"I wish I could do that."

What they don't know is that I'm drowning in payloads of grief.

With Papa gone, I've become unhinged. I feel nothing for anyone. I have no family, no one to love or share my life. Staring at the room's darkened TV set, my brain jumps over the images depicting the dregs of my existence: haunted go-go bars, massage parlors, and red-light nightmares on channel 1. Seduction and beauty on channel 2. Here's Ulysses tying himself to the mast on channel 3, but where does that leave him? Stuck here in the black-and-white fuzz of apathy and loneliness. What's the point of living like a monk, rising in the morning to pray and sing sad songs?

It's 2 A.M., and my station's finally run out of programming. Cut to static.

At the St. Patrick's Day "party" I just attended, young women in green body paint did degrading things with Ping-Pong balls for a cheering crowd of degenerate Asian businessmen and confused Western women indulging their boyfriends in a madcap "One Night in Bangkok."

"You can't get that at home!" enthused the English guy sitting next to me.

Oh, but you can, mate. You just have to know where to look. The chattel and sex slaves are everywhere, and their faces won't let me sleep.

"How are you, Aaron? Having fun in Bangkok?" My phone buzzes with a text message from a well-meaning friend in L.A. who'd like our friendship to be something more.

I feel like writing, "Actually, Liz, I don't know how many more ten-year-old enslaved children I can bear to meet. It's all too much. I'm starting to think I can't feel anything for anyone anymore . . ."

I ignore the text. Still no word from the general. I need a break, a long rest. I can no longer filter the rage, fear, and helplessness. I just need someone to listen, to help me process this information. Someone without an agenda.

Kraidejt just left. He's my connection to one of the Thai generals who has invited me to Bangkok; the same men who overthrew corrupt Prime Minister Thaksin last year and now run the country as the Council for National Security (CNS). They have won me over with their knowledge of heroin mafias and terrorist agendas and talk of helping to liberate the enslaved children and ethnic minorities of Southeast Asia. So I will work with them, hoping that our cooperation just might let some light into the desperate part of the world we're headed into. If only the generals could divorce themselves from the greed and lust for power that brought down their predecessor. The answer will never be found with guns.

I tried to convey that to Kraidejt tonight over dinner at his father's restaurant. But he was taking me out to celebrate our birthdays—not to talk politics. Born in the same week, but twelve years apart (an auspicious sign of friendship, Kraidejt said), we are bound together by the Eastern and Western astrological traditions. Yes, two grown men have built a friendship out of shared zodiac signs, and it makes as much sense as anything here does, considering the circumstances. I envy him his father.

On the surface, Kraidejt is a salt-and-pepper-haired banker who dabbles in import/export and speaks softly. But he's also the right-hand man to General Pichai, once the Royal Thai Army's second in command. Pichai is now a retired four-star general and an active CNS member. The CNS's handful of former army big shots serve as a de facto board of directors, advising their chairman (the Thai Army chief) on matters of military and strategic importance. In the world of information gathering and military maneuvering, nothing can be taken for what it seems. I've learned not to put all my trust in the social engineers, diplomats, and attachés of the world. Yet tonight, as we shared the revulsion of the sex show, I could see and feel the turmoil of that lifestyle bubbling beneath Kraidejt's smooth skin. In a different world, he would be a human rights activist.

It's been almost a year since Papa died, and I'm still rudderless. Afraid to stop and reflect, I've been doing back-to-back assessments: Poland, Czech Republic, Sudan. The past two decades of my life have been dedicated to healing myself and my entourage—Perry's and my own addictions, my mother's cancer, and my father's pain—and now I have no one to look after but myself. Although Kraidejt's gesture was touching, it has only reinforced my isolation and awareness of how much living I've neglected.

But once again, I've run out of time to feel sorry for myself. First thing in the morning we're headed into Myanmar, the repressive dictatorship still known to Americans as Burma.

Looking at my compact suitcase—which I have never really unpacked since Papa died—gives me comfort. It is the one place in my life where everything is in order. Two dress shirts, an extra pair of jeans, my favorite jacket, a Thich Nhat Hanh book on meditation, and my Bible—the one with the black cover so I can read it incognito when I need to.

My despair dissipates when I'm in motion. Contemplating the imminent rush of the mission calms me down a bit. Now I have to focus on the departure. Kraidejt's generals want more evidence of the crimes against humanity imposed by the Myanmar junta, who are more than aware of the work I've already done in the region. I can't just cross the border with a tourist visa and a smile.

I pop one of my sleeping pills, which seem to be losing their effect, and crawl under the covers with a thick stack of research on Myanmar that Kraidejt has prepared for me. He's told me that the government is using slave labor to build infrastructure in Naypyidaw, the country's sprawling new jungle capital.[1] Despite more than a decade of Western sanctions[2] against this pariah regime—the so-called "State Peace and Development Council" (SPDC)—Myanmar has stayed afloat with funds primarily from India, Russia, and China, countries that trade arms and cash for the region's rich supply of oil and other natural resources. The latter two vetoed the U.N. Security Council's January 2007 resolution urging Myanmar to stop the persecution of political prisoners and barbaric military tactics that have also been labeled "genocide" in international human rights circles.

I read on: largely thanks to China, the SPDC's army is the second largest in Southeast Asia—notorious for conscription of child soldiers and using rape as a weapon against civilians. It has repeatedly vowed to "crush" state opponents, especially its Public Enemy Number One: Nobel Peace Prize laureate Aung San Suu Kyi, the prodemocracy leader whose party overwhelmingly won a general election in 1990 but has since been terrorized and rendered largely impotent by the state. Suu Kyi has spent more than thirteen of the past nineteen years under various forms of detention. So much for its self-styled "road map to democracy"—without offering Suu Kyi the benefit of a trial, the SPDC simply extends her house arrest each time it expires.

The most damning part of the information package I have in my lap is the final three sentences. The word is that Myanmar is about to restore ties with North Korea, sign a cash deal for a Russian nuclear reactor, and has been producing and selling enriched uranium to Iran. It's hard to get this sequence out of my head, but eventually I fall into a solid sleep.

I wake up shivering from the air-conditioning and go to look out the window. The red-light district revelers are still streaming out of the sex club as I let the blast of heat in. The hot wind makes me think of the distressed children in the searing temperatures of Haiti, Cambodia, Sudan, Ecuador, and so many other places I've been. I see their faces in a swirl and say their names out loud, so as not to forget: Cecilia. Yvonne. Lin. Jonty. Jonny. Majok. Maror. Marie. Larissa. And then I can't help it—I'm flipping through my mental flash cards of all the ones we have left behind. I give up on sleep.

A few hours later, I'm shaking hands with General Pichai, who's in a hospital bed recovering from foot surgery. At Kraidejt's suggestion, we've stopped to buy Mylar get-well balloons and a small stuffed animal. I feel slightly ridiculous standing next to the sixty-nine-year-old strongman's bed grasping a teddy bear in pink overalls.

We talk about Myanmar, and then Pichai mentions his government's additional interest in some things taking shape in Laos. Just on the other side of the Thai border, he says, kidnapped Vietnamese, Laotian, and ethnic-minority boys are forced to guard heroin and methamphetamine labs for the mafias that control trafficking routes. That means, he tells me, not only that kidnapping and slave labor are rampant in Laos, but that "these mafia work closely with SPDC. Much work to do in Laos, gather evidence," he says cryptically. I can tell there's another agenda hiding in there. He obviously sees a bigger picture—he talks about Laos, Cambodia, Vietnam, and Myanmar like they are pieces on a chessboard.

I assure him I appreciate his concerns. But my primary objective is to find and document slave labor and share that evidence with anyone who can do something to stop it. Pichai smiles. "Cohen— I respect," he says, dismissing the subject. "Very political. You go Burma. You see the drugs, the slaves; other things very important. You come back pictures."

We shake hands, and I'm about to ask the general what those "other things" are but think better of it.

Pichai then reaches over, grabs my bicep, and gives it a tight squeeze: "Oooh, strong! You very courageous," he says, his voice turning serious.

"Please be good luck, my friend." Pichai folds his hands across his prodigious stomach and closes his eyes, which is my cue to leave.

As I head to the airport with Kraidejt and a few of his military handlers, I feel remarkably detached. Papa is gone, and I no longer need to worry about getting back to take care of him. There's no one else waiting for me in California—I can keep taking assignment after assignment, flitting from one trouble spot to the next helping other people escape from their suffering. Because it's the only way I know how to get away from my own.

I can't believe Papa's really gone.

In the backseat of the car, Kraidejt takes out a map of Southeast Asia. It's marked up with arrows that originate in Myanmar's Golden Triangle and flow outward in all directions, crossing into several places in Thailand. One of the darkest arrows extends due south, cutting through the Thai peninsula to Indonesia.

"Shan State is where the world's best poppy is grown," says Kraidejt, unfolding the map and touching a spot in northeastern Burma. Roughly the size of Cambodia, Shan territory borders

Laos, Thailand, and China and—like the provinces that are home to the country's other ethnic minorities such as Karen, Chin, and Wa—has been under the rigid thumb of the SPDC for decades.

During 124 years of British colonialism, hill-state people (who had been ruled separately by their own kings for centuries) were allowed to remain largely autonomous, a freedom they enjoyed even after the independent Burmese republic was formed in 1948. But since the junta took power in 1962, ethnic minorities have been given the option to assimilate—under arbitrary, often bloody military rule—or fight. The Shan and other groups that have refused to sign cease-fire agreements with the SPDC maintain their own armies and are considered rebels; therefore, they are subjected to a sort of scorched-earth policy.

Lush, mountainous Shan State also happens to contain the bulk of the country's best natural resources—gold, silver, copper, rubies, lead, and uranium. Its fertile soil also makes it ideal for growing poppy, as well as rice and tea. Kraidejt tells me that since the war in Afghanistan shifted much of the world's heroin production back to the Golden Triangle, as much as one-third of the global supply is coming from Shan State. More and more regional mafias have been taking advantage of that.

"Opium is harvested in Shan State, taken to mobile labs, and processed into heroin. It's brought down either by sea or along the eastern side of the Salween Delta to Pattani, Thailand—where terrorism is beginning to threaten our tourism industry," Kraidejt says, sweeping his finger in a circle around the outline of Shan State on the map. "These triangles you see here are the places where our police have been cracking down on traffickers."

He describes the historic path of poppy seeds and traders along the silk route—from Afghanistan across the Himalayas to Myanmar. As in Afghanistan, the drug behemoth fuels a not-so-hidden trade in drugs, arms, and humans. Which means that everyone from the SPDC to Malaysian and Indonesian terror organizations now find themselves doing business within the same trafficking networks. Globalization has enabled former small-time gang members to make big bucks doing the dirty work for rogue governments and terrorists. Vulnerable children along the trafficking routes are the collateral damage of this massive form of outsourcing.

"That's why General Pichai and I thought you'd be interested in this mission," he says, smiling slightly.

I may have gotten in over my head this time.

We fly to Mae Sot in northwestern Thailand, near the border with Myanmar. On the plane, Kraidejt points out a two-star Thai police general called Siripong—who nods politely—and a special operations commando General Pichai had mentioned would be coming along for our protection.

"This is the Scorpion," says Kraidejt, indicating a middle-aged, treelike man sitting next to Siripong. "We very lucky to have him along. He has many years of combat experience in Lao jungle."

Extracting my hand from the Scorpion's grip, I don't have much trouble conjuring up an image of him engaging in hand-to-hand combat.

We're ushered into a black sedan and quickly end up driving through a no-man's-land on the outskirts of town. This is where many refugees from the Hmong ethnic group—indigenous people from the mountains of southern China—have finally run out of luck. Political unrest and geopolitics have kept the Hmong on the move over the past two centuries through the mountainous regions of Vietnam, Laos, Myanmar, and Thailand. Denied political refugee status elsewhere despite widespread persecution in those countries ranging from mild to severe, they wait in these ghetto camps for the day when their plight will be recognized. In the meantime, open-faced Hmong girls make for easy trafficker prey. Their brothers are spirited off to work for subsistence in the bonded labor camps of Laos and Myanmar, building infrastructure or guarding drug labs for the mafias, armies, or corrupt government juntas that control them.

We stop for a few minutes to walk through the camp, but Kraidejt can see I'm getting sidetracked and ushers me back to the car. Of the handful of Hmong elders I can see, most are maimed in some way. Their missing limbs and pained expressions tell the story of the CIA's "Secret War" during another Southeast Asian era, with its own set of promises and betrayals. I can't help these people today. But I will take word of their struggle back with me to Washington, D.C., and to Christian Elliott, a human rights activist and field worker based in the U.K.

After leaving the Hmong camp, we drive through a tranquil suburb and park on a paved street in front of a modern concrete home. Once inside I bow slightly to meet the eyes of Zhao Siha, a small man who introduces himself as the Shan vice minister-in-exile. I'm not sure what I'm getting into here, but Kraidejt has decided I should interview Siha—who tells me to call him "Douglas"—on camera. Confident and mysteriously cool for a man I've just been told is on the run from SPDC assassins, Siha looks directly at the camera and delivers a monologue in polished English:

"First, maybe you want to know something about Burmese tradition and the SPDC, who are very superstitious people. There is an ancient legend still believed to be practiced even today in the art of human sacrifice—so that every time the leaders move the capital, four people are to be offered up at each of the four corners of the foundation to the facility. Human sacrifice is also carried out under, above, and on each side of each bridge crossing the moats corresponding to the twelve astrological signs, and the seven passages leading into the capital."

"What?" I call out in disbelief. "You're saying this is happening now, at the behest of the government?" It sounds like something from the final scenes of *Apocalypse Now*.

With what I detect to be a gleam in his eye, Siha turns to look at me for a second before turning his melodramatic gaze back to the camera. "Yes, well, they need to make seventy-two human sacrifices in all, preferably all foreign agents . . . anyone trying to infiltrate national security or threaten the business of the ruling party."

Is he joking with me, or possibly even threatening me? I'm not sure. I thought I was going into Myanmar to help liberate a slave labor crew who are dying in the process of building elaborate palaces and pagodas for Naypyidaw's megalomaniacal rulers. But even Kraidejt is evasive, and won't look directly at me. I'm feeling extremely uneasy. When Siha asks if I can get him arms, I stop the tape.

"I am here to help children and slaves get free," I say with an even voice. "My only agenda is human rights."

Siha looks disappointed, but not surprised. "Okay, Cohen. We eat?" He shrugs as the others trickle in, dressed in military fatigues. All except General Siripong, who has slicked-back hair with a pink oxford shirt, slim white jeans, and espadrilles.

A monk dressed in a saffron-colored robe has been sitting quietly in the corner since we started filming. He pipes up: "I assure you, Cohen, that we monks will assure your safety once you are inside Myanmar." I thank him as a young Hmong woman in traditional dress comes into the room and silently serves us dried pork rinds and hot sauce on a series of small trays. One of the men breaks out a one-liter plastic bottle full of homemade rice moonshine with some geckos floating in it. I politely refuse the pork and manage to avoid drinking the alcohol and the weak jasmine tea our hostess brings in afterward. She rolls her eyes at my refusal.

She has a nice smile, but so do all the social engineers that linger in spy circles. In real life, the poison she could slip into my noodle soup would take effect in a matter of minutes—only I wouldn't have some Bond girl to slip me the antidote. In real life, you just die. No one's going to rescue me if something goes wrong here.

After the men toast each other a few times and start smoking cigarettes, I take the opportunity to walk outside and breathe some fresh air. A vendor is selling boiled eggs on the side of the road, and I walk the few yards to her stall hungrily, grateful I still have some *baht* left in my pocket. Night is falling quickly, and she is busy lighting tea lights for the customers she hopes to attract.

This will do perfectly. It's a relief to be alone for a few minutes. I try and fail to get comfortable at one of the blue child-sized tables after feeling the tiny plastic stool start to bend under my weight. The vendor smiles and hands me her own stool, made out of wood, and pats it gently. I accept her kind gesture and then crack open the first boiled egg with my spoon, but it shatters in my hands and spurts hot fluid all over the place. Confused, I look down at the mess and am baffled at what I see inside the remains of the shell. A tiny duck—fuzzy wings, beak and all.

The vendor is laughing now, hiding her giggles behind her hand in a gesture of politeness. I crack up, too, slurping the broth and tapping out pieces of the fetus clumsily with my spoon. I try to hide my revulsion. The vendor walks around to my table and points to the dish of herbs, salt, and pepper she's put in front of me. "You haven't seasoned it!" she seems to be saying with her almond-shaped eyes. I start on the next egg, sprinkling the herbs inside this time and trying not to look too hard at the shape of the body or wonder how they go about incubating these. I need this protein—and it *does* taste like chicken, if I close my eyes and ignore the texture. I think I'll become a full-fledged vegetarian after this trip.

Five hours later, I'm in my black military fatigues and helmet, experiencing the wildest ride of my life—a winding, midnight motorcycle odyssey north across a porous section of the 1,500-mile mountainous border Thailand shares with Myanmar. We've left Siha at a Buddhist temple but have been joined by the uniformed Shan information minister and two additional military escorts on motorbikes. My Shan driver doesn't speak any English, but we're going too fast to communicate anyway.

Our bike quickly leaves the paved road and hops for hours over the rocky dirt track through the jungle, its headlamp illuminating the frequent potholes and other hazards just seconds before we hit them. Although we don't see a soul, I can feel eyes everywhere. This regime—and the one before it and the one before that—have imposed a culture of spying and fear on the last few generations. I close my own eyes and grip the driver tightly around the waist so as not to fall off. Hanging on becomes a real effort as the night wears on and the track becomes harder to follow. I feel the trees and vines flashing by, my breathing tense. The driver and I shift our weight together as we meld with the jungle. Even as our bike shrieks into the night, further into the madness and monsters lurking there, I know that I am exactly where I am supposed to be.

I'm not making this journey out of duty to country or mission. There are no friendships to ambassadors or diplomats, no tenured positions with well-appointed offices at stake. I'm riding this path away from my inability to stop grieving for my father. And for the slaves who deserve a voice.

We are well inside Myanmar now. The only thing behind me is death. A few hours more into the dense jungles—forward to the rest of my life.

When I open my eyes again, the only light is coming from the moon and a few stars in the cloudy sky. There are no other head-lights behind us, which means we have become separated from the Scorpion and Siripong. Due to the language barrier, there is no way for me to find out what has become of them. We drive for another couple of hours, until my legs are stiff and my back aches. Slowing to a halt for what I hope is a bladder break, the driver puts his hand up, indicating that I should listen. For a moment I take in the beauty of the area, all forested mountains and valleys with the backdrop of a rising sun in a deep blue sky. There is no sign of civilization.

Then there's a cracking noise, and we're suddenly in a war zone.

Shots fly from a ridge off to our left and are quickly returned from a patch of jungle on the opposite ridge. The driver motions for me to jump on the bike, and we fly ahead into the whitening sky toward some structures on the horizon. I'm not sure what's going on, but I know now that I have been brought in to document some-thing much more complicated than slave labor.

In a few minutes we pull into a base camp where a group of sol-diers wearing green Shan State Army uniforms fall into formation and salute our arrival. The overweight information minister is lean-ing up against his bike, arms folded. The Thais are nowhere to be seen. "Did you get lost, Cohen?" he asks in a mocking tone. My

Shan driver, who in the daylight I can now see is no more than eighteen years old, seems to be looking at me for permission to rest. We are both very shaken up from the ride, and the information minister is making light of it.

I touch the driver's arm in a gesture of gratitude and motion for him to sit and rest. Then I turn to deal with the information minister, whose name I cannot pronounce and don't want to learn.

"I didn't sign up for this," I tell him, struggling to contain my nerves. "I am not here to get involved in a civil war."

"We are protecting you," he says smugly. "You may as well see what we have to show you."

I see that I don't have much of a choice. If I want to get out of here, I'll have to get through this and stay calm.

I'm taken to a tent where some of the young soldiers have made room for me on the floor. They start giggling and gesturing at the difference between my height and theirs. One of them offers me his woven mat, and I gratefully settle down for a nap.

I wake a few hours later and walk out of the tent. With no sign of the Thais, the information minister has decided to start my tour without them.

With a couple of soldiers to protect us, we pile into an old jeep and rumble past some tea and coffee plantations for a few miles before getting back on the motorcycles. I put on the black helmet the Shan driver has handed me and pull the faceplate down. This is going to be another long ride.

I lean forward into the driver as we roll through foothills and jungle ravines, down long green valleys and up again to endless fields of poppies thriving in the sun. After what seems like hours, we come to the entrance of an underground bunker. The soldiers here are equipped with satellite technology, solar panels, and top-notch laptop computers. But before I can ask a question, we are back on the bikes for another forty minutes. Leaving the main track, we drive up a hilltop and dismount.

The minister explains that we are looking down at an open-pit uranium mine. Through the binoculars it doesn't look like anything unusual, though it is guarded and surrounded by a fence.

"It looks to me like it could be any old construction site," I say, hoping to ruffle him. It works, and the minister nervously shoots back, "But, Cohen, the rumors are all true!"

"What rumors?" I ask.

"The Russians have been here to extract samples, as well as Mr. A. Q. Khan, whom I'm sure you know a bit about," he says with a cocked eyebrow. I don't, but I'm sure he's going to tell me.

"Mr. Khan was the father of Pakistan's nuclear weapons program," he continues. "A scientist-turned-dealer, if you will. I suggest you research him," he says, "and then maybe you will understand why we are so upset."

He trains the binoculars on the mounds and points out the places where he says Iranian and North Korean scientists have unearthed samples. "But you, Mr. Cohen, are the first—the only—Westerner to have seen this."

"Come on . . ." Things are moving too fast for me to keep up.

"We will provide you with pictures and samples from this place, so you can prove what you have seen," he says.

"Look, I'm no uranium expert," I respond. "And it's too dangerous for me to have stuff like that on me. I'm just not qualified."

"Of course, Mr. Cohen," he says with a smile. "We anticipated you'd say that. Which is why the material will be waiting for you at your preferred hotel in Bangkok, or at your home in Costa Mesa. Is this your correct address?" he asks, pointing to a computer printout with my personal information. I don't like veiled threats.

Back at the Shan State Army base camp, the minister hands over a photocopy of Khan's visas, showing the dates he entered and left Myanmar.

"All of this should be very interesting to your connection at the Pentagon, don't you think?" asks the minister.

Who do these guys think I am? They seem to want me to be their mule. I'm going to have to listen and just ride it out.

"I'm telling you that the Pakistanis, the North Koreans, and the Russians have all been here," he continues. "And we also have evidence the SPDC is selling our Shan uranium to the Iranians, who are most likely processing it into material for nuclear weapons."

He refers to a map that was part of the dossier they had already prepared for me. The route from Shan State was clearly marked: straight through China and Afghanistan to Natanz, Iran. "There is an underground Iranian plant there," he said. "I think you'll be hearing about it again in the international press soon enough."

From the mining sites, we drive to a rebel encampment where the information minister presents me with four men he says have been enlisted to work for the SPDC. I have to rely on the minister for the translation:

"We are poor," one man says, speaking for the group. "We were once farmers, but the SPDC came, took our land to grow poppy, and mined the area. Then they told us we would work for them from then on."

"These men are ethnic Shans," the minister says, "employed as drivers for three different clandestine nuclear-processing facilities in the area. They have told us not only that the SPDC is using slave labor and overseeing the production of yellowcake [uranium concentrates used to process fuel for nuclear reactors] at these facilities, but that the materials are being transported to Natanz via an extensive courier network through China and Afghanistan, as well as by sea."

He hands me a satellite picture of the facility with its precise coordinates.

"Whether the yellowcake is for peaceful purposes or not is for you to judge for yourself," says the minister. "But either way, I have a feeling the IAEA [International Atomic Energy Agency] might be interested in this matter, which is in clear violation of the U.N. Security Council resolutions, don't you think?"

I don't know what to think. The idea of Iran having nuclear weapons is not reassuring, but I don't exactly trust this man and his rhetoric, either. I wish that Kraidejt or someone I could be sure of were here to back up what I am seeing and hearing. It's surreal. But in the puffed-up information minister's desperation to bring me around to his side, I recognize the simple desire for justice all humans share. When you are fighting for your mere existence, it's hard not to have a hidden agenda.

I decide on the spot to detach myself from my dislike for the information minister. As soon as I do this, he undergoes a remarkable transformation before my eyes.

"I can't take the nuclear material with me," I repeat. "But I will do my best to put this information in the right hands." I push record on my video camera and turn back to the Shan men. "Are you getting paid for your work?"

Their answer comes back: no.

"Are you threatened with violence?"

Two of the men smile sadly, while the others look at the ground.

"All we know is violence," one speaks up.

"We are beaten and threatened constantly," another man says. "We do not have the freedom to come and go."

Emboldened by his compatriots, the youngest man, who has yet to say anything, looks me in the eye as he waits for the minister's translation: "The Shan are a proud people. Once, we were self-sufficient. Now we are being slaughtered and worked to death. We are given nothing but scraps to eat."

"We have no choice but to fight," says the fourth man. "If we join the Shan Army we may die, but if we don't, they will kill us anyway. They will kill us all."

I load the camera into my pack. I don't know what to say. I just shake their hands and offer my condolences. Paradoxically, as we say farewell, it is these men who are wishing me luck.

The information minister listens to a command on his walkie-talkie. "The SPDC are nearby," he says. "We must be very careful getting out of here tonight. If they find out you are here, there will be trouble." The sky darkens suddenly, and I can already hear the roll of thunder in the distance.

I find it hard not to think about Zhao Siha's words about human sacrifice. "Preferably foreign agents," he had said. A loud peal of thunder underscores that thought. Why hasn't the Scorpion found us yet?

Even though it's started to rain, we leave the second camp on our motorcycles, which are less likely to be spotted than the Jeep we rode over in earlier. Now that I've heard a few first-person slave labor stories, I am determined to document my findings. But the information minister's been on his walkie-talkie all afternoon, and the vibe is tense.

Despite the heavy presence of our military escorts and the dread hanging in the air, I manage to find a peaceful state on the back of the bike, even as I prepare myself once again for battle. After an hour we stop to get out of the rain and drink some water. The minister and his men shoot rapid-fire information back and forth over their radios. The storm comes to an end with triumphant flashes of lightning in the late afternoon sky. I try to tell myself that everything will be all right. I will find a way to get the information into the right hands.

The backdrop of the rest of our ride—carpets of bright red poppy flowers backed by mountains—is dazzling under a setting sun. It's ironic that something as beautiful as the poppy plant could wind up destroying so many lives. My thoughts turn to all our friends who died from drug addictions. I say a quick prayer for the heroin junkies of the world, enslaved by their dragon master. And one for the SPDC generals, too. Maybe all they need is some compassion for their pride and ignorance. For beneath their destructive force I know there, too, lies profound suffering.

The relief I feel on the back of the bike as we near the camp almost makes it easy to forget that the former Shan inhabitants of this land have been pushed out of the area—many into the SPDC's forced labor camps. The "lucky" ones have made it across the border to places like Chiang Mai.

"You are thinking it is beautiful here, yes?" asks the information minister.

"Yes, it sure is," I say. "It's just . . ."

"Sad that there are no people," he says. "These fields were once tended by Shan, who made a good life for themselves here." He laughs bitterly. "You know how the SPDC explained its war on us, the war no one will call genocide?" He pauses to see if I will answer, but I don't dare guess.

"They declared a 'war on drugs,'" he says. "And then they took over the drug production themselves."

I wonder if the Washington, D.C., public relations firm that recommended the junta's name change to "State Peace and Development Council" was also behind that move.

"Now the SPDC controls the drug trade here from start to finish," he continues. "It gives the seeds to the remaining Shan farmers, but sends its army to collect the harvest and oversee the drug production. Distribution is handled by regional mafia."

The farmers, he explains, are allowed to earn just enough to survive as long as they keep producing opium, which is synthesized in nearby labs also run by the junta's army. All of the fields, even those where vegetables are grown, are land-mined; effectively separating the rebels from their civilian population and starving them both.[3] The land mines also instill people with fear and keep them in their homes when they're not working.

We stop by the side of the road when we see a woman tending the fields. I pass her one of the disposable cameras—subsidized by a California human rights organization—we've brought along. A baby is suckling at her breast while she harvests the poppy. So far I've seen very few people besides Shan State Army soldiers, who have control of the immediate vicinity for the time being. But now I know better. The eyes are here, too. We quickly pass around a few more cameras to the other workers, who look bewildered at first, but smile as soon as they understand our gesture. Someone cares about their situation. They begin snapping pictures of the poppy fields.

The information minister's walkie-talkie starts squawking again.

"We should leave this open area," he says. "It's not safe." And before we have started our engines, it's raining fire again. There is no time to see where it's coming from. Acting on instinct—there is no thought process now—we flee into the jungle and make our own path through the darkness, following the leader and only hoping he knows where we are headed. Holding on for my life again, up and over the jungle switchbacks, I feel free from the fear of dying or torture or becoming a human sacrifice at the pagodas of Naypyidaw. I am just the messenger.

We finally come upon a clearing in front of a large cave opening and screech right in—executing a dramatic finale to a motocross final. Entering the subterranean world is tremendous, because it coincides with a new and terrible understanding. We may be safe now, but the eyes have seen us. They know what I've seen. The slaves. The drugs. The uranium. Rumors confirmed. They will come shooting or seducing now that I've uploaded the evidence: the Israelis, the Iranians, the Russians—everyone.

When we pass through the first chamber, lit only by a candle in the center of the darkness, I watch the information minister bow to the presiding monk.

I feel relieved by his presence. Surely the head monk will be able to offer guidance and solace.

"Can you get us arms?" he says in English.

I am taken aback not only by the question, but also by the fact that this tiny and shriveled man living in a cave speaks my language.

"No! Your eminence, I am a human rights activist," I say. "I have come all this way to learn about human rights abuses, sir, and now you are asking me for arms I cannot deliver. May I remind you that you are a Buddhist monk? . . ."

I've tried, but failed, to strike the balance between being unassuming and affronted.

"It's a simple twist of fate," the old monk responds quietly. "The only way to help these people is to protect them from those human rights abuses with guns, my friend."

I nod helplessly, not knowing what to say. So I simply bow to the monk, turn and follow the others deeper down the cave. Nothing I can do will be good enough to help them.

The cave and tunnel system is infinite and mysterious. I sit and watch the information minister talk to his deputies. The soldiers have new uniforms and are surveying the movement of the SPDC Special Forces with a satellite system.

"The SPDC Army has sent an entire unit to block our exit from this territory," he says. "They are looking for us with thermo goggles." There is a short pause.

"We will spend the night," he decides.

In the dark, the young soldiers, who are still giggling at my height and taking pictures of that phenomenon with their digital camera, share their food. At first their stew turns my stomach—I'm eating alternative tentacles in a putrid fermented sauce—there's nothing else and there is little water to go around. I am grateful for their kindness. So I chew and chew and stop wondering what I'm eating. Then, exhausted by their curious eyes, I wander the caves with my headlamp and go out to meet its denizens—scorpions, snakes, and other slithering things.

I find a corner to rest and turn on my headlamp to read through the dossier I've been given. A. Q. Khan, the founder of Pakistan's nuclear weapons program, confessed in 2004 to having been the mastermind behind a clandestine network of nuclear arms proliferation that stretched from Pakistan through Europe, the Middle East, and Asia. His network sold blueprints for centrifuges to enrich uranium as well as illicit uranium centrifuges and uranium hexafluoride—the gas that can be transformed into enriched uranium for nuclear bombs.

Khan is already known to have provided complete centrifuge systems to Libya, Iran, and North Korea. He was pardoned by Pakistani president Pervez Musharraf and sentenced to house arrest after declaring on television that Musharraf's government had not played a role in his schemes. Western governments have been denied access to Khan, but the dossier includes a report by the British think tank International Institute for Strategic Studies, which indicates that Khan's network is very much alive, even without its decapitated head.

That Pakistan-Myanmar link was brought to light by a 2002 *Wall Street Journal* article detailing Myanmar's nuclear ambitions: "The program drew scrutiny recently after two Pakistani nuclear scientists, with long experience at two of their country's most secret nuclear installations, showed up in Burma after the 9/11 terrorist attacks in the United States. Asian and European Information officials say Suleiman Asad and Muhammed Ali Mukhtar left Pakistan for Burma when the United States grew interested in interrogating them about their alleged links to suspected terrorist mastermind

Osama bin Laden, who Washington believes wants to develop a nuclear weapon," I read.

It makes me think of a passage in George Tenet's autobiography I recently noted in my journal, which mentions a pattern the CIA has been tracking: "In the new world of proliferation, nation states have been replaced by shadowy networks like Khan's, capable of selling turnkey nuclear weapons programs to the highest bidders. . . . With Khan's assistance, small, backward countries could shave years off the time it takes to make nuclear weapons."

It's hard not to think that this small, backward country is trying to do just that.

"I'm sick and tired of hearing things from uptight, short-sighted, narrow-minded hypo critics," I remember John Lennon singing. *"All I want is the truth. Just gimme some truth."*[4] The truth is that the stage over Israel is being set, and the nations are coming out in full-dress rehearsal. Whether or not the play is on, I don't know, but it's not looking good from here, watching the games the Iranians have been playing with their nuclear program, and this new evidence that Myanmar is selling them yellowcake. I hope it's for peaceful purposes. But I can't help feeling that this information spells more dark times for the United States and Israel.

As I drift off into something resembling sleep, I dream of the head monk, being trampled to the ground. And softly whispering "It's a simple twist of fate," as he goes down.

Back on the surface late in the afternoon, I go through a blur of interviews with former slave laborers who have joined the rebel army. The information minister bombards me with more evidence against the SPDC. My pack is filled with maps, photographs, and tapes. In my mind I carry stories of murder, rape, enslavement, and torture.

I am about to collapse from fatigue and the weight of it all when I turn to see the Scorpion standing there in the clearing, smiling at me. "Welcome, Cohen," he says.

That's the only thing I want to hear. I say hurried good-byes to the information minister and my young soldier friends. The long ride passes in a blur. Troops are firing again, but holding on to the Scorpion's back I feel invincible. This is his jungle, and it's not our time to die.

Back in Thailand after another night ride under a pummeling rain, we pass two Royal Police checkpoints and meet General Siripong at a tea shop near the border, far from our departure point at Mae Sot, where SPDC spies might be looking for us. I am too tired to ask what happened to them on our way in.

Siripong and his translator debrief me in the SUV on the way to Chiang Rai, where I'll stay the night and rest. I hand over the uranium package for safekeeping and keep the human rights evidence for myself. I have places I can take this when I get back to the United States. These are the moments when I'm relieved I don't belong to any special interests or agenda. I can try to get this information to someone who has the luxury of putting human rights before politics.

Checked into a new hotel room, which feels like another coffin, I collapse on the bed, still paranoid. Tears stream down my face in the shower and continue to fall as I shave. But the water can't make me clean. I can't bear this anymore. I need to talk to someone who will tell me what to do. But there is no one here.

So I take one sleeping pill, two sleeping pills . . . and imagine myself still interviewing child soldiers and former slaves. I've got to tell their story to someone else, or break down completely. I was brought into this to bring the truth forward, but now I feel like burning all these bridges I've crossed. I don't know where to go now. Rash decisions, my own ignorance, and uncertainty about these people's fate weigh heavily on me. Aside from offering optimistic promises, I'm no longer sure that I can actually do something to be useful.

It's still pouring outside. I turn to the book of Job for solace and pray for sleep.

The clouds pour down their moisture and abundant showers
fall on mankind. Who can understand how he spreads out

the clouds, how he thunders from his pavilion? See how he scatters his lightning about him, bathing the depths of the sea. This is the way he governs the nations and provides food in abundance. He fills his hands with lightning and commands it to strike its mark.

AMAZING GRACE

LOS ANGELES, CALIFORNIA

March 2007

Let us not despair; it is a blessed cause, and success, ere long, will crown our exertions. Already we have gained one victory; we have obtained, for these poor creatures, the recognition of their human nature, which, for a while, was most shamefully denied. This is the first fruit of our efforts; let us persevere and our triumph will be complete. Never, never will we desist till we have wiped away this scandal from the Christian name, released ourselves from the load of guilt, under which we at present labour, and extinguished every trace of this bloody traffic, of which our posterity, looking back to the history of these enlightened times, will scarce believe that it has been suffered to exist so long a disgrace and dishonour to this country.

—William Wilberforce, speech about slavery before the British House of Commons, April 18, 1791

Through many dangers, toils and snares I have already come;
'Tis Grace that brought me safe thus far, and Grace will lead me
    home

—John Newton, "Amazing Grace"

THERE'S NO ONE TO PICK ME UP WHEN I GET TO LAX, which is probably just as well, since I look like hell and don't know how to begin talking about what I've just been through.

I'm home again, and that familiar lonely feeling is already settling in the pit of my stomach. But as the driver heads south toward Costa Mesa, I suddenly ask him to turn around and take me to West Hollywood. I need to postpone seeing the old ghosts and the empty house for a few hours longer. I get out of the car on Sunset Boulevard in front of Darrel's clothing store. He greets me with a warm smile, a huge hug, and "Welcome back!"

Darrel has been with me to Myanmar. He can imagine some of what I've just experienced. Relief washes over me. Something makes sense.

And there she is. Her green eyes are staring hard at me, but there is a softness there that makes me feel calm for the first time in months. I stumble over my bags, pushing them out of the way so I can look at her again. She smiles.

"Aaron," Darrel says. "This is Jennifer."

"Hi, Aaron," she says. "I've heard a lot about you."

I'm speechless. Darrel speaks for me. "Yeah, man, I've been telling Jennifer about your trip, and what we saw last time we were in Burma, and, well, uh, you guys are grownups, so I'll just leave you to, uh . . ." Darrel smiles and excuses himself to help a client.

Jennifer is not only beautiful, but is a human rights activist interested in advocating for trafficking victims. "I think I'd be a good mentor for some of the shelter girls Darrel was telling me about," she says.

We haven't exchanged more than a few words, but I feel as though I have always known this woman. An hour flies by, and I realize I have to get back to Orange County for a meeting. But I'm not going to let Jennifer fly out of my life.

"I want to see you again," I say. "I've got to go now, but I promise I'll call you tomorrow." She smiles, and I can sense her immense energy and compassion. "Get settled," she says, "And then we'll talk more."

I hug Darrel and then Jennifer good-bye and run out to the street, feeling a strange glimmer of hope stirring within me.

There's someone on the way to my house, ready to ask me a stack of questions. I've kept her waiting for ten days now. A couple of months earlier, an American writer based in Vietnam contacted me about a woman who had worked in victim outreach with me in Cambodia—a kindhearted Vietnamese-American who'd been thrown in a Ho Chi Minh City prison on insurrection charges and held for over a year without a trial. Christine Buckley was a New Yorker just back from three years in Vietnam, where she'd started researching that story but couldn't get any hard information in a place where investigative journalism amounted to regurgitating the Communist Party line. I had some of that information, and after we talked on the phone several times I had agreed to meet her.

Christine drove to meet me in February 2007 in Orlando, Florida, where I was to speak at an antislavery conference celebrating the premiere of the film *Amazing Grace*. The film tells the story of British politician William Wilberforce, who led the movement that finally convinced the British Empire to abolish the slave trade in 1807—exactly two hundred years earlier.

Wilberforce and journalist Thomas Clarkson followed through with what may well have been the world's first grassroots human rights campaign. It was an auspicious occasion for my first meeting with Christine, who was to figure prominently in my life.

She found me that afternoon in the hotel lobby, and I told her I could only give her five minutes, since I had to get back to the conference.

Two hours later, after we'd each had three rounds of coffee and talked about everything from eight-year-old Vietnamese trafficking victims to the role the CIA had played in the Southeast Asian drug trade, Christine started laughing.

"Are your five minutes up yet?" she said. "Because I've got my dogs in the car and I have a feeling they might need to pee."

I went back to the conference and Christine went back to her father, whom she was taking care of while he battled leukemia. I could relate to her struggle. And she, I felt, could relate to mine.

After battling freeway traffic for an hour, I finally pull into my driveway. I've been away for two weeks, and the house is stuffy. I walk around opening windows, walking to the back to check on the plants. Aside from the bamboo, they have all gone limp and brown. I give into the depressed mood, put on an Elliott Smith CD, and avoid looking at all the bills that have arrived. I've lost money on this mission, as usual, and I'm going to need to find roommates.

Without the energy to unpack, I drink some water and pass out on the bed with my clothes on. I wake to the sound of my ringing phone in the darkness.

"I'm on the 405 and it's superscary," says Christine, who is not used to driving on California's six-lane highways. "If I don't get swallowed up by these giant potholes, I'll be there in an hour."

Over the last few months, I've been telling her my story. First she listened, then she filtered, and now I've decided to let her profile me for an upcoming *LA Weekly* cover story. First, it will publicize the cause locally; and second, it might just open up other avenues for the human rights work. I can't keep going at this pace.

I shower and make coffee, trying to shake the jet lag and dark feelings that always creep in after the missions, after the excitement has faded and the fatigue sets in.

Christine knocks and opens the door at the same time, moving at New York speed and already bragging about her increasing prowess behind the wheel. She also manages a classic East Coast–style dig at Southern California. "Do you realize that to get from Hollywood to the O.C. I had to merge onto no fewer than *five* freeways?" she says with a smile. "You can't imagine how stressful that is for someone who failed the road test three, maybe four . . . Well, at least I got to listen to NPR all the way down."

She comes bearing treasure: Vietnamese-style iced coffee with syrupy condensed milk. "*Ca phe sua da!*" she cries with the obvious pleasure she takes in speaking this tonal language.

She's just spent the morning sampling the exotic delicacies to be had in nearby Little Saigon. Christine grew up with two adopted Vietnamese brothers, who had her eating fish sauce from the time she was eight. She gives me a warm hug and immediately takes notice of the red bumpy rash on my face and hands.

"Sulfur burns," I say, turning my hands over for inspection. "That's from holding a gun while being caught in the crossfire of the SPDC and the Shan State Army." I'm too exhausted to explain. But she's going to make me tell the story. All of it.

We sit in my empty living room surrounded by the maps, charts, and photographic evidence I amassed in Myanmar. I am trying to think of a way to help Christine understand the journey that has taken me from surfing on Perry Farrell's lifelong lollapalooza to wading through the world's war zones, drug dens, and brothels—and try to figure out how I am going to get out with my sanity, or at least my body, intact.

"Start from the beginning," she says.

I start to explain how I grew up reading Exodus and decoding the Book of Leviticus with my Bible-crazed mother. Papa and L.C. named me after the first high priest of the Hebrews, Moses' brother who persuaded the pharaoh to let his people go. "I guess it didn't take long for me to understand that my antislavery activism was kind of predestined—or at least expected," I tell Christine.

I go on to describe how I've been following the Jubilee dream, with the help of Perry Farrell and a handful other musicians. Digging into the Jubilee mysteries at first felt like clinging to a life preserver while I weathered L.C.'s illness and my own recovery. Then Jubilee showed me the way to tap into the decisive role that music—and narrowing the gap between rich and poor—could play in bringing about global peace. As the millennium came and went, I started to see Jubilee as a treasure map, a divine plan for times of trouble that would lead us to the big answers. As long as any of us remained oppressed, I believed, no one could truly be free. But it had taken a trip to Israel—and a later one to modern-day Iraq—for me to synthesize that vision.

Visiting children at a shelter

Meeting with a Burmese monk

Visiting with General Pichai in the military hospital before the Myanmar mission, Bangkok, 2007

Visiting with a Shan soldier who lost his leg in Myanmar to an SPDC land mine

The endless poppy fields of Shan State, Myanmar

Standing with Shan Army soldiers at their base camp

PART VI: MIDDLE EAST

ISRAEL: THE PROBLEM WITH MEN

TEL AVIV

December 2003

In my thirty years as a journalist, I've come face to face with scandals, corruption, greed and crime of all kinds. I've seen tragedy of monumental proportions—the desperation of famine, the ravages of war. I've witnessed the loss of life and hope in the Middle East and Africa . . . Yet never before have I been as struck by the senseless disregard for human dignity as I have been the last two years while researching this book.

—Victor Malarek, *The Natashas: Inside the New Global Sex Trade*

Being a trafficker [in Israel] is easier than being a plumber.

—Nomi Levenkron, human rights attorney and counsel for Tel Aviv's Hotline for Migrant Workers

MICHELE INVITED ME TO JOIN HER ON A WHIRL-wind Protection Project trip she was taking to research human trafficking. She had spent five years in Israel and spoke fluent Hebrew. Not only did she have a pretty good idea of the lay of the land, she knew the key players and was going to take a fresh look into the situation for her think tank. Michele had scheduled interviews all over the country with victims, advocates, and politicians, and I thought I could offer some valuable input based on my previous experience traveling in Israel and my work with slaves in Sudan.

In modern times, Israel is facing the same land-for-peace dilemma it dealt with in ancient history. What was fascinating to me were the parallels between today's world, in which more than 27 million people were estimated to be enslaved, and the mass enslavement of the Egyptian period—thousands of years earlier.

I had assumed that the antitrafficking movements we'd encounter in Israel would be similar, if not more advanced, than those we'd seen in Latin America. But I was wrong. One of our first stops in Tel Aviv was the office of human rights attorney Nomi Levenkron, an outspoken feminist and advocate for trafficking victims. Having read and heard about how deep Nomi's dedication ran—in one interview, she had compared the work she did to a heroin addiction—I hoped we would hit it off immediately. But Nomi regarded me warily as she shook my hand. Although she was cordial and sincere, I sensed a deep distrust.

Nomi looked only at Michele as we drove to a dense cluster of Tel Aviv apartments to talk to some former trafficking victims. "These Jewish men who exploit and rape young Russian girls should go to jail. Men . . . they're the problem," she said, without pausing for a response. "They lack compassion . . ."

"Hey, wait a minute," I said, trying to catch her eye. Surely she couldn't be serious? But the face that met mine in the rearview mirror was like a stone.

I remained silent for the rest of the afternoon, as we sipped tea and listened to the horror stories spill out of the young women gathered in a humble apartment where Nomi had organized a support group. We pulled our folding chairs into a circle as the first woman, a Ukrainian girl in her late teens, began to speak. I was the only man present, and as I listened to these women's stories of rape and abuse at the hands of men—Israeli soldiers, police officers, and Orthodox Jews among them—I felt the shame I had seen on so many victims' faces spread like a prickly heat rash over my own face. Suddenly I was the one looking at the ground, avoiding eye contact. But I'd never truly know what it felt like to be victimized in this way.

I learned that many trafficked foreign women taken from Israeli brothels were being housed in detention centers while the government decided what to do with them. Not only was Nomi doing the legal work on their behalf, she was also playing the role of social worker, counselor, and big sister to women who were falling through the gaps in the system. No wonder she was such a rock.

Later that night at one of these detention centers, we met and interviewed several more of these women, most of whom had come from impoverished former Soviet republics looking for what they thought was legitimate work. As we walked through this prisonlike setting, a parade of pained faces told their impossibly sad stories; I needed more context to understand the bigger picture.

The next day began with a big lick on my face from Sam, the standard poodle member of the family who was hosting me for a few days. Now awake, I showered and read up on the dire conditions for trafficked women in Israel, which had worsened since the breakup of the Soviet Union. Since the early nineties, an estimated three thousand women had been brought into the country annually, many lured from impoverished former Eastern Bloc countries by the promise of a better life. Although owning a brothel and pimping prostitutes was illegal in Israel, the law was rarely enforced. Prostitution was legal here,[1] which made it difficult for the authorities to distinguish between those who had willingly entered the trade and those who hadn't. I had seen that in Cambodia and Ecuador as well—all that traffickers needed to do was take away a girl's foreign identity papers, issue her a fake ID proving she was local (and therefore not trafficked) and over the age of eighteen—and they appeared to be operating within the law.

I was also shocked to learn that while sex trafficking itself had been criminalized here since 2000, buying and selling human beings for labor purposes and organ removal was still going on. I read shocking reports of women stripped and sold like livestock at slave auctions, forced to work as prostitutes for months or years only to find themselves "liberated" and victimized again by a system that treated them—not their captors—as criminals. Although important international antislavery legislation such as the Trafficking Victims Protection Act and the U.N.'s Palermo Protocol to Prevent, Suppress, and Punish Trafficking in Persons indicated that international governments were gradually coming on board, we needed to change the mind-set held by the police officers and judges who tolerated trafficking because it involved "prostitutes."

Canadian journalist Victor Malarek's research would later put the average profit a trafficker could make from one woman at around 540,000 Israeli new shekels per year ($160,000). Some of these men even bragged that "business had tripled with the Internet." The first State Department Trafficking in Persons Report, in 2001, had given Israel its lowest rating for doing "little or nothing" to tackle or prevent the problem, but the country had recently been upgraded to reflect the government's increased efforts to arrest and sentence traffickers. Malarek would cite "intense backroom maneuvering" that resulted in Israel's 2002 promotion to the TIP Report's Tier Two from the dreaded Tier Three. After all, Israel was a close U.S. ally.

Nevertheless, Malarek and Israeli women's rights activists such as Nomi found sentencing of traffickers to be a joke, largely due to indifference, ignorance, or even complicity on the part of the authorities. The Hotline for Migrant Workers, the Tel Aviv–based organization where Nomi served as legal counsel, had made a presentation the previous year to the U.N. demonstrating the collaboration between pimps and Israeli police. Not only was it common for police officers to be clients at brothels containing known trafficking victims, but some cops actually warned brothel owners of pending police raids. The previous year, an Israeli policeman was convicted of doing just that—as well as buying a trafficked woman for his personal use. He was sentenced to six months of community service after the judge accepted his plea, which of course went down on the books as a conviction.

The women were understandably wary of talking to the police; a condition that would often be used to later discredit their stories. Israeli authorities were fond of saying that women refused to come forward, implying their stories were weak or simply not true. But the reality, I was starting to learn, was that these women were not always informed of their right to testify before a judge. And even if they were aware of their rights, fear was a factor. The Russian mafia made it clear that they had access to the women's families at home. Without the offer of asylum or witness protection in Israel, most trafficked women faced being shipped back to the same place their tormenters had found them. Some were murdered soon after returning home.

I couldn't believe what I was reading.

As I continued my research, Michele had been making more visits to victim shelters and the Ministry of Justice. She called to invite me to dinner with Nomi and some other activists. Nomi, I now knew, had been unofficially accused of treason by some government hard-liners who didn't like her stirring the pot. I walked into the restaurant with a much firmer respect for the enormity of the battle she and other women here had taken on.

So when Nomi, who was pregnant, started up again, this time I was equipped to interpret the true meaning behind her words. She was tired, sad, and disgusted by what men were doing to women, and by what other men were *not* doing to help the women in need of their understanding. I was a bit nervous to speak in front of such a powerful lot, but forged ahead anyway.

"Hey, Nomi," I started, smiling so she would know my words were coming from my heart. "I heard you're going to have a son. Well, he's going to grow up to be a man, right? And your husband's a man, too . . ."

Nomi must have sensed the change in me, because this time she simply nodded and let me keep going.

"Uh, so take it easy on us. We're not all bad!" I raised my glass in a toast.

"Yah! Men are pigs!" She laughed good-naturedly, hoisting her glass in response. The other women hesitantly broke into laughter and we all toasted men and their pigdom. From that point on the tension dissolved, and we could focus on the underlying point of Nomi's statements: no matter how many girls we could retrieve, our efforts would be fruitless until we managed to decrease the demand.

After dinner, a beautiful blond Ukrainian named Anna who had been sitting near Nomi took us around the old bus station district and the diamond exchange area of downtown Tel Aviv. But this was a tour of the lowlights, not the highlights.

"I was kept in that brothel there for more than a year," she said quietly, pointing out the window as we stopped at a red light. The brothel wasn't hidden in some back alley or even concealing itself as a strip club. It was right out in the open, with a flickering red neon light illuminating a staircase that descended, I knew, into a forsaken world of cold stone walls hemming in the sex slaves just as they had for centuries, going back to the prostitutes the ancient Israelites had enslaved in shrines to worship the Baal of Peor. These promiscuous cults were probably inspired by the Egyptian god Horus, with his all-seeing eye.

One of the activists piped up from the back of the van, "A lot of the clients are Orthodox men whose wives can't have sex at certain times of the month."

"Yes, that is true," said Anna. "And it is these ones who pay more for sex without a condom. They take off their *kippah* [skullcap] before they come in, of course."

A few of the women laughed aggrievedly. For what felt like the millionth time on this short trip, I was at a loss for words.

I slept badly that night, dreaming of Russian girls held in dark red chambers. Waking from the nightmare, I decided that I had to go out and see things for myself. It was 3 A.M., and the night fright— as always—was there waiting for me.

I left the beachfront hotel and walked a short way along the boardwalk overlooking the Mediterranean shore until a taxi driver stopped to hustle me into his cab. So I headed with him to the red-light district. After talking for a while with a bartender at a club down the block from the brothel where Anna had been enslaved, I found out that the "top-of-the-line" girls could be found at a private home in an exclusive nearby neighborhood—for two to five thousand dollars a night. I had no budget to go and investigate that, but I sensed I had found a place where young Eastern Europeans were being held against their will. I could also feel the presence of a formidable mafia standing in my way.

In a second nightclub I met a young girl who told me, as had so many others, that her name was "Natasha." Israeli and Arab men wanted her to be Russian, and so she was, for the few minutes that each sad, brutal encounter lasted. We spoke in the corner of the bar about her life and her fears, until one of the Russian thugs in charge started looming over us, eavesdropping on our conversation.

I felt powerless against the dark force he represented. I knew I couldn't wait for him to escort me out, so I left of my own accord. Turning away from "Natasha," I strode four or five long empty blocks away from the source of my shame. Another soul I'd left behind. Eyes like Natasha's reminded me to keep them in my prayers. Either that or face them in my nightmares.

To take my mind off the present, that night I looked through a scrapbook diary I made the last time I was in Israel in September 1999, dancing on the beach with Perry to celebrate the upcoming fiftieth anniversary of Israel and the upcoming Jubilee . . .

It's the High Holy Days in Jerusalem. We flew in from L.A. talking scripture and Jubilee with Joey Simmons, aka Reverend Run from Run-DMC. He gets it. History feels like it's ours for the making. Perry's giving a solo performance of new material at a desert rave festival called the Prophecy, with Run-DMC and the Chemical Brothers. DJ Peretz is going to be a father, which means I'm going to be a godfather! The American rock magazines don't get what we're trying to do with Jubilee. They're freaked out by the messianic message. But most Israelis we're hearing from understand that we're talking about much more than forgiving world debts and freeing slaves. We want it all . . . peace on earth . . .

. . . At the festival, Perry and I danced all night . . . no drugs . . . This is what heaven must feel like. We're spreading the Jubilee word. Perry proved it tonight—Maybe the party's mellowed, but the music is louder than ever. Go sound the Jubilee!

Michele, who was staying a few miles away with other friends, woke me with a knock at the front door the next morning. She came bearing a tasty hummus and falafel brunch that would be our only concession to the vacation vibe that day. By midday we had driven to a new shelter for trafficking victims in Tel Aviv, housed in a three-story apartment block near the center of town. With clean rooms surrounding a plant-filled lobby, it might have been a college dormitory—were it not for the presence of round-the-clock security guards to protect the young women from violent traffickers.

Larissa, a young Moldovan with a round face and bright hazel eyes who understood Arabic, was the first girl we met that day for a taped interview. Her drawn-on eyebrows and worn facial expression made her look older than her nineteen years. Through a Russian-speaking female translator, Larissa explained how she had answered an ad in her local paper looking for dancers. She was immediately "hired" and flown to Moscow, where her new "bosses" issued her a fake Russian passport.

Although Larissa may have been suspicious that her handlers had something else in mind for her at that point, there was little she could have done once in their custody. She had fled a desperate economic situation and placed all her hopes in the possibility that the job she'd been offered was legitimate. But even if she *had* initially been willing to take a job on the fringes of the sex industry, how could anyone believe that she deserved what had happened to her next?

It reminded me of the authorities' tendency to focus on the fact that *some* women actually chose to enter the flesh trade, as though the women's so-called "willingness" could somehow explain police and government apathy. Larissa was one of too many trafficking victims who had—on top of everything else—been put in a position of justifying what had happened to her. I watched as Michele tried to assure her that none of this had been her fault.

From Moscow, Larissa and her "boss" flew to Cairo, where they were met at the airport by another Russian man shepherding a small group of young women, and driven to a remote desert location. Larissa really knew something was wrong when the Russians confiscated their real identification papers and luggage and handed them over to Arabic-speaking Bedouins from the Abu Sema Dana clan. Now the women understood that they had been sold to a criminal network. For centuries, the Sema Dana had controlled the trade of arms, drugs, and people across the stark Sinai wilderness. But in the last decade, Russian organized crime had taken over the Israeli sex industry—and they had men at every step along Larissa's journey. Her story made it clear that the Russian mafia, not the Arab nomads, were in charge of the operation.

The women were manhandled into submission and told not to speak. Larissa overheard the Arabs mention that there were police in the area and so they shouldn't really touch their cargo.

Nourished only by juice and cookies, the group of five women and their traffickers walked all night through the desert and into the mountains. A van sometimes appeared to shuttle them through parts of the journey, which took almost a week. But most of the time, they just slogged ahead on foot in the darkness. Larissa didn't even know they had crossed the border into Israel until she overheard one Bedouin tell the other he was glad they had taken a quiet route. They evaded Israeli checkpoints and hid in bunkers in the desert until another Russian thug showed up with a truck.

Larissa and one other woman were consequently driven through Beersheba and Haifa, where the group was split in two. Larissa and another woman ended up in Netanya, a midsized city on the Mediterranean coast halfway between Tel Aviv and Haifa. At that point she was transferred into the hands of people she consequently referred to as her "owners"—a Russian couple who told her she'd be responsible for cleaning their house.

Michele interrupted the narrative to ask Larissa a question: "Why do you refer to them as your owners?"

"Because they bought me," Larissa said unambiguously, pushing her glasses back up her face.

She continued with her story. "My owner, the husband, handed over some cash to the other Russian guy right in front of me." Guessing the question we were hesitating to ask, she said, "I didn't see how much it was."

Hoping for the impossible at that point, Larissa threw her heart into her new job as housekeeper and guardian of the couple's child. "If you work hard, you can earn one thousand dollars a month," the wife told her, stalling for time. A month went by: Larissa was never paid and couldn't leave the house—but at least, she told herself, she wasn't a prostitute. Yet her stint as a "maid" in Netanya didn't last long.

One morning, a female friend of the woman of the house appeared and drove her to a filthy apartment in Tel Aviv, where a small group of Eastern European girls sat frightened on a sofa. A few clients were there, speaking Hebrew, but the female trafficker spoke in her native Russian, indicating a man in the corner: "This is your client—take care of him."

Larissa, still in denial, responded, "But no, I have a different kind of job!"

The trafficker laughed and told her impatiently: "Call it what you like, but you'll be a prostitute until the end."

At this point in her narrative, Larissa looked at Michele apologetically and added: "So I just gave up because I knew I didn't have any other way . . ."

Thus began her eight months of confinement in that Tel Aviv apartment, where six girls lived in two rooms and were forced to have sex with anywhere from ten to fifteen clients a day, at all hours. "There was no day off," Larissa said, fingering her flimsy necklace. "There was just all sex, all the time—barely a moment to eat or sleep. We worked in the closet, the bathroom, the kitchen—everywhere."

The prisoners were only permitted to leave the house to service regular clients—with a minder waiting outside the door. On the rare occasion that one of the girls went out alone, something that was only allowed when there were no customers, she was watched every step of the way. Maintaining this control required the complicity of the neighbors, who received regular payments for information on the girls' movements and for keeping what they knew quiet.

"Once I tried to call home from a phone booth with a phone card," Larissa said. "But before I even got through to my mother, the owner's wife called my cell phone and told me to hang up. She was not even in Tel Aviv, but someone had seen me and called her right away."

At some point during Larissa's eighth month of captivity, her friend managed to escape with the help of a client who felt sorry for her. The woman went to the police, who raided the brothel early the next morning.

"When the police came, I thought at first they were clients," Larissa said. "They were looking in the rooms and I said, 'What are you looking for?' They said, 'We're the police.' I will never forget this happy day. It was 9 A.M. and I hadn't slept for three days. My last client had just left. All the girls were out taking care of clients and I was alone in the house. I had been praying to G-d that I could just sleep for half an hour and that no one would come . . . and then they were there."

Larissa smiled broadly for the first time since we'd met. "I felt like I was drunk when I realized the police were going to help me. I told them where the owners lived, and they were arrested at home."

The police had treated Larissa well in the few months she'd been in their custody. "They asked if I was hungry and told me about this shelter. The conditions are good—I can go for a walk or do whatever I want."

Michele had rarely interrupted, but now she stopped, touched Larissa's arm, and asked, "How did you survive this? What did you think of to keep you going?"

Larissa looked right at the camera. "I knew I had to survive and I had to go through this to save myself and other people. I had to survive for my family's sake; this gave me strength."

"Will there be a trial?" Michele asked.

"We are waiting," Larissa said. "I'll stay to the end to testify against them, even if it takes a year or two. I don't need money or anything. I just want them to be locked up so they will suffer the same way they made us suffer. When I get back to Moldova I will take revenge on the people who deceived me."

Her final words left me cold. It was natural that Larissa felt this way, of course, but it was not the route to healing, either. Instead of focusing on revenge, she should have been able to focus on getting home to her mother, getting an education, and healing herself. But the resources were just not available to her yet. I could see the Israeli government had made strides with this shelter, but that alone wasn't enough. Lucky for Larissa, she was strong, healthy, and resilient. Still, her wounds were going to take a long time to close.

Larissa's story would haunt me that night, and for many nights after I'd left Israel. I was especially struck by one thing she'd said: "I knew I had to go through this to save myself and other people." It seemed that my own struggles had brought me to the same conclusion.

Even in a utopian system with enforceable antitrafficking laws, I realized as we left Larissa that human beings would continue to be enslaved by other human beings until we all underwent a fundamental mind shift. Unless we saw each other as truly interconnected members of a global family, the desire for riches or power would translate into more chattel slavery and debt bondage, while unhinged sexual desires would continue to feed into the exploitation and enslavement of women and children for sex. If only I could find a way to help satiate the hungry ghosts and help heal the souls of those who continued to harm themselves and others. What I was also trying to do, of course, was heal myself.

While Michele was tied up in meetings on our last morning in Tel Aviv, I sat down to lunch with an Israeli Defense Forces commander and his unit from Gaza and Rafah. Commander Ephraim believed that the Sema Dana clan still ran the trafficking rings across the Sinai Desert. He was very interested in the interviews Michele and I had taped, particularly Larissa's, which implicated the Bedouins. Despite Larissa's testimony about her Russian traffickers, Ephraim was convinced that Palestinian organizations including the Muslim Brotherhood and Hamas were cooperating with the Russians in order to undermine Israeli national security.

Thinking of my discussion with Nomi the night before about the responsibility borne by brothel patrons, I decided to interject. "Ultimately it's Jewish men creating the demand for these women," I told Ephraim, "along with the Russian mafia. I don't think you can pin this one on the Palestinians. Although I'm sure they're happy to help the Russians put the noose around your neck."

Ephraim simply replied that there were all kinds of agendas at work, and invited me to join one of his covert units for a human trafficking assessment in Gaza. Although I would have loved to say yes, I knew that Michele would frown on such an idea as too politically complex. I was not in Israel to get involved in politics. Besides, the Russian mafia were notorious for making anyone who crossed them disappear, particularly in Israel. Russian organized crime had infiltrated Israel in much the same way the United States had penetrated the cocaine industry with its DEA agents. I believed the mafia were laying the foundation for future national security issues, especially in regard to an important Russian ally—Iran. I thanked Commander Ephraim and said I'd stay in touch, then jumped in another taxi to meet Michele.

I changed into a suit and tie for the meeting Michele had scheduled in Jerusalem with the Israeli attorney general, Elyakim Rubinstein. Already nervous and sweating in my warm clothes, I found my anxiety heightened by a traffic jam that almost made us late for our meeting. As we walked in, a family whose son had been killed by a suicide bomber walked out of Rubinstein's office, holding each other tightly and weeping. Rubinstein appeared a bit shaken at first, but greeted us warmly and happily welcomed Michele's praise for the progress Israel had made against human trafficking over the previous year. Michele waited until he was smiling before she diplomatically delved into the areas where she thought the country could do better.

Rubinstein was conscious of the problem and understood that the pressure, at least from an American perspective, was on. I told him some of what I'd seen in Tel Aviv's red-light district, and he nodded gravely. Michele brought forth the rest of what we'd learned so far, pointing out that conditions for victims still needed to be improved. It was clear that Israel could not fix its human trafficking problem overnight, but under Rubinstein the country looked to be making headway. As I shook Rubinstein's hand, I dared to ask his opinion of Nomi Levenkron, who'd been pretty vocal about challenging his office to do more. Ever the politician, he responded tactfully, "Whatever you think of her as a person, you have to acknowledge that she has accomplished a lot by rattling cages."

Tel Aviv deputy district attorney Itay Frost agreed with Rubinstein's assessment. Sitting with us at an outdoor café that evening overlooking the new Supreme Court building, Frost sipped from a glass of lemonade and did his best to answer all of our questions.

"I'm not happy with the way Nomi's come out against the politicians," he said. "But there's no denying she's gotten a lot done. So we're happy to have her on board. However"—he flashed a smile—"my office has prosecuted more trafficking cases than a lot of other nations."

On the plane back to L.A., I compared the way the human rights attorney, military commander, attorney general, and prosecutor each viewed this struggle. Nomi was looking through the lens of feminism and weighing the crimes that men inflict upon women. Commander Ephraim saw things in terms of national security. Frost and Rubinstein had to concern themselves with measurable progress to keep their bosses and the public happy. Shelter staff were just doing their jobs. No one, Michele and I noted, was talking too much about how the Larissas or the Annas of the world saw their own predicament.

It had been four years since Perry and I flew to Israel to announce the Jubilee, in a flood of music and good feeling. Now it looked to me as though history were repeating itself. In the same way the ancients had failed to see that keeping shrine prostitutes was a dark omen, so were the Israeli authorities missing the significance of the Russian mafia's control of their sex trafficking industry. From where I stood, the omnipotence of these cold-blooded thugs in Israel was a far more pervasive threat to the country's national security than any Palestinian terror group.

Although I was flying back hopeful that the people I'd met were making efforts to bring an end to sex slavery in Israel, I knew it was going to take a lot more of us to bring an end to all of this suffering.

The public announcement of the Jubilee to the nation of Israel, 1998. Headline reads: "From Heroin to Tefillin [Bible study]."

With Perry Farrell and our mutual friend Johnny Blista in Jerusalem before the Prophesy concert, 1998

With Iraqi KRG soldiers at the Tigris River, 2008

With Iraqi refugee children on the outskirts of Mosul

In Jerusalem, doing human trafficking investigations, 2007

With KRG soldiers in the border region of northern Iraq

This church in Amman, Jordan, more than 1,000 years old, was firebombed after our visit.

IRAQ: THEIR LAST CONCERN

COSTA MESA, CALIFORNIA

February 2008

Ordinary Americans are kind and welcoming. Many of them in fact don't like what their government is doing in Iraq. Many of them feel sorry and sad for what is happening and some of them apologized to me when they learn that I'm an Iraqi.

But still, they are all busy with their lives, their work, how to spend their day and decorate their kitchens. Iraq is their last concern. Maybe those who have lost friends or relatives in Iraq or even still have someone serving there would care.

—Ahmad Fadam, *New York Times* reporter, on a visiting fellowship to the United States

SINCE MY LAST ISRAEL TRIP I'VE BEEN TOO focused on the Jubilee and my antislavery work to think about remodeling the kitchen. And I've finally started a stable relationship with Jennifer, who's been more supportive and patient than any new girlfriend should have to be. But I've also been thinking a lot about Iraq.

Israel's neighbor and counterpart in the cradle of civilization was Mesopotamia—the land between the Tigris and Euphrates rivers cobbled together by the British into modern-day Iraq. More than five years after the American-led invasion, over sixty thousand Iraqis are dead. Four million are estimated to have fled their homes, and about 5 million children have been orphaned.

Meanwhile, Al Qaeda terrorists have traded their Afghani caves for Iraqi training camps, where the enemy is closer at hand and easier to target. Many Americans have realized that the "War on Terror" has been more about geopolitics than "liberating" a people. Greed, shortsightedness, and hunger for resources and power are once again playing into death, destruction, and slavery in the Middle East. Iraq is in tatters, and its people are still living under the threat of daily violence.

So I'm not entirely surprised when I get an email from John Eibner mentioning an upcoming CSI humanitarian trip assisting internally displaced persons (IDPs) in Iraq. I'm sitting with Darrel at his boutique, preparing for a cocktail party followed by a night out on the town.

Eibner's email details the plight of Iraqi Chaldean Catholics, a minority group that is being persecuted in a "free" yet lawless Iraq. Iraqi Muslims and Christians had begrudgingly tolerated each other for centuries up until the American invasion. Although the country's small Christian population had suffered some discrimination under Saddam Hussein, churches operated openly. Eibner goes on to tell me that religious persecution has worsened in an Iraq increasingly torn apart by sectarian violence and without any real structures to protect its citizens. The one thing upon which radical Shi'ite and Sunni militias seem to agree is that they want the Christians out. So over the last few years, the Iraqi Christian population, which once numbered near a million, has been reduced by almost half. Christians have been forced to flee, go into hiding, or be killed. Hundreds of thousands are estimated to be living as refugees in Kurdistan, Syria, or Jordan, where many bear the scars of beatings and forced conversions to Islam. Chaldean Catholics make up the majority of Iraq's Christians. Although their church recognizes the pope, it maintains its own traditions and liturgical language, Syriac—a derivative of Aramaic, the language Jesus is believed to have spoken. Their tradition in Iraq goes back to the fourth century.

The financial and political instability caused by the war in Iraq has left women and children extremely vulnerable to traffickers, a reality that's been largely ignored by the United States government and its troops. While the soldiers focus on fighting Muslim extremists, bringing oil fields back into production, and keeping themselves alive, Chaldean, Assyrian,[1] and other refugee women are being kidnapped and sold into domestic and sex slavery by the militias operating out of Mosul and in northwestern Iraq, near the Syrian border. These people's plight, it seems, is being largely ignored not only by the new Iraqi government but by a Bush administration with bigger fish to fry and an international community confused by conflicting tales of the violent Iraqi insurgency.

I feel compelled to go and see what I can learn and do. Eibner's email warns that there is no extra money in CSI's budget to pay for my trip. They'll provide for security, but nothing else.

I walk out onto Sunset Boulevard to get some air and think it over. I'm about to lose Papa's house to the bank. How can I afford to pay for another trip like this? Darrel is chatting with the well-clad West Hollywoodites rushing in and out of his boutique; people stuck in traffic are futilely honking their horns and worrying about losing their race against the clock. But I am already far away. There is a full lunar eclipse tonight and the moon is bloodred.

I am going to Iraq.

Driving home, it occurs to me that September 2007–2008 is a *shmitta* year—Hebrew for "letting go of." *Shmitta* is a Jewish tradition whereby the land is laid to rest every seven years. This land *Shabbat* symbolizes that the land belongs to G-d, not man. When the first Semites celebrated the *shmitta*, they ate from their storehouses and gave away whatever grew on their land to the poor. Debts were forgotten. Slaves were freed. Here we are in the midst of a *shmitta*—and I am headed for the world's most chaotic spot. Iraq and the rest of the Middle East arguably need a period of "letting go" more than any other region.

A month later, after having read everything I can on ancient Babylon and Iraqi history, I fly to New York to catch a flight to Amman,

Jordan. It's cold and I'm nervous about going to Iraq. The news-papers are full of stories of kidnappings, beheadings, and suicide bombings.

John and Gunnar will meet us in the field along with Ken, a journalist, and a documentary filmmaker, Rob. We all have differ-ent agendas but plan to travel together for the sake of safety and economy—in certain parts of Iraq, security costs are running as high as seven thousand dollars a day.

After a quiet dinner with the group at our hotel in Amman, I feel restless. The other guys are tired and plan to go to bed early. Of course I'm curious to see some of the city. I ask Mustapha, a friendly taxi driver I met on my way in, to give me a quick overview of the nightlife. He's been driving in Amman for a decade and tells me he knows a few places I might like.

The red-light district we cruise through is more like a refugee ghetto—and I can tell by their clothes that many of the people on the streets are homeless Iraqis. Most do not have the right to work and are wandering around like zombies or—if they are lucky enough to have shelter—sitting inside grotty apartments waiting for their future to play itself out. The heat and poverty are oppressive, even from the backseat of the cab. This is the kind of climate that breeds desperation and pushes the oppressed to do things they might otherwise never do.

I ask Mustapha if he knows a place we might find some pretty Iraqi girls. He smiles reassuringly. "Sure I do," he says. "But I'll have to take you there on foot."

We park the car and walk uphill to a pedestrian zone full of hookah bars and cafés. Aside from the international hotel bars, there are few places in Amman to get a real drink—but hookah bars are everywhere. The fruity-smelling smoke hits me in the face as we walk into the first one we see. It's dimly lit and filled with men of all ages smoking from the giant water pipes, chatting over mint tea or Turk-ish coffee. The only women are working—ostensibly as belly dancers and waitresses. Unlike most of the women on the street, these women are wearing thin see-through veils instead of heavy dark burkas. Mustapha and I sit and order a pipe and tea. As we smoke and sip, I slowly get a sense for what is going on here. Most of the girls are fairer-skinned than the Jordanians, with dark, almond-shaped eyes. Some look of age but others are clearly younger than sixteen.

By their amateur, halfhearted dancing it's obvious that the young women are not thrilled about being here. But they don't have the frightened, defeated look of trafficking victims, either. I ask one of the girls where she is from and she answers with a thick Aramaic accent. "I am Sara, an Assyrian from northern Iraq," she says, surprising me with her command of English. But she has either run out of vocabulary or is too shy to say anymore. She scurries away before I can ask how she has ended up in Amman.

"You like her?" asks Mustapha lasciviously. "No problem. You want, can have. Just talk to boss and she go with you. Not expensive." I start to wonder if Mustapha has taken me here expecting a gas coupon. It is hard to hide my disgust.

"No thanks, I'm just looking tonight. Maybe tomorrow!" I try to sound hopeful. But I'm depressed and immediately want to leave. The girls may not be trafficking victims, but the café is rife with the conditions that allow slavery to flourish. Girls like Sara are most likely hungry refugees whose economic circumstances have driven them to prostitution—a last resort. Now I see how easy it is for the militias to pluck them off the streets. If I can't help Sara, I want to find a way to prevent this from happening to other girls. But I don't yet have the resources to put forth that kind of plan. So I leave, as I have left countless places like this, countless times before—with a racing mind and a heavy heart.

The next morning I accompany Rob and Ken on a round of interviews with members of the Iraqi refugee community. I recognize the same ghetto I passed through the night before with Mustapha. Most of the people we meet are Assyrians or Chaldeans, part of the Aramaic-speaking ethnic group originally from an area encompassing parts of Iraq, Iran, Syria, and Turkey. Like many in this region, the Assyrians have long been the innocent victims of larger and more powerful political forces. Although it took place in the same time frame as the Armenian and Greek genocides, the Assyrian genocide of 1914–1920 has never officially been recognized as such—even though as many as 750,000 people were displaced or massacred. Things have not improved since the dissolution of the Ottoman Empire. More recent events like the Iranian Revolution and the Iraq War have further contributed to the already large diaspora. The United Nations has estimated that almost 40 percent of the 1 million Iraqis who have fled the country since 2003 are Assyrian.

In the first home we enter, ten people are crowded into one filthy room without a toilet or running water. A young Christian woman tells us how her brother-in-law was kidnapped by extremists who threatened to take her daughters as well. Her family fled Iraq in 2006 and has been on the move ever since. "If I go back," she says, "they will kill us."

"We pray for the phone to ring, for the U.N. to say we can go to America," she continues, gesturing at the disarray around her. "We have nothing. We are illegal here, and so we want to build our future in another country." Then she looks at me questioningly, as if to ask, "Can't you take me with you?"

All I can do for the moment is listen.

One little girl shyly approaches and blinks at me through green eyes behind a striking fringe of dark lashes. Atry thrusts a tiny pink notebook at me. "She wants you to keep it, to remember her by," says the translator. She is so sweet. I want to take her away from this uncertain future.

I promise Atry I won't forget her. How could I?

That day we log interviews with thirty or forty people. Many of their stories are similar in tone and theme to the ones I recorded in Sudan. Before fleeing Iraq, most of these Christians were forced to pay a *jizyah*, a tax levied by the militias on anyone who refused to convert to Islam. Historically a *jizyah* was meant to reflect non-Muslim subjection to the laws and power of an Islamic state. The practice has returned to Iraq in underground form with the power vacuum and chaos prompted by the U.S. invasion and subsequent sectarian violence. If a family is unable to pay the *jizyah*, they might have their home seized or even their youngest child taken.

"I am not allowed to work," says one father of three. He lives in a cramped studio apartment with his wife, children, and sister; they consider themselves lucky to have as much space as they do. When we ask how they get by, he says simply, "We live on faith and the clothes and food we get from our church." The man tells us his mother was forced out by the Baathist regime and has been living in the United States since 1994.

Another woman says she feels "lucky to be alive" after her husband was killed by one of the militias for being a Christian, a condition that the militias now associate with foreign conspiracy. "They put his name on a list of wanted men kept in the mosque," she says, rocking and sobbing as her twelve-year-old daughter serves us tea. "He had managed to get his name off that list," she says, "but they killed him anyway." Her only hope is to find her way into Canada, where her husband was once a citizen.

The next day we take a taxi to Saint Ephraim's Syrian Orthodox Church to interview some of the parishioners. When we've finished, one of them flags down a taxi for us. The driver is a young, fashionably dressed guy who offers to take us back to our hotel for only five dinars, about seven dollars.

Ken, Rob, and I nod and smile in agreement. We congratulate each other, thinking we have finally managed to stop getting the tourist treatment. My Arabic must be getting better. It cost us four times as much on the way up here.

Americans love a good bargain.

The first thing that gives me pause is the driver asking me if he can use my cell phone. "Um, I'm not sure it works here," is all I can think to say. I don't feel comfortable loaning him my phone. He persists, but we try to ignore him. Rob, who is sitting in the front seat, starts to look nervous.

When the driver subsequently stops the cab at a corner store and proceeds to borrow a friend's cell phone to make a few calls, I begin to worry. He is gesticulating and looking over at us as though we are the subject of the conversation, but he is too far away for me to make out his words.

The driver returns and gets into the car with a reassuring smile.

We resume our trek, which is clearly not the direct route to the Marriott. Frustrated, Rob starts futilely protesting in English: "Where are you taking us? We should be there by now!" Ken, who has the temperament of a combat veteran, just looks out the window.

The driver ignores Rob and continues driving us in circles. "He's planning to kidnap us," says Rob. I try to calm him down, but I am starting to think the same thing.

"We should probably be traveling with security," says Ken matter-of-factly. "Although I guess we should have thought of that earlier."

The driver comes back with more apologies and pulls out again, but now a Mercedes is following us. We make a three-point turn and start back up the hill again, toward the church. My chest feels as though it's going to burst. The hotel is definitely in the opposite direction. Ken snaps to attention.

"Let's get out of this car," he says quietly.

Rob is starting to lose it, and I can see him reaching for the knife he keeps in his backpack. His hand is on the knife, ready to unlock the blade. I'm worried the driver will notice, and tell Rob to play it cool.

The driver stalls and pulls the cab over for a fourth time, and the Mercedes slides in behind us. A crowd of local men have gathered on the pavement, talking animatedly and gesturing at our taxi. We three make eye contact, nod, and smoothly step out of the car, moving at a fast clip down a staircase to the boulevard below. The driver runs after us, screaming to his comrades, but he's not about to leave his taxi behind. We quickly evade him and flag down another cab.

Once back in the hotel, we reflect on what might have just happened. Was the driver trying to turn us over to a militia in exchange for money? Are the taxi companies here linked to extremist cells the way that the ones in Ecuador are linked to the drug cartels? It's hard to be sure, but I sense we were lucky to get out of there at all.

An hour later, as we order dinner in the hotel restaurant, word comes that the plaza in front of the church we have visited has just been firebombed.

The significance of our near-miss registers later on as I sink into the bed of yet another characterless hotel room. It's clear that our taxi driver wanted us to be near that church. It's easy enough to label him a "terrorist," and therefore "evil." But this insular approach gives the "terrorist" no voice, and no out. It also perpetuates a cycle of violence and Pyrrhic victories, the likes of which we've seen playing out for decades in the Holy Land. Feeling he has no other way to be heard, the "terrorist" uses violence against civilians in a futile effort to make his frustration with profligate Western ways heard.

So the "War on Terror" is also about ideology, and not, as many people seem to think, just about oil, although that is certainly part of it. The United States has been waging war in the name of the kind of "democracy" that no longer exists at home. Over the last few decades and especially during the Bush administration, power and wealth have been largely taken away from American citizens and consolidated in the hands of special interests. While people are busy fretting over the economy, government cronies are racking up military contracts and plotting their next conflict—in Iran or Russia.

But the economic events of the last few years and months—the real estate, mortgage, and food crises, the credit crunch, the consolidation of banks, our addiction to foreign oil—have started to wake us up. We now know that a shock felt in the United States will reverberate throughout the globalized economy. All of the participants are at risk.

What many of us have failed to notice is what Thomas Frank has called the "replacement of our middle-class republic by a plutocracy."[2] In this way, the American government of 2008 is no longer answerable to the people, but beholden to the market and those who manipulate it. Just like the ancient Babylonians, many Americans have fallen under the spell of the proverbial Golden Calf. In our case, the new idols are plasma televisions, non-fuel-efficient vehicles, and the kind of unrestrained lifestyles being peddled on "reality" TV. Distracted by shiny trinkets, we've largely failed to pay attention to the role that inflated tech stocks, diamonds, real estate, and oil have played in driving our economy. So we've found ourselves the unwitting victims of a far less tangible form of enslavement—consumerism.

I sleep fitfully and wake to the news that a sandstorm near Baghdad has altered our travel plans. Eibner tells us we'll be flying

from Amman to the northern Iraqi city of Erbil, the capital of the
Kurdistan Regional Government (KRG), and then driving through
the mountains of Kurdistan to interview refugees and distribute
emergency food packets. Ken and Rob are going to document
what we find, in the hope they can mobilize international attention and further aid.

My stomach has been fine during our few days in Jordan, but as
we get ready for the tough part of the journey it starts rumbling.
Ken, Rob, and I meet that evening with our gear in the lobby. It will
be a relief to be following Eibner's lead again. After what I've seen
him do in Sudan, I know I can count on him to keep us safe in a war
zone. We pile into a 4x4 to the airport.

A few hours later we find ourselves uncomfortably crammed
into an airport bus on the tarmac in Amman. There's a technical
problem with the plane, and everyone is hot and anxious. Eventually we're taken back to the terminal to wait some more, and I get
a good look at my fellow flyers: a hodgepodge of contractors, oil
workers, guys that look like Dick Cheney in East Coast–style business suits, Iraqi parents, American soldiers, and a few haggard-
looking journalists. Not one tourist.

We finally take off after 4 A.M.—six hours late. A hyperactive kid
behind me starts drilling my seat with rhythmic kicks, so I put away
my book on ancient Babylon and switch on my electronic escape
mechanism—Radiohead. I crank their latest album up through my
headphones and let the music transport me. *The infrastructure will
collapse* . . . Thom Yorke is talking to a potential lover, but somehow everything is filtered through the lens of Iraq. I can't forget
about the house of cards about to fall down around us—the human
trafficking explosion, predatory lending, real estate foreclosures,
markets crashing, investment banks being led to the slaughter—and
all around me *denial, denial.*[3]

I must have fallen asleep, because suddenly the air hostess is
reminding me to switch off my iPod. The sun is rising over the ruins
of Erbil Citadel as we land in the city. The soldiers and flags everywhere give a pretty good indication this is KRG territory. Kurdistan is a "federal region" of Iraq—meaning the government in

Baghdad deals with international affairs while the Kurds, who have their own language and culture, take care of their domestic agenda. The mostly Sunni Muslim Kurds have two hundred thousand troops at their disposal—roughly the same amount as the Iraqi Army, based in Baghdad.

A feisty Assyrian Kurd woman in her forties hustles over to our group, shakes each of our hands, and gets right down to business. With her authoritative countenance and designer clothing, she reminds me of an elegant Egyptian sculpture.

"Let me see your passports!" she says in a raspy voice, not wasting any time. This is Pascal Isho Warda, the former Iraqi Interim Government's minister of information and refugees. Because of the security threat posed by the extremist militias, Pascal and her men have been assigned to look after us while we're in Kurdistan. Four of her bodyguards have already been killed.

Born in the northern Iraqi city of Dahuk, Pascal was exiled to France but returned to help rebuild Iraq in the post–Hussein era. Now that she's retired from government, her main passion is the Assyrian Democratic Movement, which she helped form in response to Saddam Hussein and the Baath Party's attempts to force the Assyrian population out of Iraq. In recent months, she and her husband, William Warda, have launched a human rights organization.

Soldiers manning the checkpoints flail their arms and demand that our convoy come to a halt. But the second they notice Pascal in the front seat, they nod and wave us through. Thanks to her, a journey that might have taken over an hour goes by in a few minutes.

I'm sandwiched between one of the eight soldiers in our security detail. Kocher, the squad leader, is decked out in a suit over his bulletproof vest, plates, and a variety of guns and ammunition. He's got a walkie-talkie plastered to the side of his face. Sultan, his deputy, is a sturdy sort in camouflage, fully armed with Glocks and a few Kalishnikovs.

Pascal doesn't talk much, but when she has something to say, it comes out with passion and conviction. Her bodyguards seem to hold her in the same high respect as the checkpoint guards. While we watch her talk us through the next gate, Sultan taps my arm.

"We are very proud to serve her," he whispers. "She is very courage facing the militias, and we hope that when we protect her we also protect idea for freedom and safety in Iraq," he says.

We stop near our hotel for a quick dinner, and although the shish kebab looks delicious, my stomach won't allow me to enjoy it. I'm thankful for the comfortable hotel room that night, knowing from here on out we're going to be roughing it.

We're up at sunrise, ready to make the two-day drive across Kurdistan. Gunnar asks me to ride in his car with Sultan behind the wheel. This means not only that Gunnar has warmed up to me, but that I'll be able to partake in shared silence. Gunnar does not waste his words. Although I've enjoyed Rob and Ken's company so far, they're not the sort of guys likely to tune in to the rhythms of the landscape.

We'll be crossing the grassy plains and mountains of Kurdistan in four vehicles. Once we leave the relative safety of the KRG behind, the cost of our security detail is going to leap from three hundred and fifty to thousands of dollars a day. Sultan explains that the Ninevah Plain, the ancient center of Christianity, is now filled with hidden hazards. There are very few Westerners in the area, and for good reason.

The troop surge of 2007 boosted the number of American troops in Iraq to 140,000, which forced most of the radical militias into the Syrian and Turkish border areas just to the north of us. "Now Al Qaeda forces have surrounded Mosul," Sultan reminds us, "and the Iranian-backed Shi'ite forces are strong with the al-Sadr clan near Basra, in the south."

I remember reading about commanding general David Petraeus's "double down" strategy in the newspaper. Looking out at this inhospitable terrain now, it's impossible to see the numbers with the same detachment. Tens of thousands of Iraqis are already dead, and millions have been displaced. More than four thousand American soldiers will have been sacrificed by 2009, and to what end? Is the war part of a strategy that culminates in a successful Middle East peace accord? Or is it, I fear, a pretext to assess the quantity of oil in Iraq so that banks can set their global energy policies? No wonder Iran is getting anxious.

Not that all was well under Saddam Hussein. We are passing scores of former Kurdish villages destroyed by his regime. Now there are nothing but ruins and inhospitable desert stretching in every direction. "More than eighty villages were gassed in this district alone," says Sultan.

"Yes," Gunnar finally volunteers. "It was always hard to imagine, a village being mustard-gassed. Now here it is for us to see with our own eyes. But Sultan," he adds with a wry expression, "please slow down!"

Our convoy has been employing counterterrorism tactics by changing the lead car every few minutes. Talking about the destroyed villages has gotten Sultan's blood pressure going; I turn back to see that we've left the other cars in the dust.

Sultan chuckles and lays off the gas a bit.

Six hours later we can see the green mountains of Turkey to the north. We stop in a grassy valley to take some fresh air and break up the long journey. My sickness has heightened all my senses, and I try to tune in to the feeling of the wind in my hair instead of my irritable stomach and the gnawing fear that we'll run into a militia once we leave Kurdistan.

We soon make our way into Dahuk, which would be recognizable even from space by its Olympic-sized Kurdish flag painted on the town dam. "It's illegal to fly this flag in the Kurdish parts of Turkey, Syria, and Iran," says Sultan proudly. "But under the KRG, people are allowed to express their freedom."

I manage to get down some Turkish coffee and bread with honey, jam, and white cheese for breakfast the next morning. Now my stomach is flip-flopping just thinking about the possibility we could run into a militia.

Then we're on the road again through Kurdistan, stopping briefly at the ancient city of Elkosh and then into the countryside. Lone Sunni wearing red headdresses and Shi'ite shepherds in traditional black climb the hills after their flocks, dwarfed by the emptiness and enormity of the plains. Noting the names of the towns we're passing and keeping in mind the Iraqi refugee stories I've already heard, I know I'm watching biblical history unfold before me.

Sultan's walkie-talkie comes to life and I hear William calling out to me. "Aaron, I know how much you love scripture, and I just wanted to point out the place where Nahum wrote his prophecies," he says. "Welcome to the City of Elkosh in the Nineveh plain."

It takes me a second to process what he's just said. The squat gray suburbs of the sprawling city we're entering as we cross the Tigris bear no resemblance to the splendor of ancient Nineveh, renowned for its elaborate palace, squares, and aqueducts.

"Mosul," I say, incredulous.

"Yes," says William, over the radio. "And Nahum's prophecies look like they're about to come true. Mosul has become the city of bloodshed."

Indeed. There have been several roadside bombings around Mosul over the last few days. Militias have been kidnapping and demanding extortion money from priests, bombing churches, and confiscating Christian-owned land. Most of the city's Christians are in hiding or have fled to neighboring countries. Those who remain fear for their lives.

It's too dangerous to stop here, and so my image of Mosul is formed in a series of snapshots as we circumvent the center of the city, crouching down below the windows. Sultan explains that militia members with cell phones hover on corners, looking for kidnapping targets. By this point everyone knows I'm sick, but I'm not allowed out of the car. "Sorry, Aaron, you're just gonna have to wait," comes Pascal's decision over the walkie-talkie.

When we reach Tel Kaif, though, I have no trouble relinquishing my own physical misery to the back of my mind. These refugees have lost everything: their homes, their livelihoods, their dignity, and, in many cases, their family members.

We spend the day handing out survival kits, interviewing IDPs and touring the camp, which is in a chaotic state. Our food packets—containing a few pounds of rice, meat, sugar, and powdered milk—are enough to sustain a family for two weeks. But we run out of them in an hour, and have to turn away children and old people. Most of the men have either been killed or drafted into the army, and many of the young women have been sold to pay the *jizyah*. The smart ones, we are told, have escaped to the relative safety of neighboring countries. I think of the relative "safety" of Damascus, where the refugee women who haven't been trafficked are forced into prostitution by economic necessity. From there they are shipped all over the Gulf states for both labor and sexual exploitation.

Safely hidden in a bunkerlike conference room, we sip tea and listen to the concerns of the Assyrian community leaders. I can't locate a toilet, and have to ask one of the men to direct me to one. He assigns three soldiers to protect me on this expedition, and we head out of the camp gates into the narrow streets of Tel Kaif.

The lead soldier keeps the front clear while the man in the rear, anticipating gunfire, covers our tail. The middle guy, who seems somewhat nervous, is protecting me. We move quickly as a unit, stopping at each corner to check our surroundings. Even though the sun has dropped in the sky, it's still hot enough to faint.

The soldier in front stops a shepherd boy with his small flock and asks him a few questions. The boy's red headdress indicates he's a Sunni. And since Sunni insurgents are increasingly joining forces with Al Qaeda in Iraq, the color alone has the soldiers on guard. Scared, the boy shakes his head no a few times before hurrying off. We finally come upon a doorway leading to a squat toilet—just a hole in the ground with a couple of planks to stand on. I've never been so relieved to see anything in my life.

I can finally let myself be sick while the soldiers wait patiently outside. The exhaustion, the allergies, the heat, and the lunch we've just eaten come pouring out of me along with some involuntary tears. My body is racked with grief—still mourning Papa and missing Jennifer. I know she could make me feel better at a time like this.

The soldiers nod empathetically as I come out, and lead me to a makeshift sink next to a well. One of them hauls up a bucket of deliciously cool water and offers to pour it over my hands. I wash red dust off my face and watch it swirl down the drain. There on the stained porcelain, the faces of the slave boys and girls in Sudan, the labor crews in Myanmar, and the trio of young sisters in Ecuador are blinking up at me.

Four thousand years ago, labor shortages led to mass enslavement right here in the Shinar plain of Mesopotamia. Back then, the conquering Babylonians slowly but steadily seized the lands of people around them who didn't pay the tax, subjugated the population, and used slaves to build the ziggurats, the first pyramids, and other monuments to their glory. Many generations later, the Americas fell into a long period of men enslaving other men. Now nearly one hundred and fifty years after the Emancipation Proclamation, many of us are still trying to heal the wounds that slavery made in our collective psyche. Still, we've always consoled ourselves with the notion that we have made progress. Slavery was abolished, wasn't it? Our teachers told us it was, and we believed it. I did, too, until I set foot in Sudan and saw what was really happening.

I stand there at the sink, wanting to switch off all the memories—wanting to go back to the days of not knowing. But it is too late. I can only hope I am wrong about what it all means. I pray we are not headed for another great enslavement. But here in the Nineveh plain, stalling for more time in the shade, I know why I have come to Iraq, the final piece of my puzzle. Aramaic-speaking children are being sold into slavery while properties in Iraq and the United States are being seized in record numbers. World markets are collapsing, and economists are predicting a crisis to top the Great Depression.

One of the soldiers shakes me lightly on the shoulder, and points at his watch to let me know it's time to walk back to the compound. I've kept them waiting a long time, and it's already dark. I prepare myself for the return journey, press my head against the cool concrete wall for a second, and let my thoughts drift back to the present. I'm just so tired.

I motion for the young soldier to wait one moment longer. Dizzy and feverish, I try to focus on the night sky for strength. It's as though I'm seeing it for the first time. Feeling the wind on my face and staring up at 30 million stars, I imagine Papa walking toward me, strong and sure of himself. "I will always be with you, Aaron," he's saying. "Now I want you to go home and start living your own life. You won't forget about me, will you?"

I feel the fever start to break. "I'll never forget about you, Papa. But I've got Jennifer now."

I wipe my forehead, stand up straight, and smile at the soldiers. "I'm ready."

Sand is blowing everywhere. As we walk back to camp in formation, I say a silent prayer for all the people confined to this forsaken dust bowl, unjustly doomed to live out a reversal of ancient history. Here are the persecuted Christians, the desperate Islamic militias, and the ancient land of Babylon, collectively being violated by a new generation of barbarians—the bankers, speculators, and investors who have come to harvest the oil and privatize the industry. They've already raped the Middle East, the Amazon, and Darfur. North and South American traffickers help their governments keep the people opiated through their "wars" on drugs and terror, which serve to do little more than keep the public distracted until the next big shock.[4]

I've been following the trail of slaves long enough to recognize the unmistakable smell of oil, the taste of drugs—and see the misery in the faces of the men, women, and children being abused by the powers that keep the rest of us enslaved. I feel this misery in their souls, and in my own, as I contemplate the repercussions of all this greed. But with my one remaining sense, I can still hear the call of Jubilee, telling me I'm not alone, and that finally I am on my way home.

I've got to get home.

I see in the near future a crisis approaching that unnerves me and causes me to tremble for the safety of my country. As a result of the war, corporations have been enthroned and an era of corruption in high places will follow, and the money power of the country will endeavor to prolong its reign by working upon the prejudices of the people until the wealth is aggregated in a few hands, and the republic destroyed.

—President Abraham Lincoln, letter to Colonel William F. Elkins, November 21, 1864

I believe that banking institutions are more dangerous to our liberties than standing armies. If the American people ever allow private banks to control the issue of their currency, first by inflation, then by deflation, the banks and corporations that will grow up around [the banks] will deprive the people of all property until their children wake up homeless on the continent their fathers conquered. The issuing power should be taken from the banks and restored to the people, to whom it properly belongs.

—Thomas Jefferson, letter to the Secretary of the Treasury Albert Gallatin, 1802

AMERICAN AIRLINES FLIGHT
SOMEWHERE OVER SAUDI ARABIA

I'm organizing my wallet, ironing out my remaining Iraqi and Jordanian dinars with the fleshy part of my hand. I slip them into my souvenir envelope, an old habit from the days of going home to Papa, who loved to look at the different bills and coins I'd brought home as he sat back to listen to my faraway adventure stories. I slide the dollars out of a jacket pocket and back into my wallet.

There, on the flip side of George Washington's stoic portrait, is the image that's been haunting me: an unfinished pyramid topped by the all-seeing eye, a symbol originating in Egyptian mythology that our Founding Fathers chose to represent the Eye of Providence, keeping watch over the United States. The juxtaposition of these two ideas—a Great Pyramid built by slaves and overseen by a force that "chooses" one nation above all others—fills me with dread. Is this our destiny as Americans? Will we preside over the next great enslavement, or be its victims? Can we wake up in time to stop it?

As the plane approaches Los Angeles, this time I realize I'm going to walk over the threshold to a new life. Jennifer's waiting for me. I want to make my family's house a home. Maybe have a family of my own. But I know I have to keep walking up and down the beach, the place where I started out. In a few hours, I'll go out to the Wedge and feel the salt and the wind on my face again. And then we'll start hunting for the washed up starfish—throwing them back in the water, one at a time.

EPILOGUE

Taking a human being out of enslavement in a brothel, military compound, or strip bar brings the victim out of one kind of bondage to what can often feel like another prison—the rules and rigors of victim shelters, or the struggle to make ends meet in a tough global economy. When slaves are freed, the battle to help them reintegrate into society begins. That might seem like a gargantuan task, but it's one we've got to take on in this generation.

The human trafficking explosion is just one symptom of our much larger, more complex human dilemma. But we can't let its complexity confound us. We *can* start informing ourselves today, and within a matter of days, weeks, months, and years we'll be dismantling the traffickers' networks and shaming the consumers who buy or use the trafficking victims' products and services. In the process, we'll be reclaiming our freedom, our schools, our communities, and our ability to care for each other.

Governments may take steps for us and with us, but we have to stop looking to politicians alone to change our world. Individuals need to ask more of our elected officials while making sure we do everything in our own power to protect, assist, and empower the tired, the hungry, the poor, and the trafficked. We need to form movements, join with the like-minded, and shake up the skeptical until they, too, are walking along with us.

In many ways, it looks to me as though we are on the verge of the greatest enslavement of all time. The crisis in the financial markets and many other sectors draws inevitable comparisons to history, when widespread shortages of staple commodities led to lands being seized and masses of people being subjugated. Globalization and the Internet have made some of us freer, but have also made it easier for criminal networks to further exploit and victimize the youngest, weakest, and the poorest members of our expanding global community.

So we're left with the ultimate question:

What can I do?

GET INVOLVED

Thirteen billion a year in slave-made products and services is a lot of money, but it is exactly what Americans spent on Valentine's Day in 2005. If human trafficking generates $32 billion in profits annually, that is still a tiny drop in the ocean of the world economy.

—Kevin Bales, *Ending Slavery: How We Free Today's Slaves*

THERE ARE MORE SLAVES IN THE WORLD TODAY than at any time in history. That's the bad news. The good news is that those 27 million people estimated to be in bondage represent only 0.0043 percent of the world's population.

Most nations have passed legislation mirroring the U.S. Congress's landmark Trafficking Victims Protection Act of 2000. Governments have since signed more than a dozen international conventions banning the modern-day slave trade. Antitrafficking task forces all over the world are still being trained in how to enforce those laws. But they have so far to go. Of the seventeen thousand people estimated to have been trafficked into the United States in 2006, approximately *one hundred* trafficking and slavery cases were brought to trial. We need to do better.

The rest is up to us.

Bringing an end to modern-day slavery is within our reach. By scholar Kevin Bales's calculation, the grassroots cost of bringing those 27 million people to freedom and helping them rebuild their lives (at a cost of five hundred dollars per slave) would amount to $13.5 billion. That's less than 1 percent of the more than $700 billion

Congress approved for last year's historic Wall Street bailout—or just forty-seven dollars from the pocket of each American citizen. The income that slaves generate, while significant, is negligible compared to the size of the world economy.

But it is going to require a global mind shift to increase awareness of slavery and mobilize resources.

One of the biggest obstacles we will face is ourselves. Human beings are political animals. Well-meaning activists, policy makers, and journalists have wasted time squabbling over the definition of *human trafficking* or *slavery*, choosing sides and allowing personal agendas to get in the way of collective progress. Politicians fight for resources to combat sex trafficking while ignoring the plight of the men, women, and children trafficked into debt bondage in order to harvest American tomatoes and lettuce. Hungry for ratings, the media tend to single out sex slavery over its many less provocative forms—a huge disservice to the other slaves whose silent suffering is just as profound.

Slavery in any form is a crime against humanity, and it's going to take all of us working together instead of against each other to make it disappear. Some critics complain that slave liberators offer a shortsighted solution to a complex problem. They claim that buying human freedom creates a slave market, rewarding the traffickers and middlemen for their efforts and serving merely to decrease the length of an individual slave's bondage while ignoring the big picture. In an ideal world, the intrinsic value of a human being is not negotiable. But try looking in the face of a slave child condemned to a brutal life in a brothel, carpet factory, or slave master's home and telling her that buying her way out of there would make the problem worse. She doesn't have time to wait for a diplomatic solution.

Freeing slaves one at a time will not solve the problem, but a slave that is freed and given a chance to go to school may become a liberator herself. She then becomes part of the solution, an agent working to change the fabric of the society that created the conditions for slavery in the first place. "The example and influence of a single rehabilitated slave can dramatically alter a whole village," says Kevin Bales.

Human trafficking, modern-day slavery, and the crimes that accompany them are a complex web to unravel. Until we as a people address the root causes of this human trade, men, women, and children will continue to be sold into slavery. Working to eradicate hunger and extreme poverty is an important first step to ending slavery. The second step is holding ourselves responsible for the role, however small or unconscious, we play in allowing slavery to grow, thrive, and perpetuate. If we decrease our demand for the products and services slaves provide, the slave economy will collapse.

The responsibility falls upon everyone from the U.N. peacekeeper not wanting to know that the "prostitutes" at the brothel he likes to frequent are actually minors being held against their will, to the American consumer buying an exotic carpet that might well be made by a child slave in India. Turning a blind eye to slavery is as easy as saying "It's ubiquitous" or "It's been around since the beginning of time." *New York Times* columnist Nicholas Kristof makes this point about sex slavery: "Governments accept it partly because it seems to defy solution. Prostitution is said to be the oldest profession. It exists in all countries, and if some teenage girls are imprisoned in brothels until they die of AIDS, that is seen as tragic but inevitable. . . . If we defeated slavery in the nineteenth century, we can beat it in the twenty-first century."

Believing in a Utopia without slavery, poverty, and oppression is not naïve—as long as we are not alone. Please volunteer, donate, get informed, and write letters putting pressure on foreign governments to crack down on brothel owners who exploit children or trafficked women. Call on the president and U.N. secretary-general to act in Darfur, where the slave raiding of a decade ago has become the genocide of today. Use your freedom to help others. Pass it on. Here are some good places to start:

Abolish Slavery!

The Abolish Slavery Coalition is a registered charity founded by Aaron Cohen and dedicated to combating human trafficking and restoring dignity to victims worldwide. We organize and coordinate investigations and field operations to find, identify, and retrieve men, women, and children from slavery—and then provide for their safe aftercare and rehabilitation.

> Abolish Slavery Coalition
> P.O. BOX 5000
> Costa Mesa, CA 92626
> www.abolishslavery.org
> info@abolishslavery.org

AFESIP Cambodia

AFESIP Cambodia exists to combat trafficking in women and children for sex slavery; to care for and rehabilitate those rescued from sex slavery; to provide them occupational skills training; and to reintegrate them into the communities where they can live in a sustainable and innovative manner.

> AFESIP Cambodia
> Administration, Human Resource and
>   Communication Department
> #62CEO, Street 598, Boeung Kak 2
> Toul Kork, Phnom Penh
> Cambodia
> Phone: 855-023-884-123
> www.AFESIP.org

Causecast

Causecast is a "one-stop philanthropy shop"—a platform where media, philanthropy, social networking, entertainment, and education converge to serve a greater purpose. People want to do good, to be inspired, and inspire others to join them in giving back. Cause-cast makes this easy by providing users with the means to connect with people, leaders, charities, nonprofit organizations, and brands that inspire them.

www.causecast.org
getinvolved@causecast.org

CSI

CSI is a Christian human rights organization that helps victims of religious repression, victimized children, and victims of disaster.

CSI-USA
Christian Solidarity International
870 Hampshire Road, Suite T
Westlake Village, CA 91361
www.csi-usa.org
csi@csi-usa.org

Free the Slaves

Free the Slaves liberates slaves around the world, helps them rebuild their lives, and researches real-world solutions to eradicate slavery forever.

Free the Slaves
514 10th Street, NW 7th Floor
Washington, D.C. 20004
Phone: 202-638-1865
info@freetheslaves.net
www.freetheslaves.net

International Justice Mission

International Justice Mission is a human rights agency that secures justice for victims of slavery, sexual exploitation, and other forms of violent oppression. IJM lawyers, investigators, and aftercare professionals work with local officials to ensure immediate victim rescue and aftercare, to prosecute perpetrators, and to promote functioning public justice systems.

> International Justice Mission
> P.O. Box 58417
> Washington, D.C. 20037
> www.ijm.org

Rapha House

Rapha House is committed to rescuing young girls who are victims of slavery, sexual exploitation, and prostitution by providing them with a safe home where they can heal and receive an education, which will allow them to make good choices for their futures.

> Rapha House
> P.O. Box 1627
> Joplin, MO 64802
> www.freedomforgirls.org
> rapha@arm.org

Somaly Mam Foundation

The Somaly Mam Foundation is a nonprofit public charity working to end slavery. With the vision and leadership of world-renowned Cambodian activist Somaly Mam, the foundation strives to get to the root of human trafficking.

Somaly Mam Foundation
P.O. Box 1272
Wheat Ridge, CO 80034
www.somaly.org

Save Darfur Coalition

The Save Darfur Coalition is an alliance of more than 180 faith-based, advocacy, and humanitarian organizations united to help the people of Darfur demand an end to the genocide.

2120 L Street NW, Suite 335
Washington, DC 20037
info@savedarfur.org
www.savedarfur.org

Yinabei Mendez

Sok Lin

Jonny Thern

Jonty Thern

Proudly presenting Jonny with her diploma when she graduated from high school

Jonty and Aaron reunited at Rapha house

VICTIM UPDATES

Yinabei Mendez

Yinabei didn't stay long at the Quito convent where Michele, Ernesto, Carlos, and I left her back in fall 2004. But she had her baby anyway and wrote to let me know I was to be the godfather of little Alison, who's now five years old. Yinabei and her husband work together at a beauty salon where she's a beautician. Although she says it's sometimes hard to make ends meet, Yinabei has not given up on the hope of a bright future. Here's an excerpt I've translated from a letter she sent me:

> I've been working in the salon as a beautician and doing administration. . . . In October, God willing, I'll enter university to study languages and follow a career path based on that. These are my mid- and long-term goals—to have decent work and be able to study peacefully, following my heart.

Sok Lin

Eight-year-old Sok Lin first found me on the streets of Phnom Penh, where she was selling books for a living. Charmed by Lin's energy and outgoing nature, I ended up meeting and sharing lunch with her whole family that day—a happy, supportive lot. Before leaving, we walked Lin, her brothers Snar and Rina, and her mother to the International School and paid for two years' tuition. Of all the children I met in Cambodia, Lin was the last one I would have thought would be vulnerable to human traffickers. Nevertheless, before leaving, I asked some of my shelter contacts to keep an eye on her. In 2006 I got word that Lin had disappeared; there was little my friends in the nonprofit community could do but keep looking and hoping they would find her. They later discovered that Lin had been sold into a sex trafficking ring by a street gang. Authorities arranged to get her out and retrieve her from harm. Lin is now twelve, out of danger and growing up in the shelter system. We talk on the phone from time to time and I visit her at the school. Her caretakers are giving her a good education, and she is even more fluent in English than she was the last time I saw her. But it's hard to accept what she has had to go through. Her rehabilitation involves helping to keep her brothers off the streets and in school.

After leaving Cambodia in November 2004, I traveled to southern Thailand to rest for a week and write up a report of what I had learned. I made friends with the locals before flying home to check on Papa. Two weeks later, a tsunami triggered by a massive earthquake in the Indian Ocean hit the coastal communities of Indonesia, India, Sri Lanka, and Thailand. Two hundred and thirty thousand people were dead or missing, including many of the new friends I had made in Phuket and Koh Phi Phi. So the call I received a few days later was especially devastating. I listened in disbelief as Juliette, the French aid worker from the AFESIP shelter in Phnom Penh, recounted the events of the previous three weeks. The Cambodian police had finally raided a hotel they had long known was being run as a brothel and exploiting children for sex. The hotel's inhabitants had been brought to the shelter for police questioning. Many were underage and frightened. But the shelter couldn't protect them from the mafia. The next day, an armed gang showed up at the safe house and, as corrupt police officers looked on, forcibly removed all of the girls who had been taken from the hotel, along with several Vietnamese girls who had been rescued on the raids.

It all felt so hopeless, but I couldn't forget those faces. I returned to Cambodia several times in 2005 to search for Thai girls who had survived the tsunami but had subsequently gone missing, suspected to have been trafficked to the Cambodian border region. While night-frighting a karaoke parlor, I met two teenaged sisters, Jonty and Jonny, who came in to dance for me with a group of young Vietnamese girls. I filmed the solicitation on my cell phone and took the tape to Pastor Dear Sorum, the Cambodian director of a shelter called Rapha House. The next day, the chief of police, accompanied by the pastor, took the sisters and their young friends out of the brothel and to a new home at Rapha House. Since then, I've stayed in touch with the girls as they adapt to a "normal" life.

Jonny Thern

This lovely young woman was trafficked from Cambodia to Thailand when she was only thirteen years old. She escaped and returned home, only to be sold by a family member into the Battambang karaoke parlor/brothel where I found her working with her younger sister, Jonty. Now seventeen, Jonny blossomed at Rapha House, learning to read and write. She graduated from the high school program in 2007, and I returned to Cambodia to present Jonny and some of the other girls I'd found with their graduation certificates. It was a proud and emotional moment for us all. The girls' mother, Mrs. Thern, was introducing me to family and friends as their godfather. Today Jonny is managing a beauty salon and mentoring young girls considered at risk of being trafficked.

Jonty Thern

Jonty was only thirteen when I met her at the karaoke parlor/brothel where she was enslaved with her older sister. I worked hard to sponsor her and stay in her life over the years. But while Jonny thrived at the shelter, Jonty cut class and became more and more withdrawn and depressed as she struggled with depression and an addiction to methamphetamine. When I went back to watch the other girls graduate, I could tell that Jonty was in trouble. We had a long talk, and she promised she would go back to school. But it wasn't that simple. Jonty had e-mailed me a month earlier asking for money, and I told her I'd send her something in exchange for her own autobiographical narrative. I never got it. The last thing Jonny said to me that afternoon was, "Can I have fifty dollars?" I gave the money to her mother and kissed Jonty good-bye.

In September 2008 I got the terrible news that Jonty had died in a Vietnamese hospital of drug complications after having run away from the shelter. Her liver had failed. When I went back to comfort the family and speak at Jonty's memorial service, her mother told me that she had been having a recurring dream that I was bringing Jonty back to her. Mrs. Thern cried as Jonny and I held her and grieved for the loss of this young life. Her tragic death is a reminder of the emotional and physical trauma enacted upon victims of human trafficking and slavery. Sometimes all the love in the world is not enough to repair the damage done to these lives.

NOTES

PART I: CAMBODIA

NIGHT FRIGHTING

1. Translation courtesy of the documentary *S21: The Khmer Rouge Killing Machine* (2003), directed by Rithy Panh.
2. Louise Brown, *Sex Slaves: The Trafficking of Women in Asia* (London: Virago, 2000).
3. The United Nations Transitional Authority in Cambodia (UNTAC) has officially had a Cambodian presence since 1992.
4. Statistic courtesy of the 2004 Cambodia Socio-Economic Survey and the World Bank.

IN THE FACE OF DARKNESS

1. Henri Mouhot, French explorer and naturalist in Cambodia from 1858 to 1860. Quoted from a presentation made at the Khmer-Canadian Buddhist Cultural Centre by Venerable Vodano Sophan Seng.
2. Cambodian national police chief Hok Lundy, a close ally of Prime Minister Hun Sen, had already become notorious for his involvement in drug and human trafficking, extrajudicial killings, and organized crime before my first visit to the country. But his reputation only got worse thereafter. After a December 2004 raid, conducted by AFESIP, he reportedly ordered the release of several human traffickers before an investigation could get under way. This act was grounds for the U.S. State Department's refusal to grant him a visa in February 2006. Yet a month later, the FBI awarded him a medal for his support of the U.S. "global war on terrorism." In April 2007, the FBI invited Hok Lundy to a seminar on bilateral counterterrorism cooperation. Human Rights Watch called on the State Department to cancel his visa, with its Asia director stating that "the FBI should be investigating him, not hosting him. . . . Treating Hok Lundy like a respected law enforcement officer is like something out of *Alice in Wonderland*. He represents the absolute worst that Cambodia has to offer and should never have been given a U.S. visa." See http://hrw.org/english/docs/2007/04/16/usint16717.htm. Lundy died in November 2008 after his helicopter caught fire and crashed in

Cambodia's Svay Rieng Province. The crash, attributed to bad weather, has provoked much speculation in a country where many have cause to believe his death was not an accident.

PART II: CALIFORNIA
SCREAM

1. Lyric from "Pigs in Zen," *Jane's Addiction* (live studio album), 1987.

DROP THE DEBT

1. See www.guardian.co.uk/world/2002/mar/18/usa.debtrelief.
2. From *Three Days*, directed by Carter B. Smith, 1997.
3. Interview with Jay Babcock for *LA Weekly* www.jaybabcock.com/perry.html.

PART III: SUDAN
PRELUDE TO DARFUR

1. Reprinted in Human Rights Watch report "United States: Diplomacy Revived," August 21, 2003.
2. Bill Berkeley, *The Graves Are Not Yet Full* (New York: Basic Books, 2001), p. 196.
3. At the time of my first visit to Sudan, government-sponsored raiding was concentrated in the south, then a war zone. The second civil war would rage on until 2003, at the cost of approximately 2.2 million lives. Since the majority of Sudan's southern population had been displaced by the time the peace agreement was signed, the government began to target Muslim Africans in northern provinces like Darfur.
4. Sudan is more than 70 percent Muslim, with the rest of the tribes a mixture of animistic and traditional religions. Most estimates put the Sudanese Christian population at about 5 percent.
5. http://en.wikipedia.org/wiki/John_Garang.
6. www.nytimes.com/2004/11/11/international/europe/11serb.html?scp=2 &sq=srebrenica%20massacre&st=cse.
7. www.everyculture.com/Africa-MiddleEast/Nuer-History-and-Cultural-Relations.html.
8. strategyleader.org/profiles/dinka.html.
9. www.sudan101.com/baggara.htm.
10. This designation would only come in July 2008, when an International Criminal Court prosecutor finally filed genocide charges against Sudanese president Omar al-Bashir. It was the first time the ICC charged a sitting head of state.
11. www.hrw.org/campaigns/sudan98/sudfam.htm.

THE TIME WHEN THE WORLD WAS SPOILED

1. Dinka collectively refer to the Turco-Egyptian period and the Mahdist rule that followed as the time "the world was spoiled." For more detail see Francis Mading Deng, *War of Visions: Conflict of Identities in the Sudan* (Washington, D.C.: Brookings Institution, 1995), p. 73.
2. Amnesty International: www.amnesty.org/en/library/asset/AFR54/001/2002 /en/dom-AFR540012002en.html.
3. At the time the middlemen's profit averaged about $10 per slave, according to Ian Fisher, "Selling Sudan's Slaves into Freedom," *New York Times*, April 25, 1999.

ALLEZ, ALLEZ, ALLEZ!

1. Although the Los Angeles police listed Smith's death as a suicide, the coroner could not conclude that his wounds were self-inflicted. See www.rollingstone .com/artists/elliottsmith/articles/story/5936000/smith_autopsy_inconclusive.

PART IV: LATIN AMERICA

SI DIOS QUIERE

1. By the Paul and Lisa Program (a Connecticut-based nonprofit that works to prevent the commercial sexual exploitation of women and children), which cosponsored the trip.
2. Approximately half were killed by Shining Path; the rest died in reprisals by government security forces or by other militias/guerrilla groups (2003 Peru Truth and Reconciliation Commission Report, cited by Human Rights Watch, August 28, 2003).

SOUR LAKE

1. Since many of the countries on Tier Three—including Myanmar, North Korea, Sudan, and Cuba—are already subject to U.S. sanctions, critics have been quick to call the threat ineffectual.
2. Part of the U.N. Convention against Transnational Organized Crime, the Palermo Protocol was signed by 147 countries and ratified by 141 (out of 195 countries in the world). Countries that have signed but not ratified the Palermo Protocol include Greece, Ireland, Japan, India, Iceland, Korea, Indonesia, Syria, Iran, Jordan, and Vietnam. See www.nybooks.com/articles/20654.
3. Mariana Sandoval Laverde, "Executive Summary," in *Magnitude, Characteristics, and Environment of Sexual Exploitation of Girls and Adolescents in Ecuador* (Lima: International Labor Organization Regional Office for Latin America and the Caribbean, International Program on the Elimination of Child Labor, October 2002), reprinted in Protection Project report on Ecuador: www .protectionproject.org/human_rights_reports/report_documents/ecuador.doc.

4. BBC News, "Colombia's Rebels: A Fading Force?" February 1, 2008; International Crisis Group, "War and Drugs in Colombia," January 27, 2005.

5. Western oil companies actually pulled out of the country for a while, replaced by China (Michael Backman, "Bribery Helps China Buy New Friends," *The Age*, April 26, 2007). There have been reports that employees of the country's oil company Petroecuador, which left OPEC in 1992, aided drug traffickers in siphoning off "white gas," which is used to make cocaine (Kelly Hearn, "Drug Cartels Siphon Pipelines," *Washington Post*, June 4, 2008), and Stephen Kueffner, "Petroecuador Finds Evidence of Widespread Corporate Corruption," Bloomberg.com, January 7, 2008). FARC actually attacked oil pipelines from the late 1990s: www.pbs.org/wnet/wideangle/uncategorized/farc-guerillas/570/.

6. www.cofan.org.

7. www.amazonwatch.org.

8. In response, ChevronTexaco has said its Ecuadorean subsidiary operated within local laws when it dumped contaminated water directly into the ecosystem, as opposed to the more expensive reinsertion of waste water back into the earth, as required by U.S. law. Doing it the right way would have cost a few dollars a barrel, but instead the company paid $40 million to "remediate" the sites after it left. See www.texaco.com and www.texacotoxico.org.

9. "New oil spill reported in Ecuador," Xinhua News Agency, June 20, 2008.

10. Catherine Worth, "Refugees of an Endless War," Spring 2001, www.elander.com/back/spring01/stories/story_colombia.worth.html.

11. 2004 *CIA World Factbook* figure: the average salary in Ecuador was $3,300 a year, or about $9.04 per day.

PART V: MYANMAR

A SIMPLE TWIST OF FATE

1. In 2005, the junta's paranoid generals relocated the capital overnight from Yangon, formerly Rangoon.

2. The United States cut off all political and military assistance to Myanmar in 1988. Trade sanctions began in 1997, when Congress banned all business investment.

3. According to a Human Rights Watch report, in 2006 the SPDC was the only government in the world to use antipersonnel mines on a regular basis.

4. John Lennon, "Gimme Some Truth," from *Imagine*, 1971.

PART VI: MIDDLE EAST

ISRAEL: *THE* PROBLEM WITH MEN

1. Prostitution is legal in most parts of the world, including Canada, Australia, most of Europe, South America, and Asia.

IRAQ: THEIR LAST CONCERN

1. Chaldeans consider themselves a distinct ethnicity, while Assyrians maintain they share the same ethnic makeup. The U.S. State Department refers to both groups simply as "Chaldeans." For more detail, see www.unhcr.org /refworld/country,,USCIS,,IRQ,4562d8cf2,3f520de14,0.html.
2. Thomas Frank, "Obama's Touch of Class," *Wall Street Journal,* April 21, 2008.
3. Radiohead, from "House of Cards," *In Rainbows,* 2007.
4. For more on this theory, see Naomi Klein's *The Shock Doctrine.*

FURTHER READING

Bales, Kevin. *Disposable People: New Slavery in the Global Economy*. Berkeley: University of California Press, 1999.

——. *Ending Slavery: How We Free Today's Slaves*. Berkeley: University of California Press, 2007.

Bowe, John. *Nobodies: Modern American Slave Labor and the Dark Side of the New Global Economy*. New York: Random House, 2007.

Brinkley, Joel. "A Modern-Day Abolitionist Battles Slavery Worldwide." *New York Times*, February 4, 2006.

Clark, Michele. "Prevention and Vulnerability in Combating Trafficking in Human Beings: The Need for New Paradigms." Background paper for UN-GIFT International Forum to Combat Trafficking in Persons, February 2008.

——. "From Policy to Practice: Combating Trafficking in Human Beings in the OSCE Region." Organization for Security and Co-operation in Europe (OSCE), Vienna, Austria, September 2006.

Ehrenreich, Barbara, and Arlie Russell Hochschild, eds. *Global Woman: Nannies, Maids, and Sex Workers in the New Economy*. New York: Metropolitan, 2003.

Glenny, Misha. *McMafia: A Journey Through the Global Criminal Underworld*. New York: Knopf, 2008.

Kristof, Nicholas. "A Heroine from the Brothels." *New York Times*, September 24, 2008, in addition to numerous articles and blog postings over the years.

Malarek, Victor. *The Natashas: Inside the New Global Sex Trade*. New York: Arcade, 2003.

Saviano, Roberto. *Gomorrah: A Personal Journey into the Violent International Empire of Naples' Organized Crime System*. New York: Farrar, Straus & Giroux, 2007.

Skinner, E. Benjamin. *A Crime So Monstrous: Face-to-Face with Modern-Day Slavery*. New York: Free Press, 2008.

With my mother, L.C.,
Annapolis, Maryland

Ruthie, Arthur, and me

Walking with Papa after
a water polo game

Papa and me

ACKNOWLEDGMENTS

Thank G-d for my mother and father, for my Jennifer, for my brother Arthur and my sister Ruthie, for Kirsten, Tom, Daniel, Matthew, Sarah, Joseph, Michael, Anna, David, Francis, Naomi, Hannah, Mary, Ellen, Johnny, Crystal, and Tina. I'm grateful to my father's caretakers Maxima and Juanita, and to Lois and Doc Beshore. Special thanks to Tricia Boczkowski, Cara Bedick, Jennifer Robinson, Kerrie Loyd, and Jen Bergstrom from Simon & Schuster. Big hugs to David Kuhn and Justin Manask for believing in this project. Thank goodness for Bill Silva and the management team at Bill Silva Entertainment, including Ryan Chisholm, Larry Butler, Eric Herz, Eric Nordon, Josh German, and Allyson Spiegelman. Blessings to our Causecast family, including Joanna and Ryan Scott, Levi Felix, and my friend, Brian Sirgutz. Thanks to my mentors John Eibner, Sharon Payt, Mohamed Mattar, Michele Clark, and Pastor Hans Stückelberger. I'm grateful for attorney James Feldman, for my friends Allyce Engelson, Julie Weiss, Darrel Adams, Tom and Tony Adams, Alex Mouracade, to Linda and Glen Megill for grounding me, and I'm appreciative to Dave Masters for his help with financial matters. Many thanks to Sandra Kirkpatrick for her support, to Cindy Castano, Pam Kefi, Lauren Konigsberg, Eric King, Ene Taylor, Tommy Calvert, Dear Sorum, Sokhang, Soklin, Stephanie Freed, Jonny Thern, Kerry Decker, Cindy Cafferty, Nichole Shive, Drew Tewksbury, and Aaron Frankel for his pictures. I'm indebted to Nora and Todd Hathaway for sharing William Walker and their home with me. Thanks to Michael Maccoby, to Kraidejt, General Pichai, General Hogbin, General Siripong, Christian Elliott, Terry Wade, and Peter

Lowes. I'm thankful to Mikel Dunham, Sonny Smith, David Fox, Tina Hoffman, Joyce and Rob Marcarelli, Sandy Kikerpill and Richard Leger, Ken Timmerman, Gunnar Weibalck, Brendan Hawkins, Tommy Davis, Jesse Baker, Eric Lubitz, Jeff Smith, Malysa Wilson, Daniel Yovan, Scott Clowes, Gregory Simms, Dave Harris, Brandon Marlowe, Troy Westergaard, Andrew R. Tennenbaum, Bruce McKenna, Archie Bell, Joanna and David Itzikman, Rob and Paula Boyer, Phil and Julie Castillo, Christine and Yobel, Tom Kennedy, Mel Thoman, David Imbernino, Trudy Green, Jerry Fowler and the Save Darfur Coalition. Thanks to Gary Haugen and The International Justice Mission for the vision and inspiration to free captives, really. Thanks to Ron and Flo Speers, Gina and Pete Peterson, Rabbi Langer, Rabbi Schwartz, Rabbi Jonah, Bob Schupp, Rick Roland, Terry Schroeder, Bill Barnett and Tony Hawk. Special thanks to Cynthia Ryan, Daryl Hannah, Bianca Mead, Michael Lohan, attorney Hugo Harmatz, Robert Eliseo, Mireille Bravo, Jose Luis Vega, Ricky Martin, Amber Heard, Tasya VanRee, Demi Moore, Ashton Kutcher, Jack Healy, Richard Kamsai Lee, and special thanks to Etty and Perry Farrell.

Words cannot express the gratitude I have for my co-writer Christine Buckley, for her tireless work, intellect, and compassion.

—AARON COHEN

There are many people who helped make this book happen. First and foremost was my *LA Weekly* editor Tom Christie. Tom moved mountains to help me tell the whole, complicated thing, and editor-in-chief Laurie Ochoa granted me the space to do so. Later on, David Kuhn, Justin Manask, and Billy Kingsland found Aaron's book a home and brought me onto the project. I've been grateful for their advice and support along the way. Thanks also to Trish Boczkowski at S&S for taking a chance on this book, and to Cara Bedick and Lisa Healy for their patience and willingness to let us delve into territory not usually covered by SSE. This is a much better book thanks to their hard work. Much gratitude to Elisa Rivlin for her keen eye and to Thomas Pitoniak for his top-notch copyediting.

Two more brilliant women did the behind-the-scenes work that allowed us to cover so much territory on a tight deadline. Cynthia Gonzalez transcribed like a speed demon, offered excellent input, and never complained about the salary. Mary Bowers—research assistant, fact checker, and now friend—amazed me with her energy, insight, and ability to ferret out the essence of complex issues.

I am indebted to many writers whose work inspired and shaped my understanding of various forms of modern-day slavery—especially John Bowe, Nicholas Kristof, Kevin Bales, Victor Malarek, Barbara Ehrenreich, and Ben Skinner. I spoke with many on the front lines of the abolition movement, who took precious time away from their schedules to talk to me about their work. Of that group, Michele Clark, Tommy Calvert, Michael Cory Davis, and Dottie Laster stand out.

Un grand merci to the dear friends, family, and colleagues who have housed and fed me, read chapters, and put up with my nomadic ways and long periods of enforced solitude, especially Jennifer Orth, Avery Sumner, Lisa Miller, Amy Selmès, Karen Pedlow, Steffie Nelson, Cécile Vazeille, Millie Casper, Chris Calhoun, Ngô Kim Anh, Tiphaine Massari, Pierre Lapeyronnie, Régis Taranto, Matthew Kay, Eric Pape, Jim Rutman, Dama De, Lisa Mouallem, Rich Garella, Marc Roussel, Brice Dunwoodie, Zeth Dubois, and my brother Hòa.

And finally, to Gaëtan Kandzot: The readiness is all! I'd like to dedicate my part of this book to my father, who made me laugh, and my mother, who made me strong.

—CHRISTINE BUCKLEY

ABOUT THE COAUTHOR

 **Christine Buckley** was born in New York and is a graduate of Boston College. Her travels have taken her to five continents and taught her to shear sheep, cultivate rice, sail without a GPS, and edit a state-run newspaper with a straight face. Christine's *LA Weekly* cover story on Aaron Cohen was a 2008 L.A. Press Club and Maggie Award finalist. She has contributed to National Public Radio, the *New York Times*, Russian *Newsweek*, and Current TV, among others. Her reporting has also won her an Associated Press award. Currently based in Paris, in 2009 she plans to return to Southeast Asia to work with human trafficking victims.

ABOUT THE AUTHOR

Aaron Cohen is a human rights activist who draws his inspiration from the Jubilee, the ancient law of debt forgiveness and slave liberation. Cohen has established a modern-day Jubilee movement to forgive debts and free slaves around the world, Abolish Slavery. Cohen was awarded a Commendation from the County of Los Angeles for his efforts to combat human trafficking. On his international missions to Nicaragua, Israel, Egypt, Ecuador, Iraq, Colombia, and Myanmar (formerly Burma), Cohen worked undercover and assessed the slavery phenomenon from the inside. He received the World War II Memorial Foundation/The Immortal Chaplains 2008 Prize for Humanity, and has been honored with a U.S. Congressional Certificate of Merit for his public service.